international interiors | 6

international interiors 6

JEREMY MYERSON

Co-ordinating researcher
JENNIFER HUDSON

LAURENCE KING

PUBLISHED 1997 BY LAURENCE KING PUBLISHING
an imprint of Calmann & King Ltd
71 Great Russell Street
London WC1B 3BN

A catalogue record for this book is available from the British Library.

ISBN 1 85669 105 5

DESIGNED BY PRICE WATKINS, LONDON

Printed in Hong Kong

Frontispiece: Oxo Tower Wharf Restaurant, London (see page 75). Photograph: Timothy Soar.

Acknowledgements. The author and the publishers would like to thank Helen Castle for editorial work on the book; all the designers and architects involved; and the photographers whose work is reproduced. The following photographic credits are given, with page numbers in brackets:
Peter Aaron, ESTO (181 right); Archipress (48–51, 53); Architekturphoto Busam/Richter (204–9); courtesy of Emilio Ambasz (178 right); courtesy of Atelier Mendini (145–7); Hedrich Blessing (45–7); Luc Boegly, Archipress (78–83, 241–3); Andrew Bordwin (37, 105 right); Brakke/Scagliola (180 right, 190 left & centre); Donatella Brun (54–7); Richard Bryant, Arcaid (8 left & centre, 178 left); Rory Carnegie (121, 124); Earl Carter, Belle/Arcaid (68 centre); Jean-Philippe Caulliez (11 centre); Robert Cesar, Archipress (68 left); Chris Chapman (69); David Churchill, Arcaid (129 right); Niall Clutton (88–91); Keith Collie (8 right, 9 centre); Peter Cook, Archipress (111–15, 194–8); Peter Cook, View (179); Stephane Couturier, Archipress (116–19); Richard Davies (221–3); courtesy DEGW (11 right); courtesy of Design System (106); Carlos Dominquez (128 centre); Franck Eustache, Archipress (131–3, 135); Mitsumasa Fujisuka (70–3, 191–3); Chris Gascoigne, View (160–3); Dennis Gilbert, View (9 right, 120, 123, 125, 180 centre, 186–7, 189); Richard Glover, Arcaid (148); Jeff Goldberg, ESTO (13–17); Roland Halbe (59–61); Jiri Havran (18–21); Timothy Hursley (182–4, 216–17, 219); courtesy of Massimo Iosa Ghini (126 left & centre); Conrad Johnson (129 centre); Nicholas Kane, Arcaid (63 top, 64–5, 67 right, 68 right); Barbara Karant/Karant & Associates (22–5); Jon Keenan (136–9); Toshiyuki Kobayashi (210–15); John Edward Linden, Arcaid (149–51); Marco Lorenzetti (10 right, 100–1, 103–5); Rainer Mader (237–9); Peter Margonelli (36); Peter Mauss, ESTO (39); Trevor Mein, Arcaid (67 left & centre); Tom Miller (63 bottom); courtesy of Ministry of Defence (10 left); Michael Moran (165–9); Nacasa & Partners (84–7, 170–3); courtesy of Nardi Associates (128 right); John O'Brien (128 left); Tomio Ohashi (230–3, 235); courtesy of Pentagram (127 right); Eugene Pons (153–5, 200–3); Jo Reid and John Peck (40–3); Christian Richters (30–5, 130, 140–3, 224–9); Tomas Riehle, Contur (156–8); Phil Sayer (97–9); Schinkenchiku-sha (107–9, 180 left); Shotenknchiku-sha/Shinichi Sato (127); Timothy Soar (75–7); Mark Steeke (175–7); Morley von Sternberg (66 left & centre); Paul Warchol (92–5); Nathan Willock (27–9).

contents

The ambitious scope and diversity of more than 75 interior design projects discussed in *International Interiors 6* reflects a profession that is fast rediscovering the sources of its creative credibility

introduction

THE interior design profession has been forced to tread on eggshells through much of the economically brittle nineties. In *International Interiors 6*, however, there are sustained signs of renewed confidence, restored technical belief and reinvigorated creative vision.

Insecurities about work, technological change, the future of our cities and the fragility of our environment remain evident throughout the world. Nevertheless, interior designers and architects of interior spaces are, increasingly, being regarded as agents of change, as they suggest ways we can live and work in the next century, rather than just decorators of the status quo.

In this pre-millennial period of flux – the age of both the Internet and of the eco-warrior – it is clear that the ability of interior designers to create a material sense of place, and to articulate the aspirations of both companies and communities, is of a significance beyond the dimensions of physical space. As Derrick De Kerckhove, director of the McLuhan Program at the University of Toronto, has observed: 'It is to artists and designers that more and more people will turn to ask for an intelligible and livable technological environment; it is artists and designers that they will ask to be comprehensive in their approach to reality.'

How interior designers ultimately measure up to this responsibility will decide their value as a professional group. As staging posts on the way towards a new and changed world, the interior design projects shown in this book are encouraging in that they reflect an appetite for engagement with the big issues in design and society.

Our selection spans a two-year period from autumn 1994 to autumn 1996, a time of accelerating activity, eclectic ideas and often contradictory signals in design. To capture this sense of growing complexity and richness in design schemes, we have greatly expanded the introductions to each of the four main sections of the book – Work, Leisure, Retail and Public. This editorial innovation has enabled us to look briefly at around 30 further projects in addition to the 48 we have selected for detailed case-study analysis.

Setting nearly 80 projects in their social, cultural and economic context puts a larger frame around our biennial overview of interior design expertise and provides more opportunity to trace and analyse trends. The main case studies are shared out among 11 different nations. It is no surprise that work in the USA, UK, Japan, Germany and France should figure so prominently. There are, however, also engaging entries from Iceland, Mexico and Hungary, illustrating what a global phenomenon leading-edge interior design has become.

What does *International Interiors 6* tell us about national design trends? In the workplace, American designers and corporations continue to lead the way in rethinking the form and style of the office. Some of the most radical ideas are emanating from the 'fast company' hothouses on the East and West Coasts. In retail and leisure, Britain has re-emerged as a creative powerhouse, with London setting the pace as a city of exciting new regenerative schemes. In public environments, Japan continues to leave the rest of the world trailing in its wake in terms of the scale of its investment. The Tokyo International Forum is just the latest and largest in a line of schemes which combine awesome technological accomplishment with genuine artistry.

What does *International Interiors 6* tell us about global design trends? A much-heralded return to Modernism has been consolidated in a body of work which interprets its universal values in a welcome variety of ways, from the delightful Mondrian composition of Bramante Architects' Citizens' Advice Bureau in the UK to the clever Corbusian styling of a music school in Weimar, Germany, by Thomas van den Valentyn. Minimalism in hotels, shops and public spaces is part of this new modern attitude, perhaps as an antidote to an increasingly information-cluttered world.

There is also a counter-trend to the temple-like 'minimum' style espoused by John Pawson, Anouska Hempel *et al*. 'Maximum' style is, in the word of its champion Nigel Coates, about 'orchestrating spaces so that they reflect the multiplicity of life itself'. Coates, Professor of Architecture at the Royal College of Art in London, believes that 'we are at a special moment historically, in which the challenge is not so much to control our environment but to develop it to let go, to release sensual currents instead of hide them, as so much design does'.

Coates's surreal scheme for the triple-height Glasgow pub Bargo in this volume powerfully demonstrates his ideas that 'each project is a potential stage, a world in which relationships are developed dynamically so that no object or space is trapped by its own use'. Other schemes equally elevate the role of fantasy and metaphor – from the clownish nightmare scenarios of Philippe Starck's Theatron nightclub to the evocative thirties Hollywood styling of Gensler's Lincoln Square movie complex for Sony. Even such brand-led retail developments as Fitch's Planet Reebok or Studio Mendini's Swatch Store invite the customer into a dynamic mental landscape of their own making.

It is perhaps in the tension between the rational analysis of the problem-solver and the more subjective, sensual forays of the dream-maker that interior design is currently regaining its creative resonance and credibility. For every scheme in this book which correctly frames its objectives – the Paris office of Andersen Consulting, for example, which is set to save $1 million a year in property costs, or the German lighting showroom of Zumtobel-Staff, which spatially interprets a technical light diagram – there are others which delight in physically expressing the ambiguities, contradictions and illogicalities of life itself.

1 workspaces/offices/studios

Cordless, creative and collaborative, the new workplace is shedding its old bureaucratic traits and embracing more ambitious spatial concepts aimed at bringing people together in dynamic city-like communities

work

THESE are exciting times for workplace interiors. Advances in cordless technologies, new thinking about management change, and a growing belief that barriers to improvements in staff productivity, communication and morale are physical, have combined to unleash a new wave of creativity in office design. Once the rationalist, repressed poor relation of interior design, workplace environments are now bristling with fresh ideas.

The project that really got the ball rolling was designed by Italian architect Gaetano Pesce late in 1994 for the Chiat/Day advertising firm in New York. Pesce remodelled the 38th floor of an anonymous Manhattan tower block into a colourful and convincing 'virtual office'. The total effect was to radically reconfigure our idea of what a workplace could be like.

Since then, Pesce has returned following Chiat/Day's merger with TBWA to extend the key-design themes to the floor below. For the young, techno-literate agency team, with their mobile phones and laptop computers, each day is a new adventure in

1

2

a surreal landscape of resin, rubber and felt. They work where they choose, according to the demands of the current task. Nothing could be further from the traditional territorial office.

Pesce's controversial workspace experiment has attracted worldwide attention at a time when management frustration with conventional office-space planning solutions has reached its peak. Business theorists responsible for encouraging downscaled corporations with flatter hierarchies, have turned their back on the corporate slickness and cellular neatness of the status-oriented modern office. They want more fluid, free-form work environments capable of responding flexibly to changing market conditions. Pesce's metaphor of the office as city, with its alleys, streets and central piazza for social interaction, captured the imagination at the right time.

Chiat/Day's playful, zestful, artful lessons – primarily that the workplace should not be dull and should aim to inspire some measure of 'feel good' social cohesion – have not been lost on office interior designers and architects over the past couple of years. In Fernau and Hartman's scheme for Nickelodeon, the children's cable TV company, there is a similar sense of exhilaration in the layout of parks, streets and neighbourhoods, with distinctive micro-architectural landmarks and chalk-board surfaces bearing friendly messages in public areas.

The head office of the Union Bank of Norway in Oslo, expertly refurbished by Narud-Stokke-Wiig, does much the

1/2 BANK OF LUXEMBOURG, LUXEMBOURG
Designed by Jean-Michel Wilmotte
The spartan elegance of Wilmotte's interior style complements the strong lines of the bank's architecture, designed by Miami practice Arquitectonica. A wedge-shaped tower bisects two blocks in the scheme, creating some powerful interior spaces.

3/4 MICHEALIDES & BEDNASH OFFICE, LONDON, UK
Designed by Buschow Henley
This office for a small media company on the third floor of a former Art Deco factory in central London takes the team working theme to its zenith: a single working table 66 feet long for all staff, supplemented by two quiet rooms. The idea of the office as singular 'resource centre' is reinforced by simple materials – wood, steel, glass, concrete.

5 HYPO BANK, LONDON, UK
Designed by Bernhard Blauel Architects
This 2,500-square-metre scheme for one of Germany's major banks in the City of London has generous reception and circulation areas which provide exhibition space for a fine collection of modern art.

same thing for better social communication, but respects the more conservative culture of a bank with a more restrained palette of materials. A second remodelling of a bank, Pentagram's conversion of the 1913 Lincoln Trust Bank on Fifth Avenue in Manhattan, reflects another decisive trend in office design in the late 1990s: team-working. Pentagram's studio places the partners of the design company on an elegantly suspended mezzanine level in the main banking hall, close to team tables just a few feet above or below, but that is tame stuff compared to other spatial solutions which accommodate collaboration between members of staff.

In Germany, Kauffmann Theilig & Partner's scheme for a company of building engineers, with its transparency and interior criss-crossed by bridges and walkways, is a powerful metaphor for an interdisciplinary mode of working; in London, Buschow Henley's office for a media-strategy company reduces the teamwork setting to its essentials – one long table shared by all 20 employees.

'Work smarter' could be the motto for many of the projects, from the elliptical 'energy-bursts' at corridor intersections in Valerio Dewalt Train's scheme for US Robotics, designed to encourage spontaneous interaction among employees, to the chic finishes of Andrew Chadwick's Parisian office for Andersen Consulting, which is set to save the client a million dollars a year in property costs through the time-metering control of space.

HOK's interior for Catellus, a United States real estate company, typifies many schemes in its concern to unify space using strong architectural forms. The Oklahoma offices of the Ackerman McQueen advertising agency perform a similar task using intriguing forms of artificial light. It would, however, be wrong to suggest that every project is about creating a greater sense of openness and unity. The London headquarters of PolyGram, for instance, exploit the narrow linear shape of the plan to create a series of individual fiefdoms for film and music divisions with cellular office accommodation.

It would also be misleading to conclude that in the last two years innovatory workplaces have been confined solely to the private sector. In France, local mayoral authorities have commissioned a series of signature buildings and interiors, while in Britain there have also been some quality public sector offices, most notably DEGW's refurbishment of the Department of Trade and Industry at Victoria, in London, and Percy Thomas Partnership's giant green work campus at Abbey Wood, in Bristol, for the Ministry of Defence.

The British public sector's finest workplace is its smallest. Gabriele Bramante's Citizens' Advice Bureau at Chessington, Surrey, is an exquisite jewel-like environment on a tiny site that crosses a Mondrian painting with the aesthetic principles of Japanese garden design. This project shows just how far workplaces are responding to the individual, not just the bureaucrat.

1

2

3

work projects

1 MINISTRY OF DEFENCE PROCUREMENT EXECUTIVE, ABBEY WOOD, BRISTOL, UK

Designed by Percy Thomas Partnership

The largest and most ambitious Government office relocation scheme in Britain for a generation. This green work-village cost £273 million to build; it accommodates 4,400 staff in 1.3 million square feet of space, most of it open plan. Particularly striking are the public areas – piazzas, cafés, atria, internal glazed streets, village squares and a circular drum library in the best traditions of Alvar Aalto and Gunnar Asplund.

2/3 CATELLUS DEVELOPMENT CORPORATION, SAN FRANCISCO, USA

Designed by HOK

This 35,000-square-foot scheme for a Californian real estate company on two floors of San Francisco's Gateway Building uses strong architectural forms and subtle colours to enhance the irregular geometry of the building's footprint.

4 SYBASE HEADQUARTERS, PARIS, FRANCE

Designed by Studios Architecture

The headquarters of this software company incorporates a customer centre and training centre in a scheme which skilfully accentuates Sybase's corporate identity.

5 DEPARTMENT OF TRADE AND INDUSTRY, LONDON, UK

Designed by DEGW

This major regeneration scheme for the Victoria HQ of a large Government department incorporates a state-of-the-art conference centre accessed via a new glass and steel entrance.

1.1 fernau & hartman architects
nickelodeon headquarters
new york, usa

Internal streets, piazzas and parks turn the Manhattan base for a children's cable-television channel into a playful setting for social interaction at work

THE entertainment business is infiltrating the corporate heartland of midtown Manhattan. In an area once occupied exclusively by law firms and banks, the offices of a children's cable-television network, Nickelodeon, injects colour and creativity into four floors of a 1970s high-rise close to Times Square. The scheme by architects Fernau and Hartman – dubbed 'the hybrid newsroom-playroom' by *New York* magazine – deliberately sets out to encourage spur-of-the-moment creativity by eschewing the traditional formality of office layouts in favour of a light-hearted spirit of social interaction.

This is achieved by designing the workplace on the model of the city – with internal 'streets', 'parks' and 'piazzas' in which staff can meet on an impromptu basis and exchange 'neighbourhood' ideas. There are more than 20 differently scaled and sized meeting rooms, painted in bright colours and clad in a range of contrasting materials, from perforated aluminium to papier mâché and ribbed steel. The largest is the 'town hall', with a glazed garage door. Passageways are not dead spaces but extending message-boards hung with cork, chalkboard and magnetic metal surfaces, so that people feel they 'belong' in the public spaces beyond their immediate work areas.

Vibrant and refreshingly non-hierarchical, this is a scheme with democratic ideals rarely achievable in such a large space with 400 employees. The designers have tapped into the inherent feel-good factor of the company's own product by achieving a childlike quality and enthusiasm in this project, with its chalkboard doodles, casual clusters of giant bouncing balls and 'history corner', displaying props from Nickelodeon TV shows.

COMPLETED **Summer 1995**

COMMISSIONING CLIENT **MTV Networks**

TOTAL FLOOR SPACE **120,000 square feet**

NUMBER OF FLOORS **4**

RIGHT: The Mediaplatz, one of Nickelodeon's communal spaces, has a chalkboard wall for messages and a galvanized sheet metal Refrigerator Tower (right) with dubbing rooms inside.

EXIT
SMUD
2000LB

ABOVE: The office of the director of on-line services is a mock control room, an ironic gesture in a scheme dedicated to communal working.
ABOVE RIGHT: One of the scheme's many varied meeting rooms with a glimpse beyond of the community outside.
RIGHT: The axonometric shows the overt architectural elements within the plan.

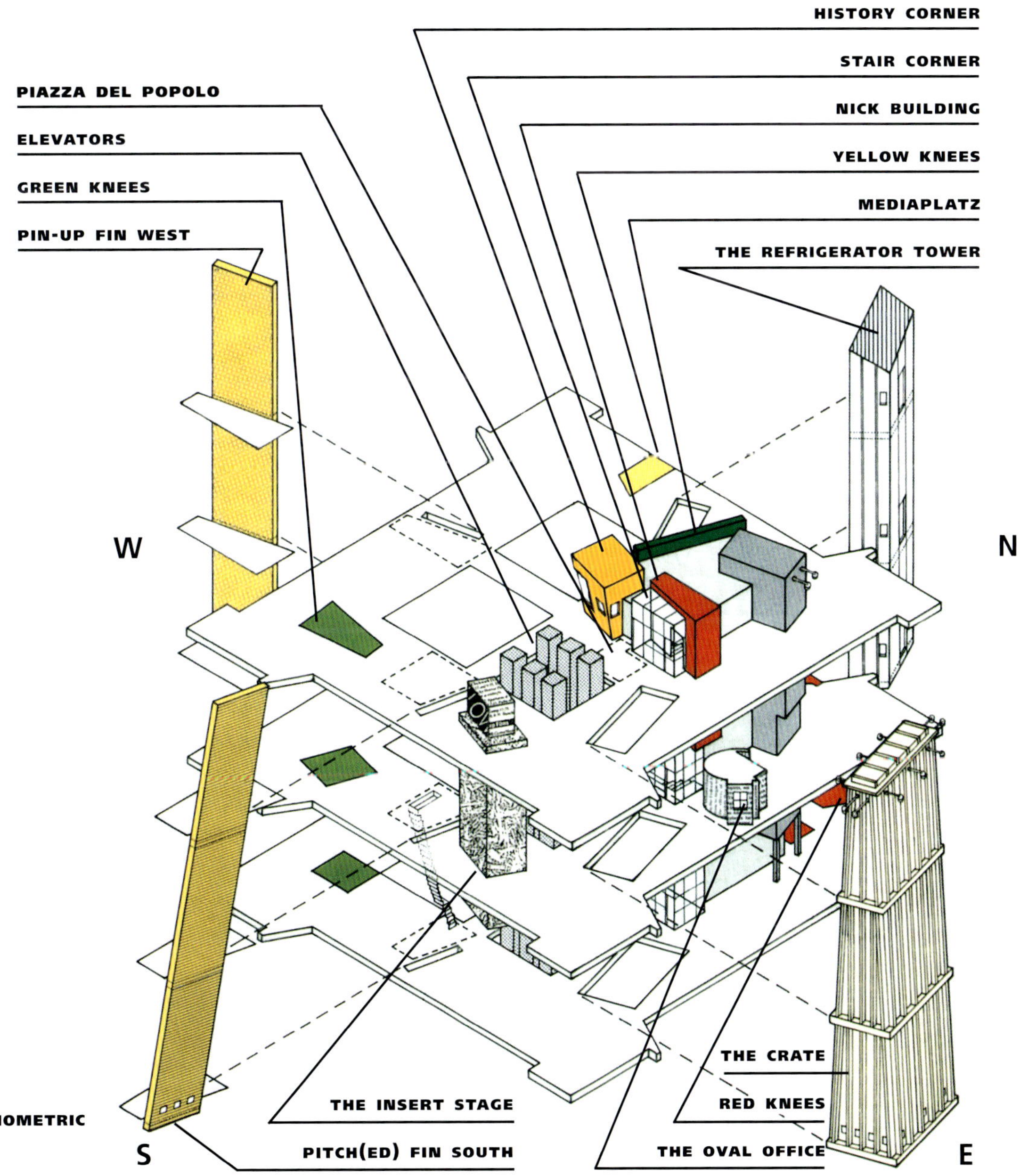

AXONOMETRIC

NICKELODEON
11
KID WASH

LEFT: View from staircase of The Crate, a giant truncated pyramid unit which houses three stacked conference rooms and gives the illusion of a single volume within the space. **BELOW:** The top of The Crate, lit from above, shows the uppermost conference room. **BELOW RIGHT:** The idea of the office as city is expressed in a series of buildings within the building.

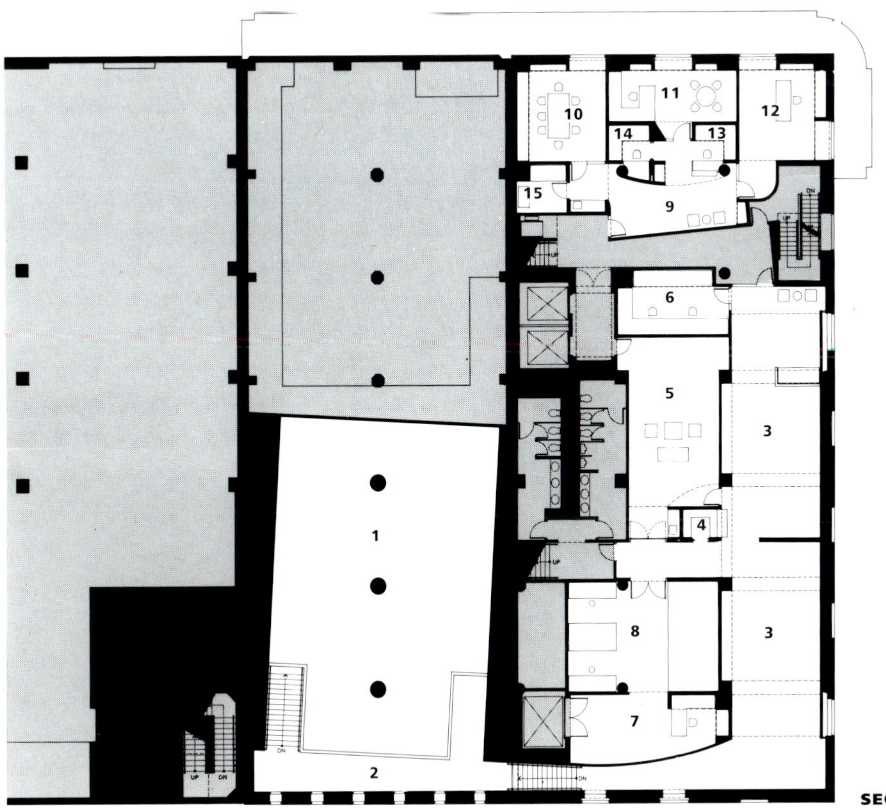

KEY

1 Open to below
2 Balcony
3 Gallery
4 Control
5 Private viewing gallery
6 Photography
7 Receiving
8 Storage
9 Office reception
10 Conference/library
11 Assistant director
12 Director
13 Assistant
14 Registrar
15 Copy

SECOND-LEVEL PLAN

1.2 narud-stokke-wiig a.s. architects

union bank of norway head office

oslo, norway

The careful restoration of existing elements combined with the sensitive introduction of new materials has created a balance between tradition and modernity in this Norwegian bank

SCANDINAVIAN workplaces are renowned for reconciling economic efficiency with humanity and openness. This refurbishment of a distinguished 1920s building in central Oslo by one of Norway's leading architectural practices is no exception. The scheme relocates 650 employees of the Union Bank of Norway to an environment which uses the existing building fabric to suggest the decorum and substance of a financial institution, but introduces new fixtures and materials – oak veneers, glass walls and modern luminaires – with restraint to suggest a contemporary and progressive flavour.

The social heart of the project is a grand double-height banking hall on the ground floor whose original roof glazing had been crudely panelled over to stop leaks. The domed-atrium roof light has now been reglazed to allow daylight into the generous volume of this meeting, restaurant and orientation space. Many other original features have also been retained but subtly reinvented. The banking hall's green marble cashiers' counters, for example, have been redeployed as reception desks; a central expanse of marble flooring has been extended to contrast with new oak flooring for corridors, and marble columns reclad.

One of the main objectives of the scheme, to link the public and more private aspects of the interior, is achieved primarily through the use of a horizontal band of glazing within the timber partitioning system. This allows continuous views throughout almost the entire headquarters, reflecting the democratic principles of participation on which the culture of Scandinavia's workplaces is firmly based.

COMPLETED **January 1996**

COMMISSIONING CLIENT **Linstow Eiendom AS (on behalf of Union Bank of Norway)**

TOTAL FLOOR SPACE **17,900 square metres**

NUMBER OF FLOORS **6 plus 2 basement levels**

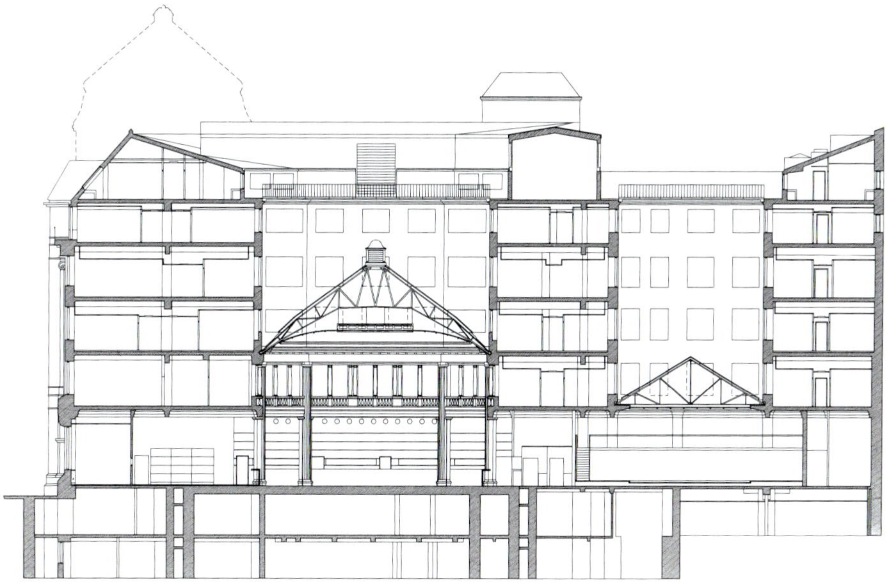

SECTION

ABOVE: The original banking hall designed by Waldemar Hamsteen in a late Art Nouveau/early Art Deco style has been expertly restored to create a light and airy glazed arena for social interaction.

FAR LEFT: New marble flooring on the ground floor creates a sense of continuity, while new luminaires, fixtures and materials suggest a more contemporary spirit.
LEFT: This meeting area with oak-veneered partition walls combines formality and intimacy.
BELOW: A glazed partition unit enhances the project's commitment to creating as open an office environment as possible, despite the bank's obvious need for security.

GROUND-FLOOR PLAN

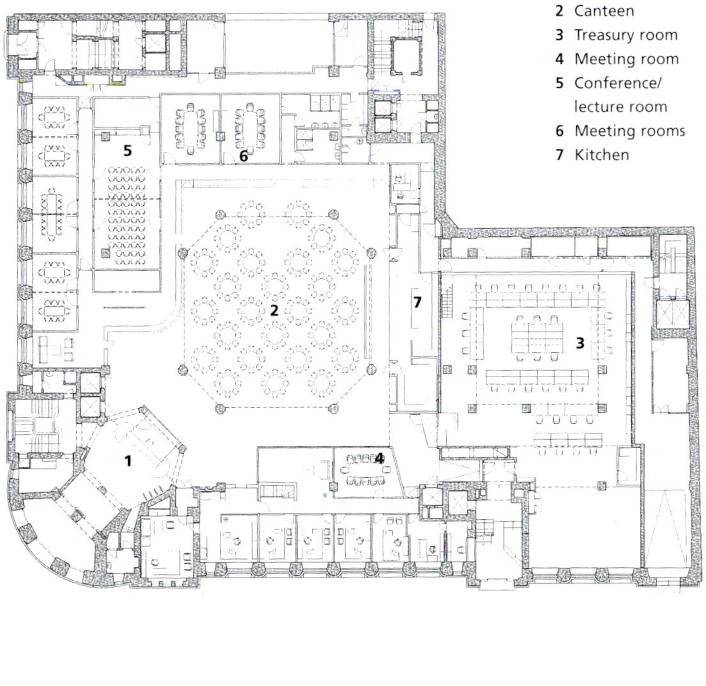

KEY
1 Entrance foyer
2 Canteen
3 Treasury room
4 Meeting room
5 Conference/ lecture room
6 Meeting rooms
7 Kitchen

1.3 valerio dewalt train

ustate us robotics

skokie, illinois, usa

A boxlike office has been transformed into a vital, fast-moving workplace by a series of super-corridors, which create 'energy bursts' at points of intersection through the use of challenging geometries

THIS Illinois interiors project was carried out for the personal communications division of US Robotics, a fast-growing high-tech company. The previous set-up was such that the staff were continually attempting to create social interaction in conditions that were hardly conducive to meeting and greeting colleagues. The scheme involved renovating the very ordinary boxlike premises of the Allstate Insurance building, a typical dehumanizing scientific management workplace of 1958 with its office 'factory floor'.

Designers Valerio Dewalt Train decided to 'invent significance' where none could be found. They created a grid of 'super-corridors' and corridor intersections through the plan to allow people to stop, talk and interact at predetermined 'energy points'. Old acoustical ceilings were excavated to expose the structural concrete deck along these brightly lit 11-foot-high internal circulation streets; and partitions and soffits were added to define specific areas. At the point where these 'super-corridors' meet, there is a geometrical collision of elliptical forms with the rectilinear grid to express the idea of energy bursts. Walls lean, soffits curve and surface patterns change in support of this concept.

The oval shape of the reception area – the visitor's first encounter with this powerful, high-energy environment – is repeated in a series of conference rooms at corridor intersections. The overall effect is hardly reflective or tranquil, but the almost-out-of-control look is a deliberate response to the requirement of capturing the imagination and harnessing the energy of US Robotics employees.

COMPLETED **Autumn 1996**

COMMISSIONING CLIENT **US Robotics Corporation**

TOTAL FLOOR SPACE **42,500 square feet**

NUMBER OF FLOORS **2**

TOTAL CONTRACT COST **US $765,000**

LEFT: The elliptical form of the reception is reiterated throughout the plan at corridor intersections. **ABOVE:** Slots of light in the corridors and exposed ceilings differentiate public thoroughfares from private offices and workstations.

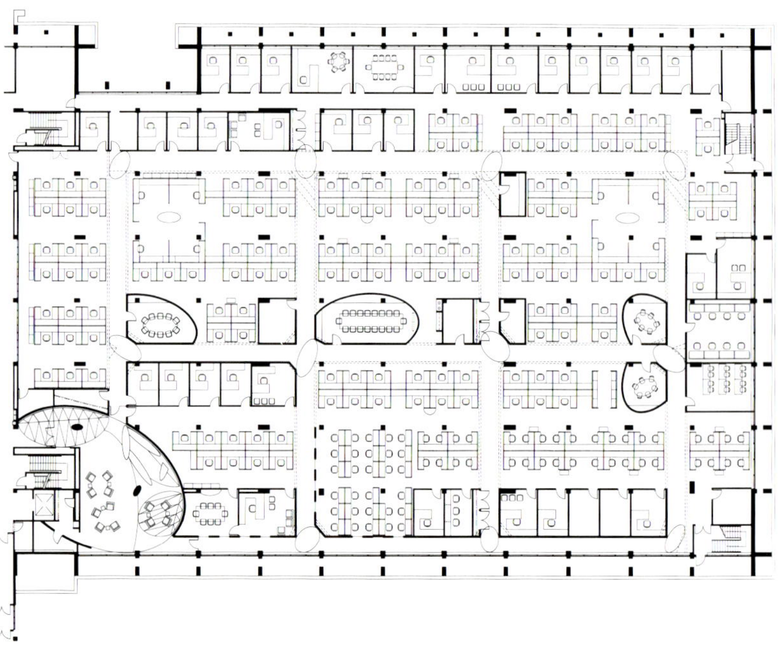

FLOOR PLAN

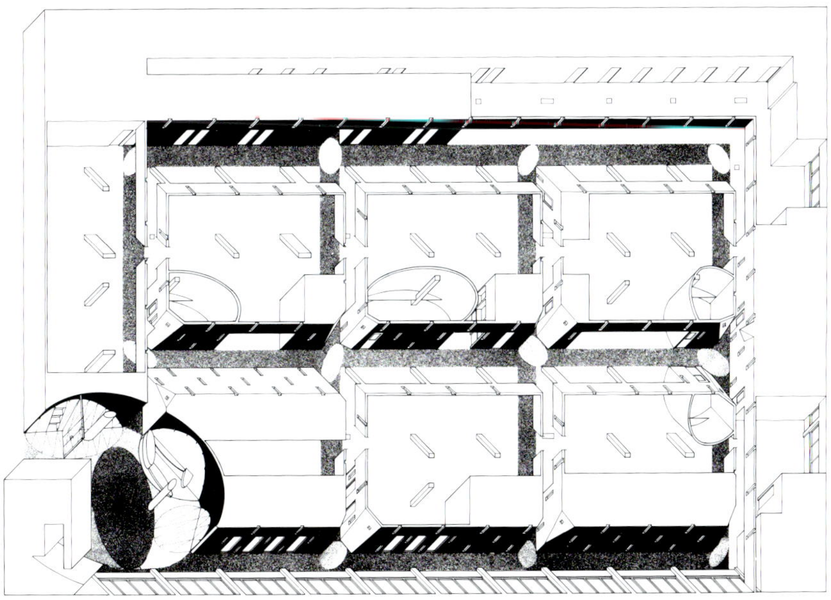

AXONOMETRIC

ABOVE LEFT AND RIGHT: The oval-shaped 'energy bursts', which punctuate the main circulation corridors, are expressed with oval light fittings, furniture, surface patterns and ceiling cut-outs. These combine to create public areas where colleagues can meet and chat.

FAR LEFT AND LEFT: The floor plan shows the elliptical focal elements at key intersection points. The axonometric expresses the powerful pattern of super-corridors which divides the plan into six areas.

1.4 chadwick international
andersen consulting
paris, france

Highly mobile management consultants are given a smart new drop-in office in the heart of Paris, where nobody owns their desk and all space is bookable for a given time

THERE has been far more talk about the 'virtual' office than there have been implemented projects. This relocation scheme, however, in which 1,200 employees of Andersen Consulting have been moved from the windswept campus of La Défense to a new office with 30 per cent less space, closer to the centre of Paris, brings the concept vividly to life. The move is set to save the company $1 million a year in reduced property costs, while giving staff a smarter working environment.

The new headquarters at 55 Avenue George V, close to the Champs Elysées, has seven floors, which fit around a semicircular atrium in an awkward triangular plan, speculatively designed by architect Jean-Michel Wilmotte. If conventionally occupied, the building would only accommodate around 350 people, but UK design consultant Andrew Chadwick has achieved the seemingly impossible by creating the ultimate non-territorial 'space-time' office. Nobody 'owns' their own desk, and space is meted out on a strict booking system. A smart-card entry system to the facility tells employees which fellow staff are in and which spaces are available for use. A sophisticated, concierge system books space on each of the four main consultants' practice floors. The other three floors are given over to reception, support, meeting and client spaces.

In the ground-floor reception area, there is no reception desk. Instead two hostesses dressed in custom-designed couture Balenciaga uniforms stand at minimalist pulpits. The rather ascetic tone of the building, with its hard palette of etched glass, polished aluminium and wood, is softened by the glimpses of Parisian life which seep into the building and are best viewed from the seventh-floor client suites, which include a roof terrace, restaurant and a rotunda.

COMPLETED **January 1996**

COMMISSIONING CLIENT **Andersen Consulting**

TOTAL FLOOR SPACE **7,000 square metres**

NUMBER OF FLOORS **7**

TOTAL CONTRACT COST **25 million French francs**

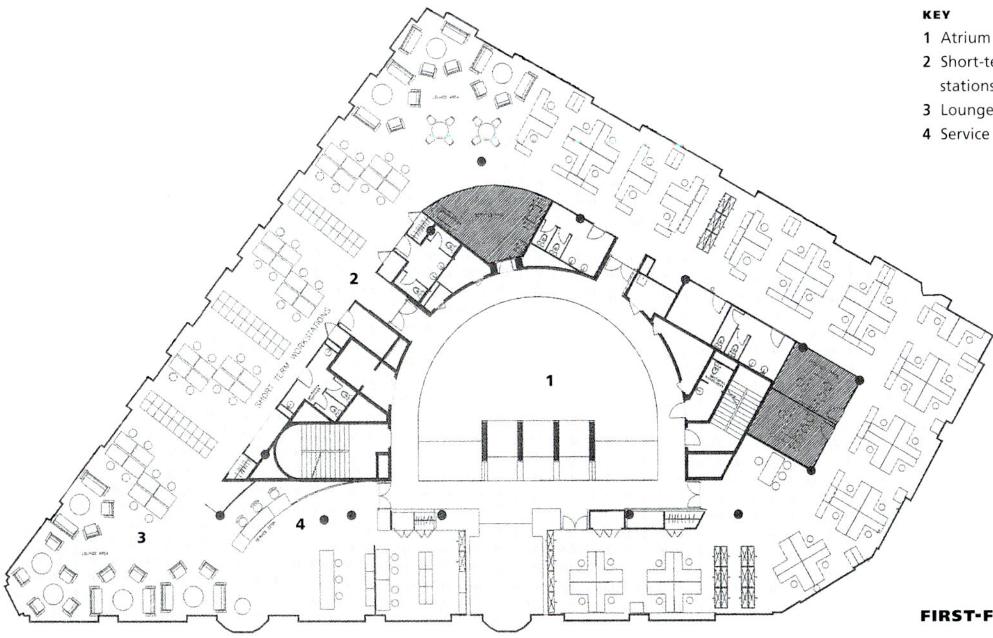

KEY

1 Atrium
2 Short-term work-stations
3 Lounge area
4 Service desk

FIRST-FLOOR PLAN

ABOVE LEFT: Visitors are greeted by two couture-costumed receptionists at the foot of a glass-banded seven-storey semicircular atrium.
ABOVE RIGHT: View of the glazed roofing at the top of the atrium from a roof terrace, with a distant view of the Eiffel Tower.
LEFT: First-floor plan shows a typical practice work environment tightly shoe-horned into an awkward triangular form around the atrium. The lounge, meeting and workstation facilities are all on a strictly timeshared basis.

LEFT: A meeting area on a practice floor. Etched, lined glass divides many spaces, providing acoustical privacy while maintaining a sense of openness. **ABOVE:** The concierge desk at the entrance to the first-floor practice lounge. The idea of the comfortable 'office hotel' is expressed in this environment. Individual spaces within the scheme are named after French philosophers, poets and inventors as part of the move to culturally re-engineer the workplace.

1.5 e.e.a. erick van egeraat associated architects

andrassy boardroom

budapest, hungary

In the debate about Budapest's architectural future, this pod-like extension to a classical building refuses to take sides between the forces of local conservatism and foreign investment

THE architectural tension between the artistic heritage of Eastern Europe's old capitals and the post-communist influx of foreign money and design is vividly captured in this Hungarian office scheme, designed by Dutch architects Erick van Egeraat and Maartje Lammers. A white, classically ornamented building in the centre of Budapest has been respectfully restored, and then topped with a futuristic whale-shaped blob of a boardroom, which protrudes on to the skyline in a stark and thrilling contrast to the original building.

The development is by Czech-born Paul Koch of Nationale Nederlanden, part of the Dutch ING financial group. In the context of Budapest's cautious planning policies, the 'Whale' – as the rooftop boardroom is known – makes an outrageous statement. It also makes a stunning interior space, comprising 26 laminated timber ribs that are hung on to the main load-bearing steel structure. The skin of the room, which has 103 different glass elements, is analogous with shipbuilding in construction. It is lined with linen on the inside and finished with zinc on the outside. The Whale sits on an expanse of glazed roof like a giant lantern, allowing natural light to penetrate deep into the stairwell of the original building.

The marriage of new and.old is inescapable, but the mix is not antagonistic. Erick van Egeraat claims that the more he respected the hundred-year-old building on Budapest's Andrassy Ut, the more he wanted to add 'pure space', which neither represented a repressive conservatism nor automatically resorted to developer's high-tech. The Whale's intervention challenges both extremes in the debate about the architectural future of Budapest and other similar East European cities.

LEFT: Front view of the classical white 1884 building on Andrassy Ut, giving no hint of the drama on its roofline.
RIGHT: Inside the 'Whale'. The board-room is constructed using a series of 26 ash ribs. Each span is slightly different to the next. This is due to the shape of the roof in relation to the main structure.

COMPLETED **Autumn 1994**

COMMISSIONING CLIENT **Nationale Nederlanden**

TOTAL FLOOR SPACE **7,830 square metres**

NUMBER OF FLOORS **10**

TOTAL CONTRACT COST **£32 million**

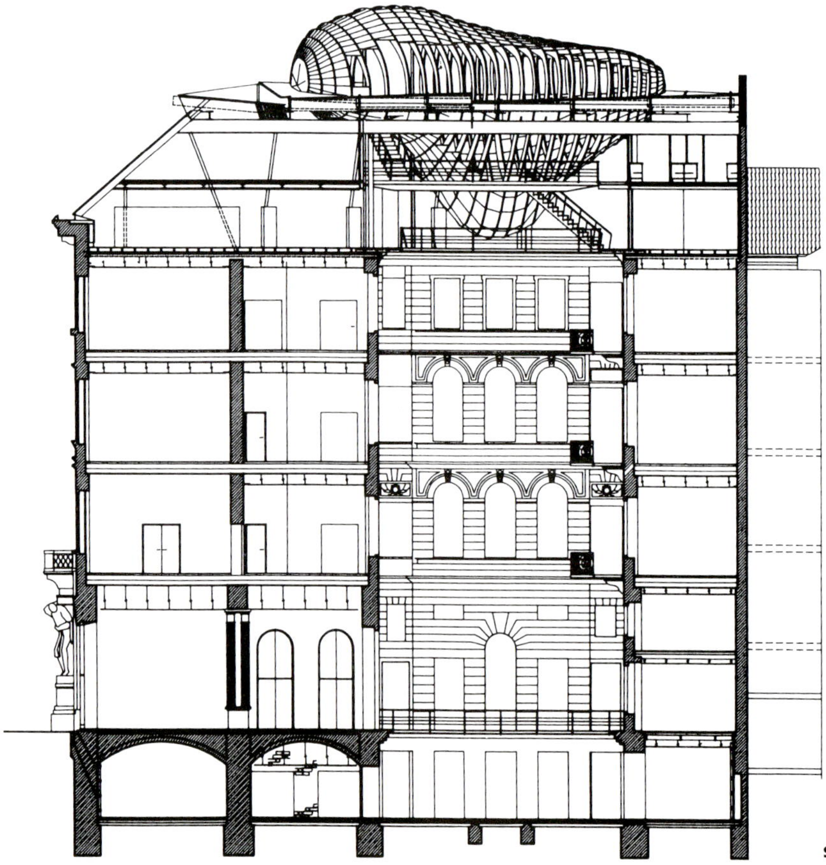

SECTION

PAGES 32–33: The rooftop boardroom at night, sitting like a lantern on a glazed roof. Its glass planes are only supported by glass beams, without any metal frames; the load-bearing glass beams are supported by adjustable stainless-steel forks.
FAR LEFT: Upward view from the ornate, original interior. The wrought-iron banisters frame the protusion of the rooftop Whale.
CENTRE: The boardroom's futuristic form penetrates the building, in a manner described by its architect as 'powerful but not overbearing'.
LEFT: The luminous design of the Whale allows light to penetrate deep into the 10-storey building.

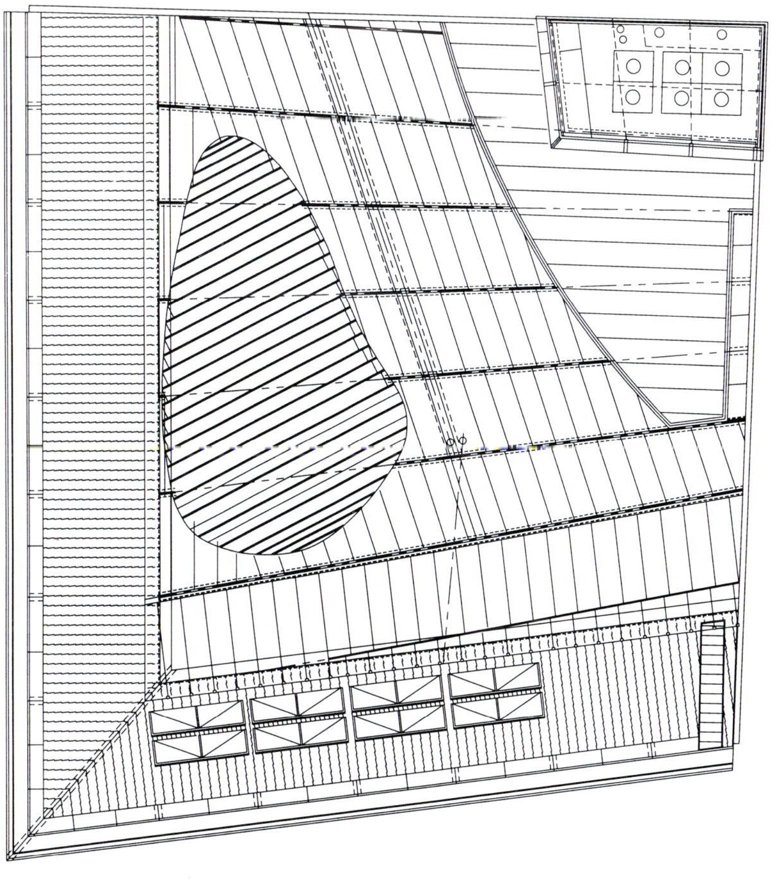

ROOF PLAN

1.6 pentagram architecture design offices new york, usa

A former Manhattan banking hall has been turned into an open and lively design atelier, with the Pentagram partners never more than a few feet away from their teams

BEING your own client is never an easy business. Having five graphic design partners breathing down your neck makes life even harder. James Biber, Pentagram's architectural partner, however, has made light work of the task with this new studio for the New York branch of the world-famous design practice. Number 204 Fifth Avenue is a limestone-façade building, originally designed by C. P. H. Gilbert for the Lincoln Trust Bank in 1913. Since then, it has been a clothing store and a nightclub. Today, the building hums with the activity of design consultants for whom teamwork and community have been the keynotes since Pentagram began in London in 1972.

To maximize the culture of collaboration, Biber turned the original banking hall into a 25-foot-high main studio, an atelier with 'team tables' on the ground floor and an upper mezzanine. The partners sit in a long row of desks on a mezzanine level in-between, either a few feet above or below their team. There are no private offices, although an array of private spaces for teamwork or meetings can be found on every level. As you move between levels, everything is visible to the client. Messy cut-and-paste tasks are confined to team tables in the steel vaults of the basement, where a workshop and archive of printed work is located. The scheme also includes a kitchen, staff dining room, exercise room and library.

There is what Biber describes as 'a careful, almost surgical fit' between Pentagram's design philosophy and the neo-classical robustness of the original building. This is enhanced by graphic wall displays and by the simplicity of fixtures, furniture and finishes, signifying that utilitarian workspace can also be stylish.

ABOVE: Pentagram's Fifth Avenue offices are based in a former bank designed by C. P. H. Gilbert in 1913.
RIGHT: The original banking hall is now the design firm's main studio, a colourful atelier with team tables. The partners are based on the mezzanine level above.

COMPLETED **May 1995**

COMMISSIONING CLIENT **Pentagram Design**

TOTAL FLOOR SPACE **13,000 square feet**

NUMBER OF FLOORS **4**

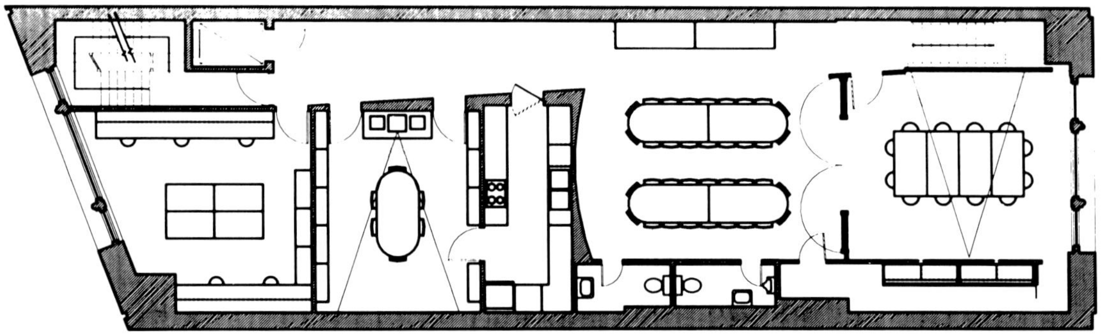

THIRD-FLOOR PLAN

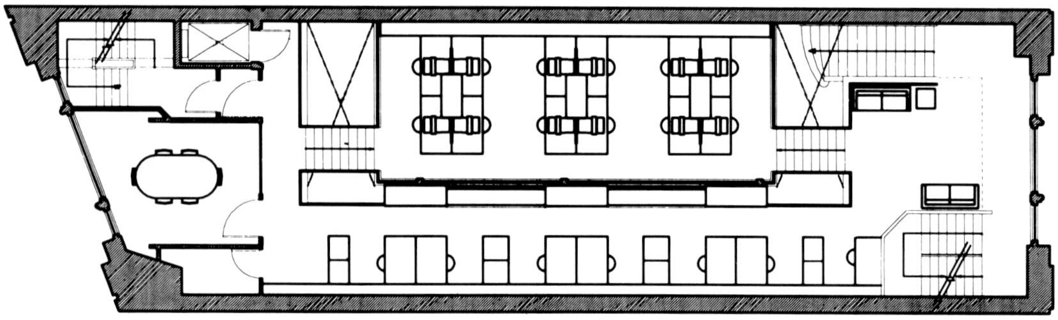

SECOND-FLOOR PLAN

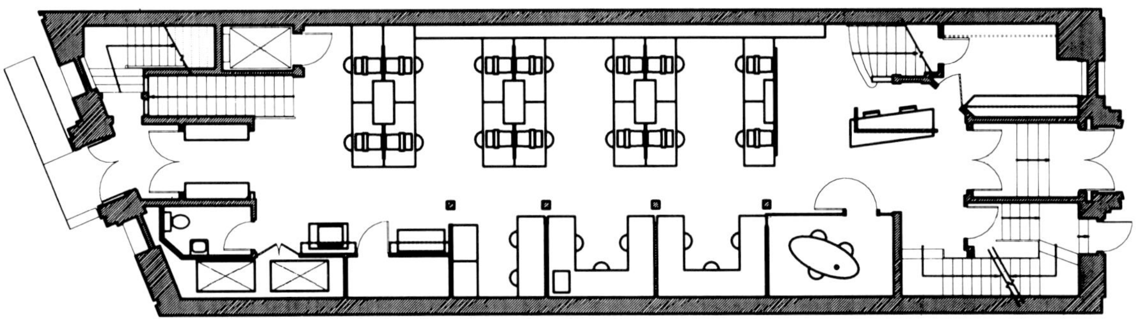

FIRST-FLOOR PLAN

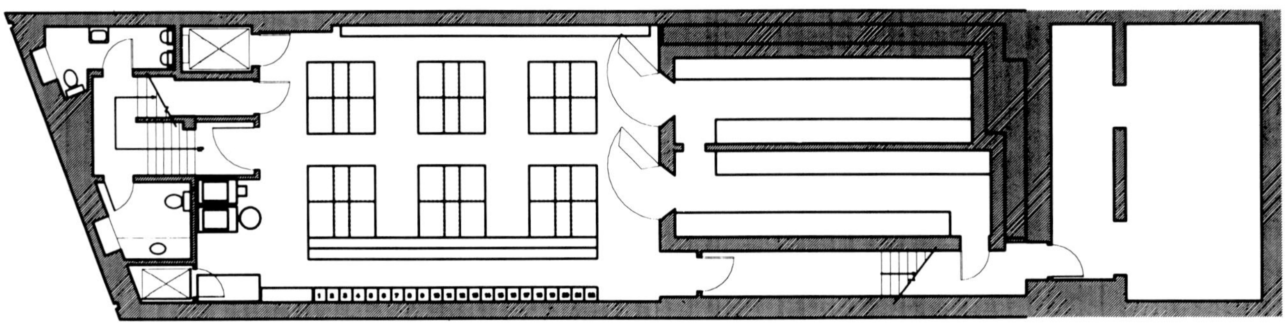

BASEMENT PLAN

ABOVE: In the basement, the former bank vaults make a convenient archive store. Team tables are reserved for messy work.
RIGHT: The view through the open studio reveals an arena for creative interaction as well as a gallery for graphic artworks. The interior features customized furniture and lighting solutions.

1.7 jestico & whiles architects
polygram international offices
london, uk

Behind the sober façade of a wartime Ministry of Labour building, a dramatic steel and glass intervention slices through the ground floor of this scheme for a music and entertainment company

BEHIND THE bland Georgian-style façade of a St James's Square building, designed in 1940 by Angel & Curtis for the Ministry of Labour, architects Jestico + Whiles have struck a highly contemporary note in creating a new headquarters for the music and entertainment conglomerate PolyGram International. The clue to the transformation of the building's dark and difficult interior is in its massive, oversized 7-metre-high solid oak door. This opens on to a long, narrow double-height internal street, which extends past a reception desk aligned to the side wall, across a glass-block suspended bridge with small coffee terrace below, to a rear lightwell.

This dramatic, glass and steel intervention slicing through the length of the ground floor is the unifying feature of a scheme in which the requirement to allow each of PolyGram's activities to create their own independent mini-community was more important than providing a total interior design unity.

The eight-floor building was chosen for its long, narrow, linear form, which invited the subdivision necessary for PolyGram's different departments to inhabit autonomous areas. Finishes and details vary from department to department and reinforce the distinctive identity of each mini community – a zingy, metal laminate and etched glass for Pop, a more traditional veneer for Classics. The fourth-floor senior management area is a sleek cocoon of custom furniture, curved-glass walls and soft-beige carpeting. The spacing of windows at intervals of three metres also assisted the plan, enabling the design of single-person offices with windows that can be opened by individual users.

COMPLETED **1995**
COMMISSIONING CLIENT **PolyGram International**
TOTAL FLOOR SPACE **4,650 square metres**
NUMBER OF FLOORS **8**

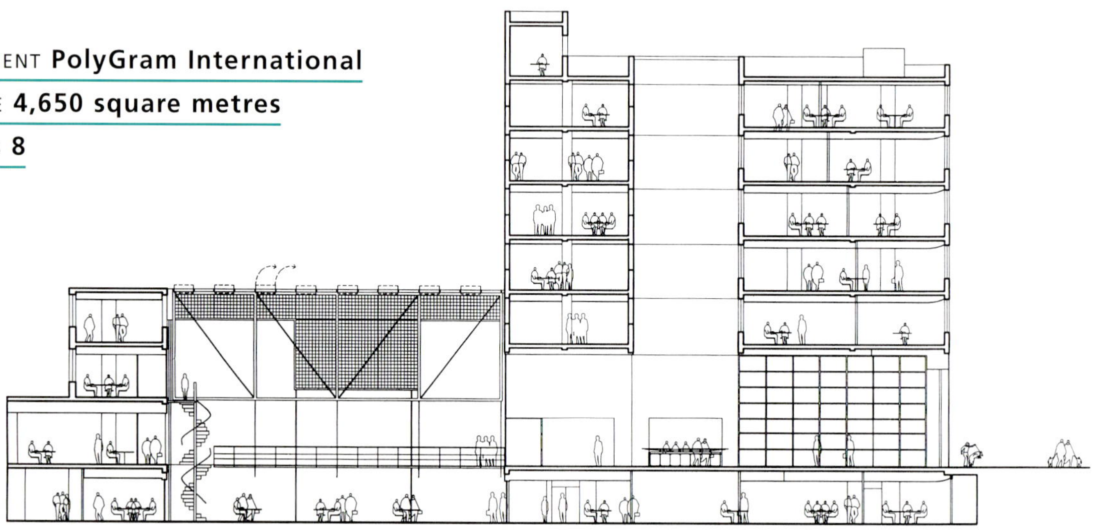

SECTION

ABOVE: This bland 1940 office building in St James's Square appears unexceptional, until you notice the oversized, solid oak door (bottom right), which is the only clue to PolyGram's interior transformation.
RIGHT: View from the lightwell at the rear of the narrow ground-floor reception lobby back towards the front entrance. This dramatic glass and steel intervention is the unifying feature in a scheme otherwise dedicated to giving different departments their own recognizable territory.

AXONOMETRIC

LEFT: A view of the coffee terrace underneath the glass-block suspended bridge. The narrow interior plan was preferred to other offices because of the ease with which it could be subdivided.
ABOVE: The axonometric shows the insertion of the glass bridge and spiral staircase elements into the building within a double-height framed structure.

LEFT: Each office washroom has two spun, stainless-steel washbasins, rimmed with neoprene strips and set below a counter of 19-millimetre-thick etched, toughcned glass which rests on tapered steel channels. These glass fixing details are repeated in glass screens fitted on to cellular offices to enhance views and light.

BELOW: The fourth-floor plan illustrates how the linear form facilitates the creation of cellular office and private meetig space for senior management.

FOURTH-FLOOR PLAN

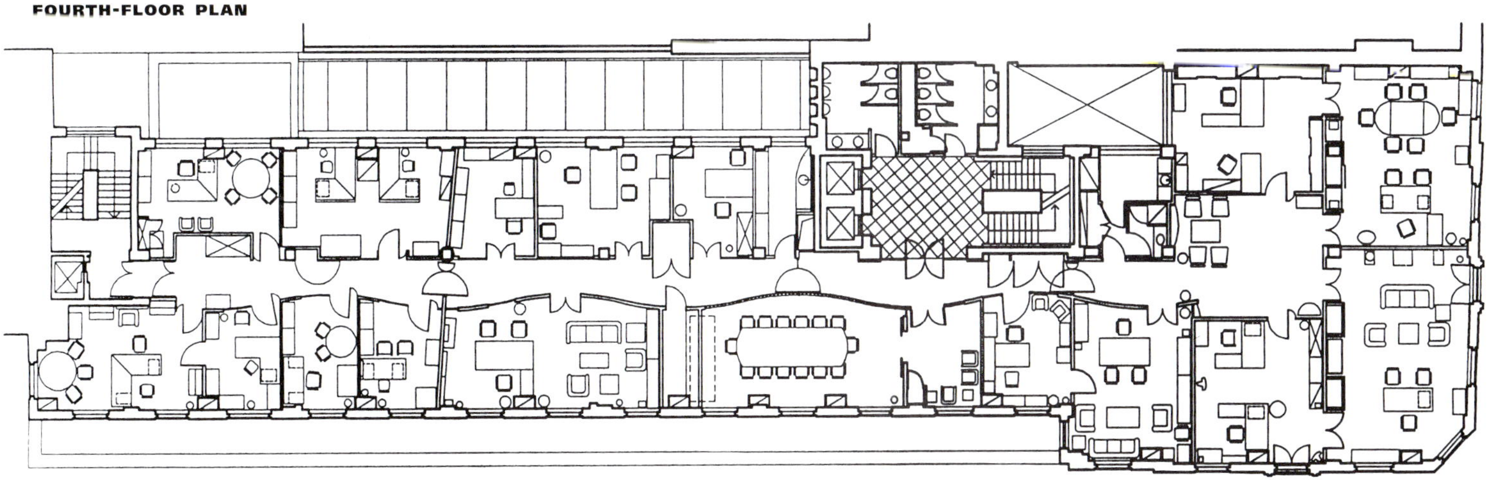

1.8 elliott & associates architects

ackerman mcqueen advertising

tulsa, oklahoma, usa

An office for an Oklahoma advertising agency explores the themes of creativity and ideas generation within concrete-framed interior volumes, full of unexpected spatial surprises

THIS office for a Tulsa advertising agency has been fashioned as a 'dramatic studio for creative thought'. Architect Rand Elliott has conceived his scheme as a stage set expressing what it feels like to be 'on the inside of an idea'. The location on the 12th floor of a 1917 office block, which was once an oil-company drawing room, supports this daring concept. Its poured-in-place concrete structure, with ceilings of 14 and 18 feet high, skylight openings, clerestory windows and structural braces, creates an environment full of unexpected spatial surprises.

Elliott has maximized the opportunities afforded by this unusual structural skeleton to embrace the verticality of the interior volumes. In particular, he has worked with lighting-designer Phil Easlon of Hunzicker Brothers to shape forms and surfaces with light as an expression of the client agency's creativity. Use of clear, etched and black transparent glass complements this layering of messages through space.

A reception desk, with bands of ebony and blue-stained oak, and the company logo, projected as light on to a concrete X-brace, greet visitors. A long gallery space, punctuated with light-filled portholes along a perimeter wall, features a sculptural light box displaying randomly taped campaign images. This gallery connects to a videoconferencing centre at the heart of the project, with 18-foot-tall etched-glass light towers, which glow in the dark, and blue-rope lighting that 'floats' down from a black-ceiling grid used to hang promotional materials and banners. The creative department adopts a different mood: natural light pours into an atelier which imitates an early artist's studio. This is a scheme that is archly self-conscious in its exploration of the act of creativity, but completely natural and liberated in its use of light, structure and texture.

COMPLETED **1994**

COMMISSIONING CLIENT **Ackerman McQueen**

TOTAL FLOOR SPACE **18,700 square feet**

NUMBER OF FLOORS **1**

TOTAL CONTRACT COST **25 million French francs**

RIGHT: The company logo projected on to a concrete structural brace welcomes visitors to the dramatically lit offices of this Tulsa-based advertising agency. 'Lines of communication' are created using light and glass panels within the unusual structural framework.

AM

LEFT: The videoconferencing centre at the creative heart of this scheme is a stageset with blue rope lighting and luminous glass towers which accentuate the verticality of the entire project. **RIGHT:** Poured-in concrete structural elements frame a view of the sculptural light box in the reception area which has advertising campaign images taped to its surface. Despite the seemingly random imagery, the total effect is one of studied calculation.

KEY

1 Elevator lobby
2 Entry
3 Gallery
4 Conference
5 Library
6 Videoconference
7 Art editor's reception
8 Art editor's office
9 Office
10 Art director's office
11 Art production
12 Art workroom
13 Traffic
14 Traffic manager
15 Shipping/receiving
16 Media reception
17 Accounting manager
18 Files
19 Copy
20 Telephone
21 Corridor
22 Mechanical

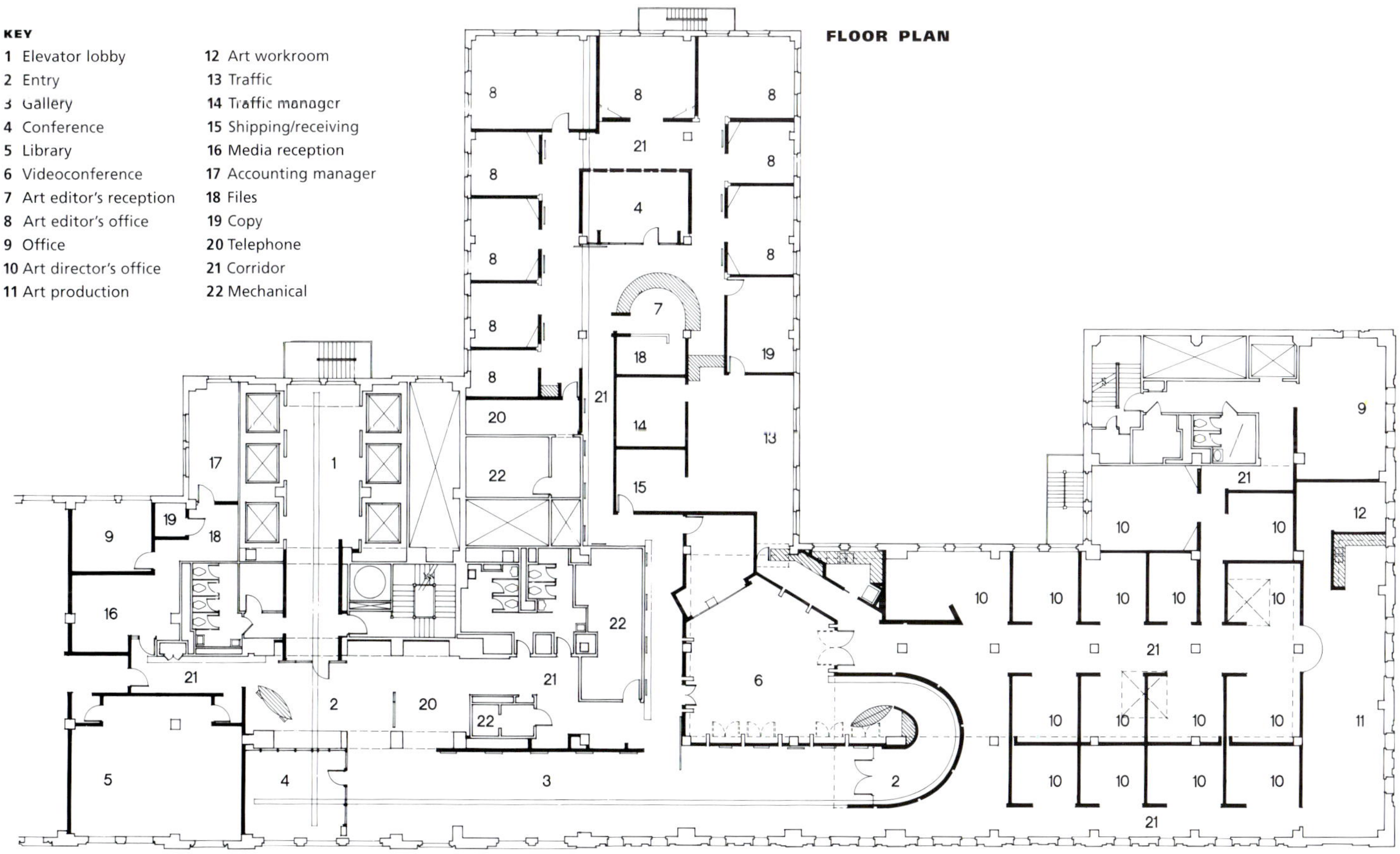

FLOOR PLAN

1.9 reichen & robert architectes
nestlé headquarters
noisiel, france

The architects of Nestlé France's relocated headquarters, on the site of the famous Menier chocolate factory near Paris, turn the tension between the newly built and industrial heritage to their advantage with a series of quality spaces

NESTLÉ France's unification of its business units within a single corporate headquarters has been realized on the site of the old Menier chocolate factory at Noisiel, just 18 kilometres from Paris. This landmark project has relocated 1,800 head-office staff to a setting that benefits from a new-town infrastructure, while evoking a past era of technical innovation. Some of the greatest French architects and engineers of the late nineteenth century worked on the Menier factory, including Gustave Eiffel and Jules Saulnier.

Reichen & Robert's intelligent scheme, which breathes new life into the site, is two-thirds restoration and one-third newly built – a delicate balancing act between industrial heritage and modern business that yields interiors of undeniable quality and interest. The original site – a succession of buildings along the River Marne – has been developed into a green-edged village community with a network of streets, squares, galleries, bridges and quays. Covered walkways and meeting points link a closely knit complex: a group of new buildings to the east of the site adopts the layout of the old Noisiel workers' estate layout and Saulnier's famous mill has been skilfully restored.

Nineteenth-century Noisiel lives again in the architects' carefully researched interior design: extensive study of period colours and original details has produced a vivid spectrum of brick, ochre plaster-work, stone, tile and blue metalwork. Modern elements and insertions avoid the shock of the new by emphasizing elegant lines, sober forms and authentic materials – stone, wood, stainless steel and glass. This is a scheme of many parts, including three restaurants, a cafeteria, gymnasium, shops and individual workstations for every member of staff. If some of the new white and grey offices lack the grand style of the period interiors, then that is only to be expected.

COMPLETED **December 1995**

COMMISSIONING CLIENT **Nestlé France**

TOTAL FLOOR SPACE **60,000 square feet**

NUMBER OF FLOORS **various**

TOTAL CONTRACT COST
620 million French francs

RIGHT: Interior view of Jules Saulnier's famous mill, expertly restored as part of the total rehabilitation of the Menier factory site.

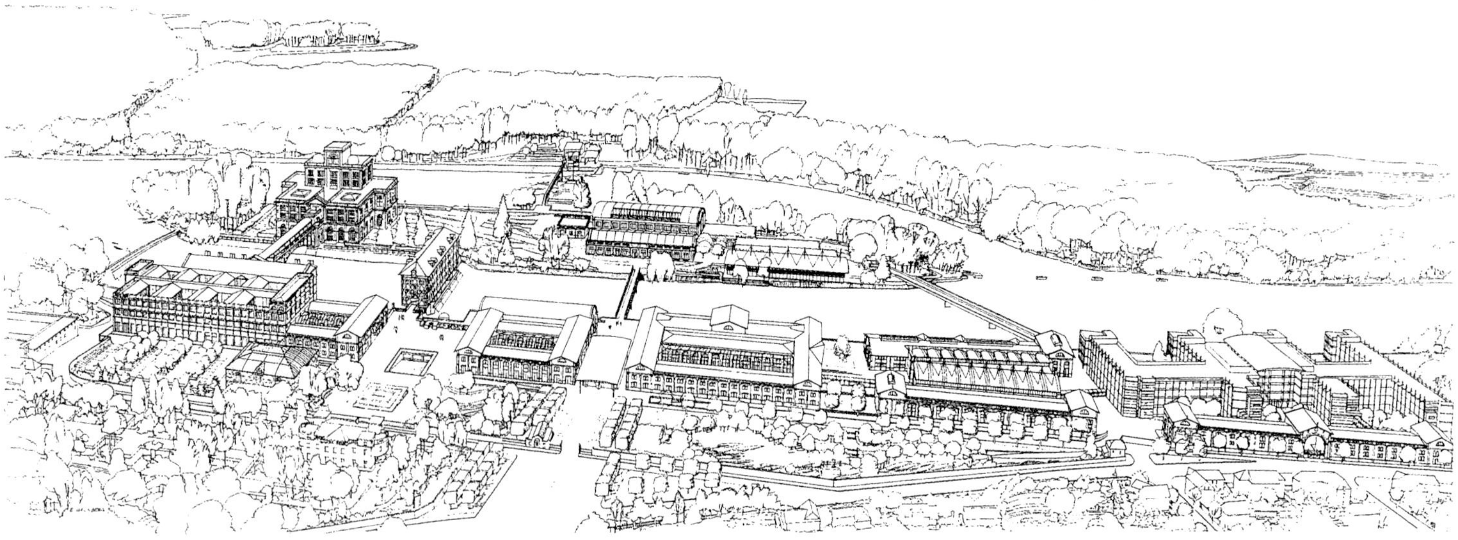

AERIAL VIEW OF NOISIEL SITE

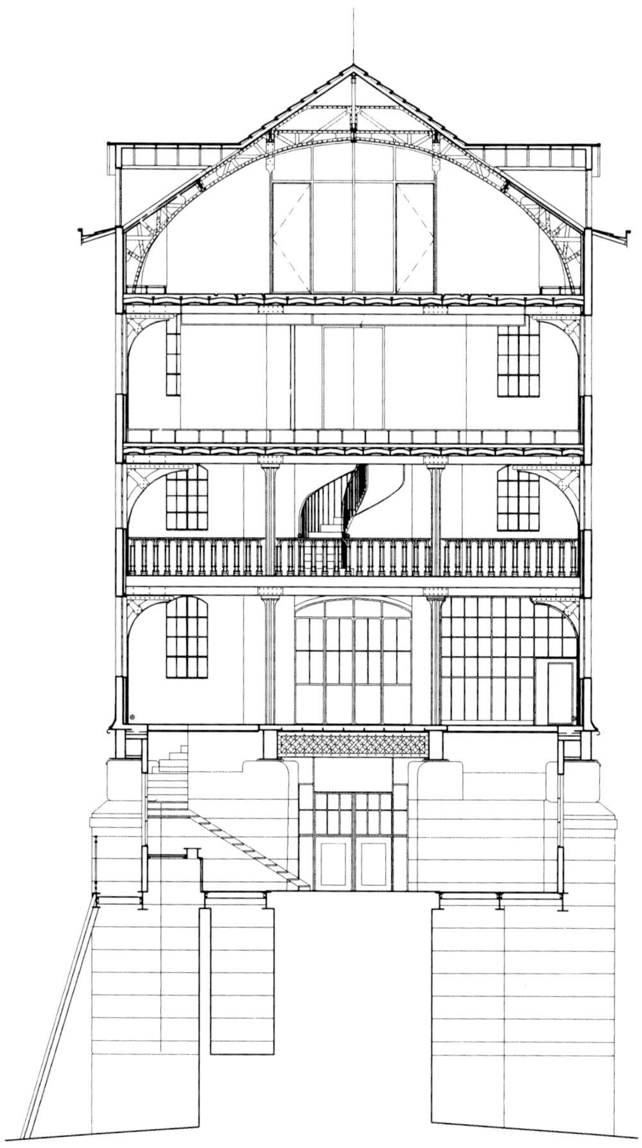

PAGES 50–51: Aerial view (left) shows the coexistence of newly built elements with the traditional decorative architecture of the Noisiel estate. The entire site has been reconfigured as a networked waterside work village. The sinuous spiral staircase (right) is a focal point in Saulnier's restored mill.
RIGHT: Engineering ingenuity and expertise expressed in the restored Eiffel Hall. Like Saulnier, Eiffel was one of a number of great architects and engineers associated with the Menier chocolate factory. It is the heritage of technical innovation that the designers of Nestlé's new headquarters have sought to emulate.

SECTION OF SAULNIER'S MILL

1.10 gaetano pesce
chiat/day advertising offices
new york, usa

Gaetano Pesce's Manhattan advertising office – now extended on to the floor below following an agency merger – is a colourful and provocative trailblazer for the virtual working of the future

GAETANO PESCE'S appearance at the forefront of workplace management theory on account of this innovative 'virtual office' scheme is not entirely a surprise: we have learnt to expect the unexpected from an architect who has combined a fine-art career of often violent and shocking images (dripping blood, disembowelled animals) with a parallel life in industrial design, where he has explored the qualities of resin, rubber, polyester and felt in a highly individual way. Even Pesce himself, however, must have been amazed at how much attention his Chiat/Day workplace has received around the world.

The 38th floor of the Continental Center, a typically anonymous office block in Manhattan's financial district, was first remodelled by Pesce in 1994 in ways which completely reinvented the traditional office and provided a vivid, abstract setting for non-territorial working. It is full of saturated colour and dynamic finishes, the 25,000-square-foot shared space for the mobile, laptop-carrying agency team based on the idea of living in a city with alleys and lanes converging on a central piazza. The entire floor was conceived as a single artwork of poured and brushworked resin.

Since then, Pesce has returned to the project for a second phase in which the 38th floor has been partially remodelled to accommodate a stairwell linking it to the floor below – a further 25,000 square feet of office space was required following Chiat/Day's merger with TBWA. The new floor has large open art and media departments, an evening clubhouse, a post office, a video-production room and other facilities, including private lockers. What was dismissed by many as a 'boutique' project aimed by client Jay Chiat at amassing publicity for his agency is now much bigger, more substantial and more grown-up – even if such original features as a felt playpen, punchbags for staff and brick structures, comprising resin-dipped videocassettes and VCR controls, remind us that Gaetano's view of work remains full of childlike whimsy.

COMPLETED **May 1996**

COMMISSIONING CLIENT **TBWA Chiat/Day Inc Advertising**

TOTAL FLOOR SPACE **50,000 square feet**

NUMBER OF FLOORS **2**

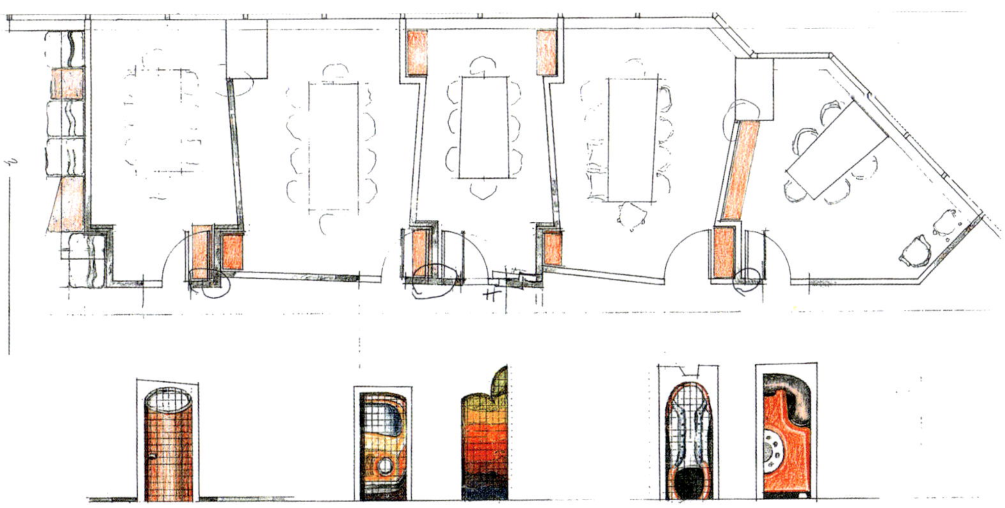

ABOVE: The mobile 'work anywhere' culture of Chiat Day expressed in colourful, free-wheeling public space. The entire floor level of the 38th floor was conceived by Pesce as a single artwork of poured and brushworked resin. **LEFT:** Private rooms are devoted to client projects rather than staff. Pesce designed doors to these rooms as idiosyncratic message-carriers which say something about the nature of the client business.

38TH-FLOOR

MODEL OF THE OFFICES ON THE 38TH FLOOR

TOP LEFT: Pesce's model of the 38th floor reveals its design in terms of a complete artwork offering a range of different spaces to explore. He likens office life to 'living in a city – you are familiar with the area, you aren't intimate with the details'. **BOTTOM LEFT:** A door opens into a client project room for a drinks manufacturer. **ABOVE:** Movable staired float in the office's central piazza. Staff make speeches from it and eat their lunch on it. Evidence of Pesce's vibrant material invention is everywhere.

1.11 kauffmann theilig & partner
house of engineers
herrenberg, germany

This airy and transparent office for a group of building-engineers creates a relaxed and informal network of bridges and walkways that encourages interdisciplinary collaboration between colleagues

THIS unusual multi-level workplace for a German building consultancy is an engaging essay on the materials and techniques of construction. Its sense of transparency suggests how the different elements of an environment fit together, as well as providing a pleasant collaborative space for engineers from different disciplines to work together. It was commissioned by Helmut and Monika Wetzstein, whose consultancy had expanded from electrical engineering to embrace a whole range of building services. The brief they gave to the architects was for an office with easy internal communications to promote co-operation across specialist fields.

This has been interpreted as an angular glass structure filled with natural light, and traversed by a complex arrangement of walkways, bridges and a spiral staircase offering views into all corners of this exceptionally open building. Glass-panelled interior office spaces are fitted with wooden-framed casements, which can be opened to allow colleagues to chat. To balance the needs for group-meeting space and private areas where people can work undisturbed, each floor is dissected by a right-angled network of walkways of different widths. The main walkway runs along the building's central axis, widening into an atrium under the glass roof at its centre.

Given the expertise of the consultancy, the building's heating, lighting and ventilation make optimum use of natural-energy sources. State-of-the-art building controls provide a technological counterpoint to the simple, studded-wood panels that face on to public areas and other low-tech delights, such as exotic plants, an artificial pool and a sea-water aquarium – all contributing to a relaxed environment.

COMPLETED **1994**

COMMISSIONING CLIENT **H & M Wetzstein**

TOTAL FLOOR SPACE **3,500 square metres**

NUMBER OF FLOORS **3**

TOTAL CONTRACT COST **approx. DM 9 million**

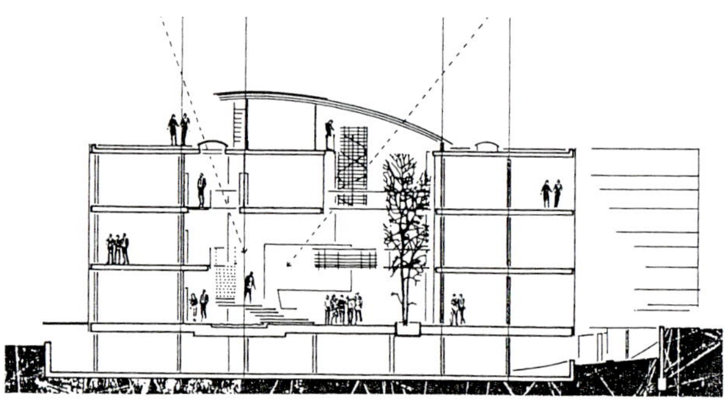

LEFT: Section through a building designed to encourage more open ways of working.
RIGHT: A lightweight spiral staircase and bridge-walkways draw the eye in the main atrium space.

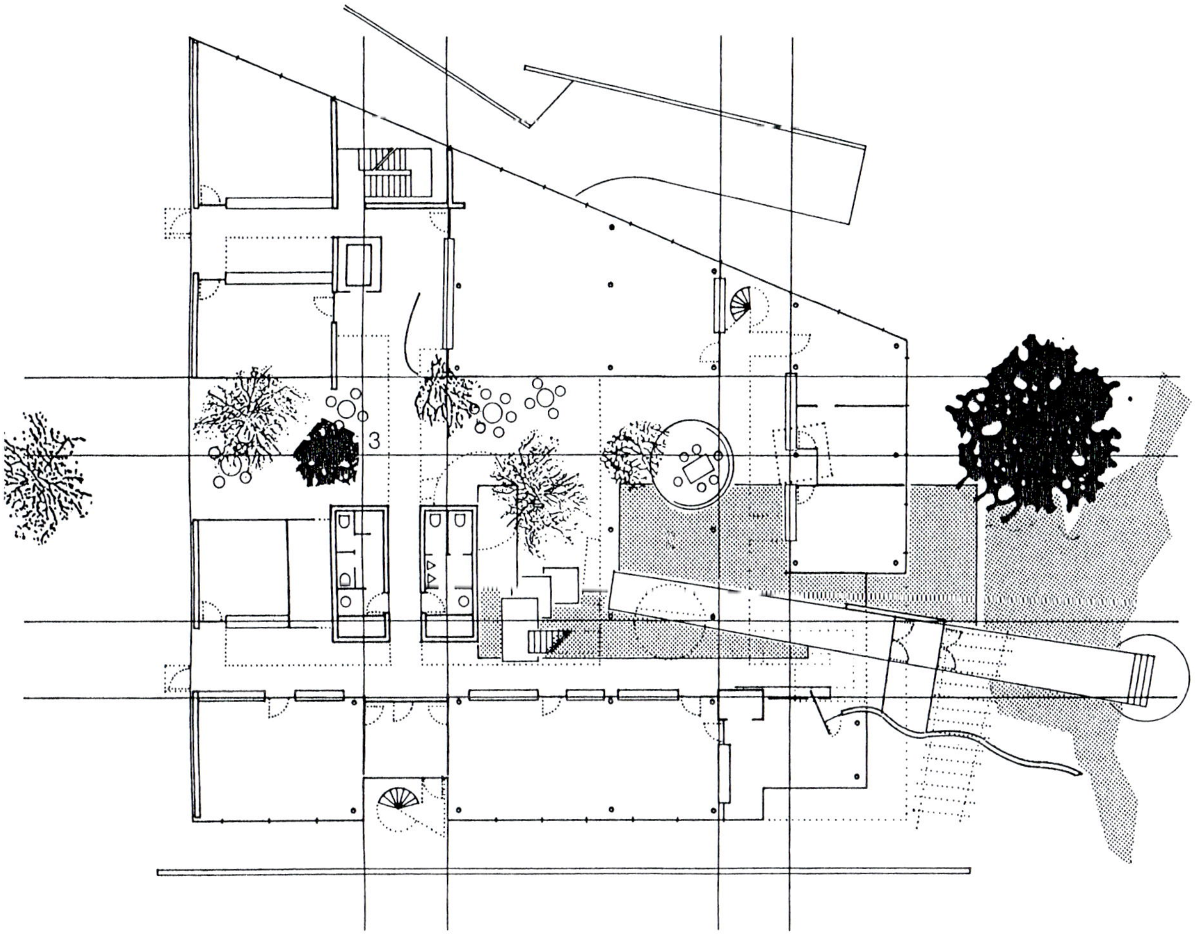

GROUND-FLOOR PLAN

LEFT: Glass-panelled office with wooden partitions offers a mix of openness and privacy.
ABOVE: The floor plan shows a typical linear work floor enabling different engineering disciplines to collaborate. Areas are linked by a network of walkways.
RIGHT: Looking up into the spiral staircase. The scheme delights in creating simple constructional elements.
BELOW: Conceptual sketch showing the office building as an open landscape.

1.12 bramante architects
citizens' advice bureau
chessington, uk

A jewel-like Modernist box on a very constrained site yields interiors of surprising generosity and quality in a project inspired by the proportions of Japanese garden design

SEEKING advice in a Citizens' Advice Bureau has traditionally been a dark, dirty and depressing experience. Lack of funding has created a culture of make do and mend. Architect Gabriele Bramante's achievement, however, in creating a jewel-like building on a tiny 10-metre-square plot of land in Chessington completely changes perceptions of what the interiors of such facilities can be like.

Despite many constraints – the site was hemmed in on three sides and the budget required that the designers themselves raise some £200,000 in cash, as well as free materials and labour towards the project – the new environment is a light and welcoming public building easily accessible to disabled people. Bramante was inspired by Japanese garden design, in which tiny spaces create the illusion of the whole universe, and applied its aesthetic principles. These are especially apparent in the layering, transparency, melodic progression and proportional logic of the interior spaces, and what she describes as 'the glorification of the glimpse'. No dimension or detail is arbitrary in this carefully crafted environment.

Despite its scale the Bureau is an 'intelligent' building which promotes new technology and uses high-tech sensors to control light and heat. A continuous honeyed-stone plane links the external and internal floor, while the seamless sense of unity is further expressed by built-in beech joinery and furniture. From the outside, the building is a steel-framed modern glass box with coloured panels inserted like the composition of a Mondrian painting. Internally, however, the Modernism becomes less European and more Japanese, creating delicate, sensual, and surprisingly generous spaces.

ABOVE: View into the Citizens' Advice Bureau through the south wall reveals the seamless progression from exterior to interior spaces of exceptional clarity. **BELOW:** Beautifully detailed, beech pigeon-holes are a central feature of the double-height resource area for administration and information storage.

COMPLETED **September 1995**

COMMISSIONING CLIENT **Kingston Citizens' Advice Bureaux Service**

TOTAL FLOOR SPACE **200 square metres**

NUMBER OF FLOORS **2**

TOTAL INTERIOR FIT-OUT COST **£127,800**

STARLITE CLEANERS

GROUND-FLOOR PLAN

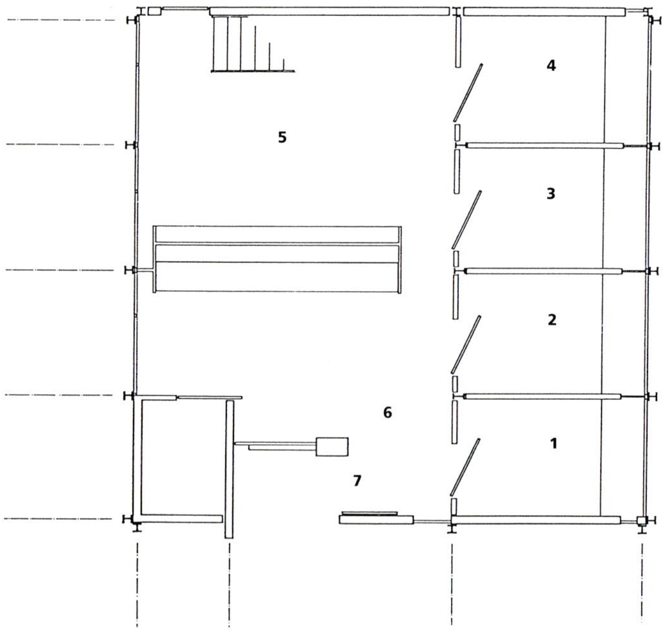

FIRST-FLOOR PLAN

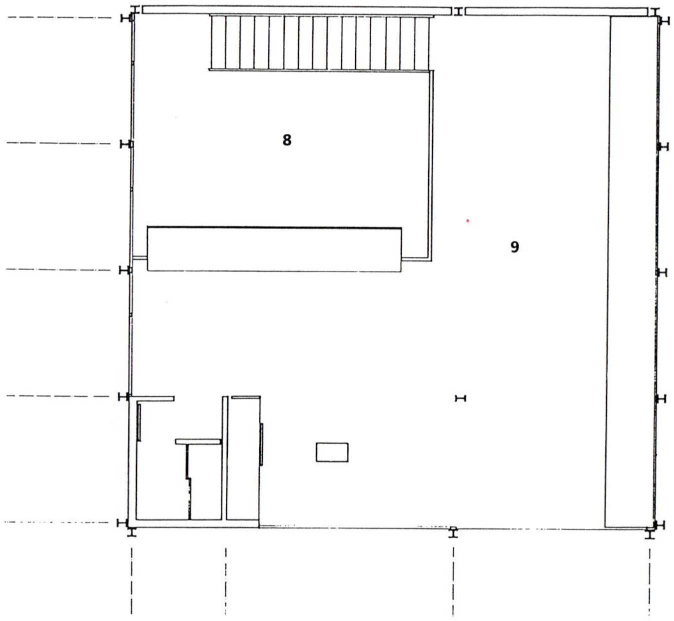

KEY

1 Interview room **2** Interview room **3** Interview room **4** Interview room **5** Meeting room **6** Waiting area **7** Entrance **8** Office **9** Void

LEFT: Artemide desk lamps and high quality beech joinery express the simple, uncluttered finesse of an upper work area. **RIGHT:** Coloured columns form part of the scheme's Mondrian-like composition. The yellow column disguises a service riser.

2 restaurants/cafés/bars/clubs/hotels

leisure

The big restaurant revival in swinging London has set the tone internationally for more confident leisure interiors which put the accent on metaphor, fantasy and role-playing in designer hotels, stylish bars and quirky nightspots

LEISURE interiors struggled in the early 1990s as worldwide recession hit consumer spending and designers were forced to eke out their fantasies on limited budgets. In the past couple of years, however, leisure environments have made a strong comeback, not on the triumphalist scale of a decade ago, but in the upper register of the bold and brassy.

Nowhere is this recovery of nerve more apparent than in London, recently given official status as the world's hippest city by *Vanity Fair*. The 'Big Restaurant' is back on the menu as London once again pulsates. Architect Julyan Wickham's 220-cover Bank – showcased in our selection – follows on from Terence Conran's Mezzo, Rick Mather's Avenue, Ron Arad's Belgo Centraal and Marc Newson's Coast in format. They all serve ultra-contemporary design, glamour, theatre, noise, art and that most intangible and necessary of ingredients, buzz – and yes, they even dish up food, but that's rarely the real issue.

Bank entertains its diners with Hopperesque murals and vibrant colours beneath a continuous horizontal chandelier

1

2

of greenish-glass fins, resembling a slowly melting glacier. The narrative quality of London's new restaurant landscape is augmented by refurbishments of such famous venues as Bertorelli's, given a poppy 1950s-retro style by Harper Mackay; by smaller schemes by younger architects, for example the finely crafted Soba noodle bar by David Adjaye and William Russell; and by the continuing regeneration of sites along the River Thames for eating and entertainment. Conran's spectacular gastrodome close to Tower Bridge at Butler's Wharf draws more and more people, while the remodelling of the Oxo Tower has yielded a popular riverside café designed by Apicella Associates, as well as a Harvey Nichols-branded restaurant by Lifschutz Davidson above.

Add to all of that a new wave of designer London hotels such as the Hempel and the Metropolitan, and the emergence of stylish sports clubs, in such unlikely urban nooks as the six arches of Cannon Street Station, and you can see why *Vanity Fair* chose to announce: 'London finds itself cast once again as the Futura 2000 of cities, the place to which we must all look to learn how to act, think and dress.'

Interior designers have played their full role in this renaissance, exporting this metropolitan buzz to animate the nightlife in other large British cities. In Manchester, Oliver Peyton – the restaurateur behind Coast – has opened a new 40,000-square-foot food palace called Mash, again designed by

1/2 HEMPEL HOTEL, LONDON, UK
Designed by AHD
This small, 43-room designer hotel in the Bayswater area of London was developed by Anouska Hempel Designs to create an oasis of minimalist Oriental calm in the heart of the metropolis.

3/4 THE CAPITOL, MELBOURNE, AUSTRALIA
Designed by Kovacs Architecture
Changing coloured light, washing over sinuous form, is the characteristic of this abstract Melbourne nightclub designed by Tom Kovacs in a 2.8-metre-high basement space.

5 BERTORELLI'S RESTAURANT, LONDON, UK
Designed by Harper Mackay
One of London's most famous Italian restaurants, opened in 1913, has been refurbished in a vibrant retro-1950s style to compete with the new wave of design-led eateries in the city.

3
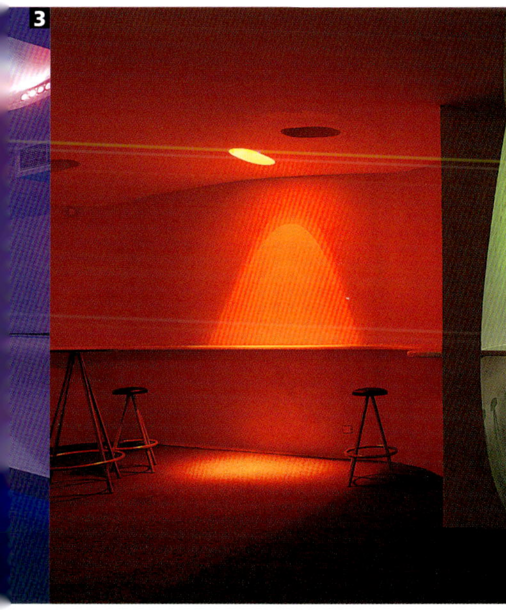

4

5

Marc Newson. In Glasgow, designated City of Architecture and Design for 1999, Branson Coates's Bargo for brewer Tennents in the city's former Cheesemarket reinvents the British pub as a piece of pure social theatre in a spectacular triple-height space.

Meanwhile, offshore sits the QE2, the world's best-known cruise liner and once a symbol of classic 1960s British design by Dennis Lennon and James Gardner. Today, it too is back in shape – rescued from being a period piece by MET Studio's sympathetic master plan, which gives its public areas a more contemporary style while simultaneously evoking the pre-war glamour of luxury liners.

The role of metaphor and fantasy on board the QE2, and in such schemes as Bargo, where timber frames, steel plates and greenish light seeping through portholes create the aura of the dockside factory, cannot be over-emphasized. British designers, however, do not have a monopoly in this area. David Rockwell's Tapika Restaurant, for example, introduces Texan ranch motifs and prairie wheat to midtown Manhattan in an ironic way. Another New York project, Gensler's giant Sony film-theatre in Lincoln Square, captures the golden era of the American movie palace of the thirties in a glittering sequence of gilded palm trees, Decoesque counters and replica studio-lot gates.

Gensler's work is historically accurate, especially in its recreation of entrance detailing from Hollywood's old Loews Theatres, now owned by Sony. Some leisure environments, however, do not need to lean on such overt symbolism to create a mood. Lighting effects alone can paint an entire leisure environment, as Tom Kovacs' Capitol nightclub, in Melbourne, and Tsujimura Hisanobu's Ricordi Café, in Kyoto, demonstrate.

Kengo Kuma's transparent Japanese guest house, sitting on a high coastal bluff above the Pacific Ocean, stands apart from the crowd in that it requires neither symbols nor theatrical lighting to define itself. Its concern is only to frame and filter the exterior view; it suspends three glass-walled rooms on a water-filled roof above the waves, creating a seamless unity between exterior and interior.

At the other extreme, projects by two French designers in our selection go out of their way to dictate the terms of an enclosed fantasy world without reference to exterior context. Andrée Putman's starry-night themed Sheraton Hotel interior at Paris's Charles de Gaulle Airport insulates itself from its surroundings – the external noise and vibration of a transport nexus – which demand a calm oasis. Philippe Starck's extraordinary Theatron nightspot in Mexico City takes the clubber on a descent to the 'edge of insanity' in perhaps the most extrovert scheme in our selection.

London may currently be upstaging Paris in the style and gourmet wars, but as Theatron and the Delano Hotel in Miami demonstrate, in Starck the French still have interior design's most potent weapon.

leisure projects

1 CAFE RICHELIEU, THE LOUVRE, PARIS, FRANCE
Designed by Jean-Michel Wilmotte
Wilmotte collaborated with artist Daniel Buren to create the black-and-white striped theme which extends from furnishings to ceramic tableware in this scheme.

2 DELANO HOTEL, MIAMI, USA
Designed by Philippe Starck
The latest in a line of hotel-renovation collaborations between Starck and former Studio 54 impresario Ian Schrager, which has already given New York the Royalton and the Paramount. The Delano's Deco style on the Atlantic seafront receives a calm, classic, simple treatment which defines the soulful, whiter-shade-of-pale *Zeitgeist* of the late nineties, just as the Royalton's colourful swirls expressed the having-it-all late eighties. The interiors use 40 different shades of white.

3 COAST RESTAURANT, LONDON, UK
Designed by Marc Newson
The creamy contours of Newson's interior design for restaurateur Oliver Peyton set the mark in the London designer restaurant wars. Its highly contemporary composition seats 150.

4 SOBA NOODLE BAR, LONDON, UK
Designed by Adjaye and Russell
This Japanese noodle bar in Soho reflects David Adjaye and William Russell's interest in playing with structure, space and light in a filmic way. Soba means 'close to you' as well as 'wheat noodle' in Japanese.

3

4

2.1 kengo kuma & associates
water/glass villa
atami city, japan

High above the Pacific Ocean, this corporate guest house acts as a frame and filter to the natural environment and reconnects modern Japanese design to a tradition of well-crafted, translucent serenity

THIS CORPORATE guest house, 180 kilometres south-west of Tokyo, stands on a bluff high above the Atami coastline overlooking the Pacific Ocean. Its designer Kengo Kuma has exploited this spectacular natural setting with a transparent structure in lightweight materials – primarily glass sheathed in a slender steel frame – which expresses the Japanese traditions of delicacy, serenity, craft and translucency in a highly contemporary way. A sense of history permeates the site, not least because Kuma's new villa stands next door to the Huga Villa, the only architectural work by the German Bruno Taut to survive from his six-year stay in Japan during the 1930s.

The centrepiece of Kuma's design is the top floor, which dissolves all sense of interior and exterior by 'floating' three glass-walled spaces – two rectangular guest rooms and one jewel-like oval lounge – on a 15-centimetre-deep artificial pond constructed in cantilevered steel and granite. This water-covered section unites the building with the ocean. Inside the oval lounge, gently lit from beneath, transparent furniture designed by the architect enhances the quiet sense of reflection and translucence.

Kuma conceived his design as a bridge to the natural environment, rather than as an obstacle to it. His work can be seen as turning the clock back for Japanese interiors. The postwar Japanese architectural movement, led by Kenzo Tange, made monumental statements in concrete according to Western models. Kuma is seeking to recapture the purity and calm of an indigenous design culture which is centuries old.

COMPLETED **March 1995**

COMMISSIONING CLIENT **Bandai Corporation**

TOTAL FLOOR SPACE **1,125 square metres**

NUMBER OF LEVELS **3**

ABOVE: Night view towards the oval lounge from the guest room. The transparency of the entire project is expressed by the under-lit flooring which dissolves all barriers between the villa and its dramatic natural surroundings.

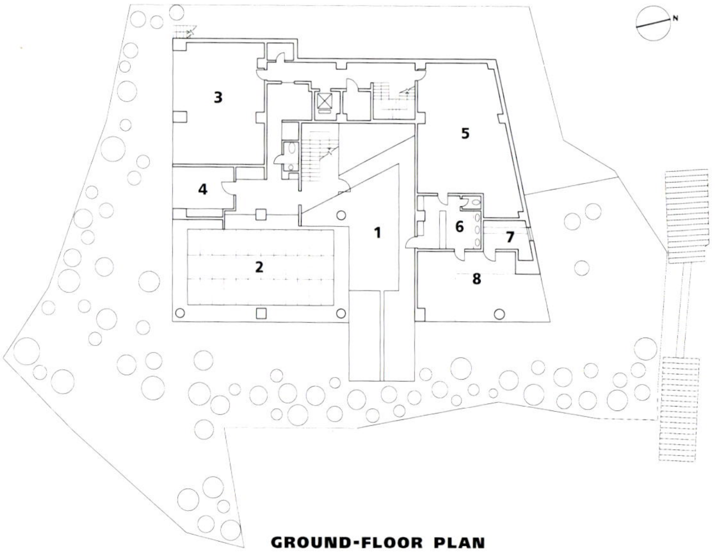

GROUND-FLOOR PLAN

KEY

1 Pool
2 Japanese-style room
3 Administration office
4 Meeting room
5 Machine room
6 Dressing room
7 Sauna
8 Bath

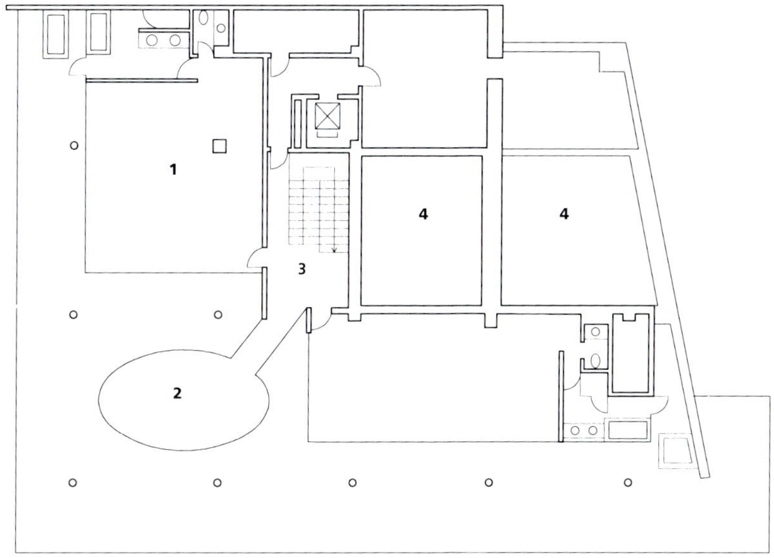

SECOND-FLOOR PLAN

LEFT: Three glass rooms 'float' on an artificial roof pond. The elliptical lounge, with furniture custom-designed by the architect, is a viewing platform for the Pacific coastline. The villa takes advantage of its position on a rocky bluff to play visual tricks with water, light and glass. **BOTTOM LEFT:** The glass bridge connects the translucent upper portions of the project to spaces which explore more conventional Japanese interior preoccupations. **BELOW:** Bedroom facilities for guests on the villa's waterfront.

KEY
1 Guest room
2 Lounge
3 Hall
4 Open

2.2 apicella associates
oxo tower wharf restaurant
london, uk

The dark and narrow space of a South Bank riverside warehouse has been converted into a bright and colourful riverside café with some of London's most spectacular views of St Paul's Cathedral

THE MIXED-USE redevelopment of the Oxo Tower Wharf, on London's South Bank, has given a shot in the arm to the idea of riverside regeneration in the capital. There has been much debate on ways to reanimate the river corridor through the centre of the city: the Oxo Tower's new second-floor restaurant has given the local community and office workers in the area an amenity with outstanding views across the Thames to St Paul's Cathedral and the Embankment.

The scheme was conceived as a natural extension of the public riverside walk. Indeed, it is intended that the restaurant will eventually have direct access down to a centrally positioned pier or jetty, in the tradition of the grand pavement café. However, the creation of a light, airy and inviting eaterie was challenged initially by the dark, tunnel-like structure of the original warehouse space, its tight column grid and an even tighter budget.

The solution by Apicella Associates respects the constraints of the column grid by organizing the three main elements of the interior – canteen servery, refectory area and café space – into three narrow longtitudinal 'strips' or 'lanes', which extend throughout the venue. The inner wall is lined with nine serving counters – one to a bay – with steel-roller shutters. The central refectory area has long, bespoke refectory tables and benches oriented north to south so that nobody sits with their backs to the windows. Closest to the window is the café area with its line of circular aluminium-topped tables, which are complemented by Arne Jacobsen's ubiquitous, stackable Series 7 chairs in vibrant colours. These colours are repeated on plasterboard casings around the entire space by the interior structural columns, in a scheme that skilfully animates the environment overlooking the river in an accessible and non-elitist way.

COMPLETED **April 1996**

COMMISSIONING CLIENT **Coin Street Community Builders**

TOTAL FLOOR SPACE **850 square metres**

NUMBER OF FLOORS **1**

SEATS **350**

TOTAL CONTRACT COST **£330,000**

RIGHT: Vibrantly coloured plasterboard casings around structural columns have turned one of the scheme's main drawbacks – the tight column grid – into one of its principal attractions. Long refectory tables and benches ensure every diner has a river view.

ABOVE AND RIGHT: Round café tables and Arne Jacobsen chairs create social clusters in each bay window. The view of St Paul's Cathedral across the Thames is spectacular, as designer Lorenzo Apicella extends the idea of the public riverside walk into the café. **BELOW:** The axonometric reveals the long, thin, tunnel-like structure of the original warehouse, which is broken up by the colour-coded window bays. The inner wall is lined with nine serving counters.

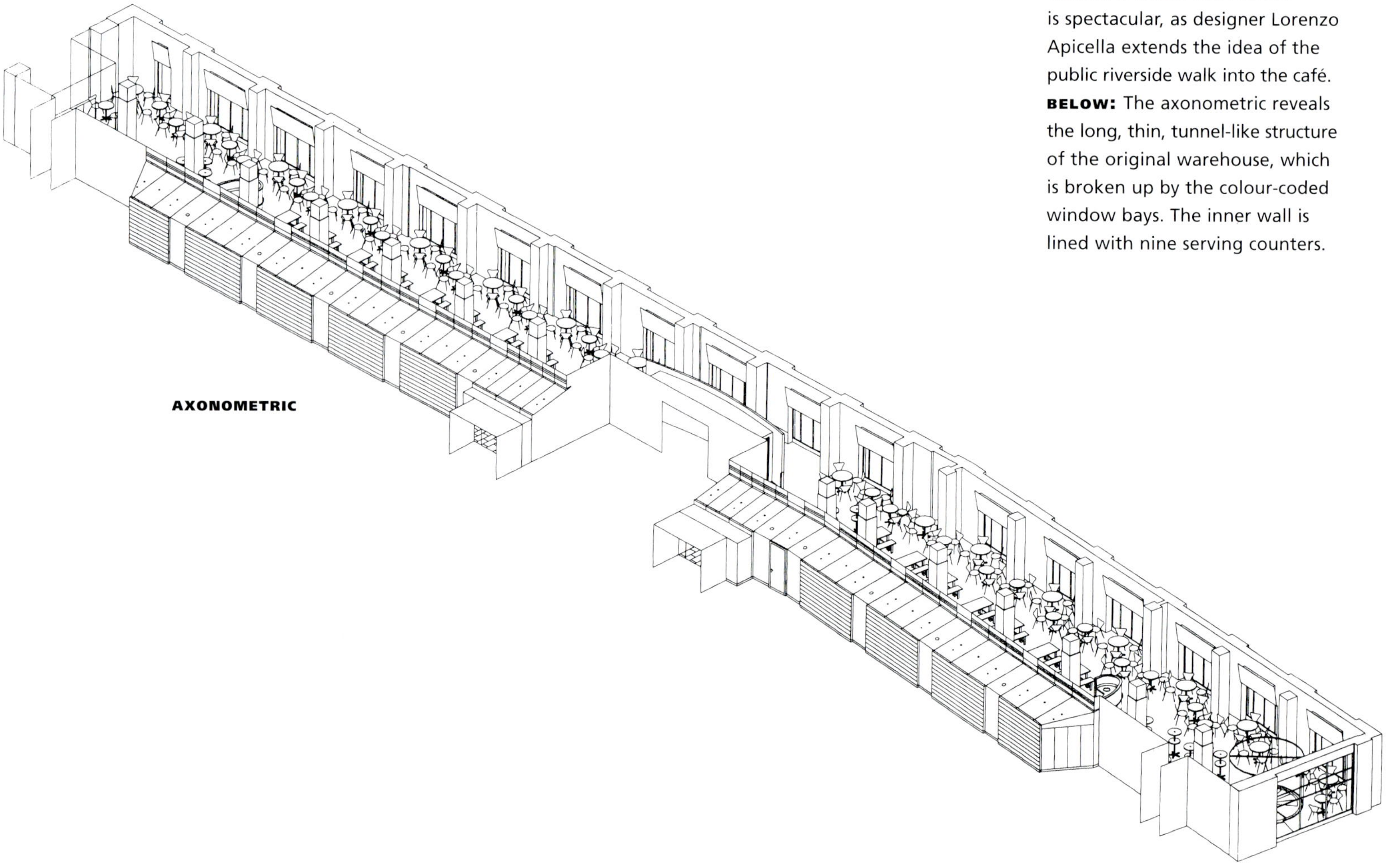

AXONOMETRIC

2.3 ecart
sheraton hotel
paris, france

This airport hotel sitting on top of a busy transport junction at Charles de Gaulle Airport takes the 'milky way' as its interior theme and creates an abstract, ethereal mood – reaching for the stars

ABOVE: The wedged-shape exterior of the Sheraton Hotel, designed by architect Paul Andreu. The building is ringed by motorways with trains below and aircraft above.
RIGHT: Despite all the adjacent transport, the hotel interior designed by Ecart is an oasis of calm. Guest rooms are arranged on four floors around a glass-roofed atrium, with an elliptical column repeating the exterior forms.

COMPLETED **February 1996**

COMMISSIONING CLIENT **Sheraton Hotels**

TOTAL FLOOR SPACE **10,000 square metres**

NUMBER OF LEVELS **4**

ROOMS **256**

TOTAL INTERIOR COST **30 million French francs**

AIRPORT hotels have been synonymous with bland anonymity for too long, as if the proximity to the technology of flight and the imminent departure of guests automatically deprives such facilities of design expression. This hotel, with interiors designed by Andrée Putman and Ecart, is an exception. Its unusual location atop a vast, complex transport junction, amid Terminal 2 at Paris's Charles de Gaulle Airport, and its imposing white-wedge form by Martinet Architecture, demanded a richer vocabulary for its interior.

The hotel's position above a transport nexus means its lower levels are given over to a glass-roofed TGV railway station, which can be viewed by hotel guests from above. Special soundproofed, double-glazed windows and springs in the main building supports have been installed to protect visitors from the noise and vibration of road, rail and air traffic all around the hotel. Ecart's theme of the 'milky way', using frosted glass and the colour blue to unite lobby, walkways, bar and restaurant introduces a more creative, ethereal environment than can normally be found within the Sheraton's international design guidelines.

A central feature of the lobby areas is an elongated, glazed, light-filled pod, like a berthed spaceship, which houses the hotel's technical services. Bedrooms are arranged on four floors around a glass-topped atrium which floods the space with natural light. Putman's customary stylish economy is evident everywhere – inside the bedrooms a writing desk converts into a dressing table at the flick of the wrist and in the public areas sparkly lighting, blue-armchair fabrics and a large circular carpet reflect the abstract intergalactic theme.

PAGES 80–81: An elongated, light-filled pod disguises the hotel's technical services in the main lobby areas.
LEFT: Guest bathroom. Putman's restrained, modern approach is chic and stylish.
RIGHT: Restaurant area. Ecart's exploration of subtle blue patterns of lights on frosted glass expresses an ethereal, other-worldly theme.

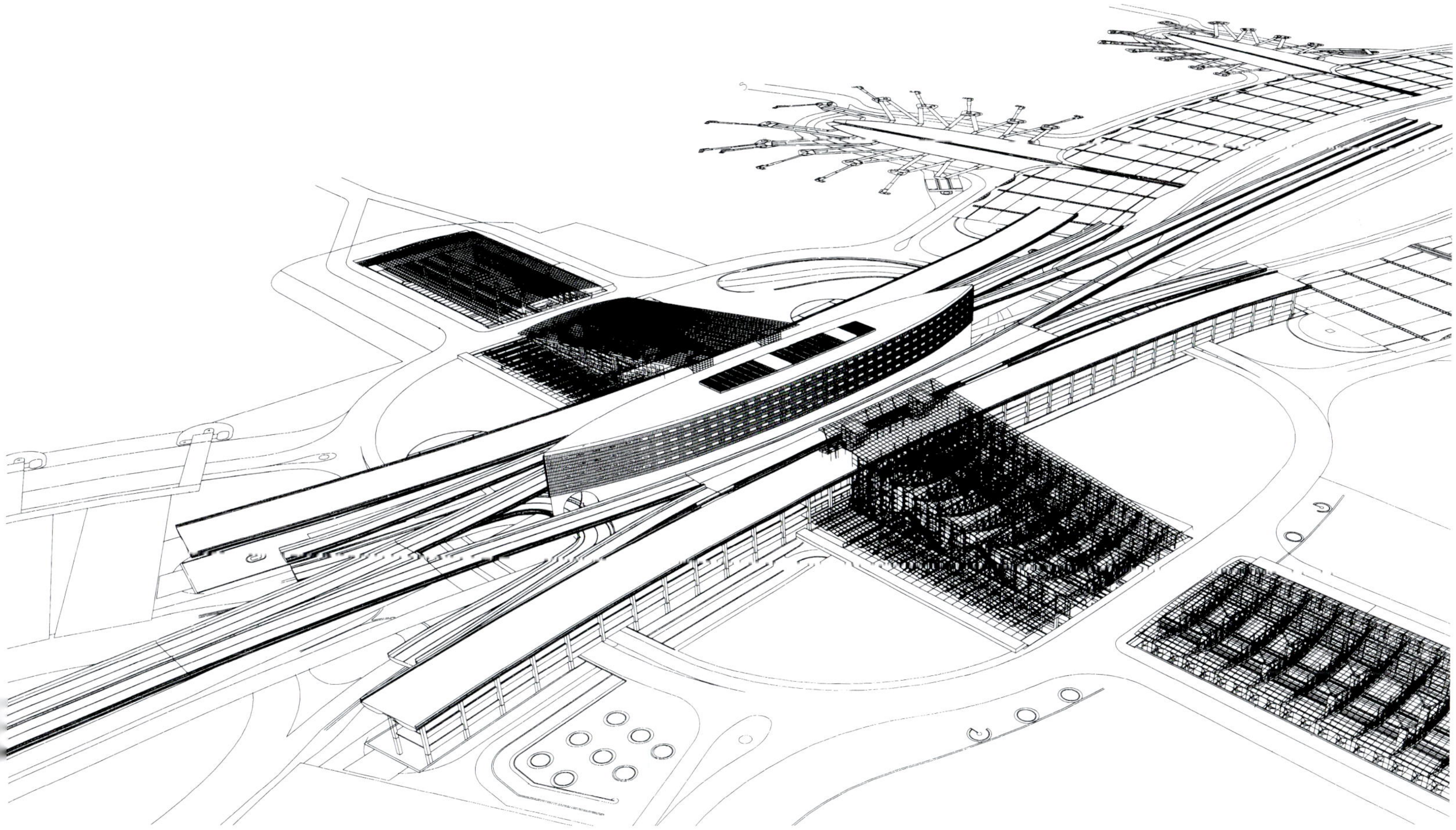

ABOVE: An aerial view of the Sheraton Hotel site shows its position at the centre of a transport nexus. Measures to protect rooms from noise and vibration are central to the project.

2.4 tsujimura hisanobu design office
ricordi café
kyoto, japan

Forget the cosy atmosphere of a Tuscan trattoria. This Italian restaurant in the historic city of Kyoto is a multi-purpose performance space washed with variable light

THE RICORDI Café is one of those odd cross-cultural hybrids – an Italian restaurant in the commercial district of one of Japan's most historic cities. Japanese perceptions of what an Italian restaurant should look and feel like are, of course, very different to those of London, Cologne or Chicago. Designer Hisanobu Tsujimura has chosen to conceive it not as a Tuscan trattoria all decked out in red, white, green and wicker but as a floating, ethereal space doused in light.

There are perfectly good reasons for adopting this strategy. The restaurant's ceiling height is extremely low compared to the 101-square-metre floor space. The design scheme draws attention away from the ceiling to the light-filled walls and floors. The lighting was planned to create no shadows, enhancing the dreamy neutrality of a venue dedicated to film shows, art exhibitions, fashion shows and concerts, as well as Italian food and wine.

More than ten different types of lighting are to be found in the interior, including halogen, fluorescent and low-voltage sources: a yellow-greenish hue is cast on to the white-painted walls and ceiling, and orange accents provide focal points for the eye behind the bar and create a luminous end grid-wall. Brightness can be varied to emphasize the depth of the space and lightfittings are changeable so as to respond to different events. Semi-transparent sunken floor lights with opal glass filter additional light through the space. Classic Arne Jacobsen furniture, from Denmark, adds a further cross-cultural note to the project. This is hardly the cosy ambience of the local pizzeria we have come to know and frequent in the West, but it is a definite attraction in the busy Gion area of Kyoto.

COMPLETED **December 1995**
COMMISSIONING CLIENT **Shigeo Mashiro**
TOTAL FLOOR SPACE **70 square metres**
NUMBER OF LEVELS **1**
TOTAL CONTRACT COST **US $32,000**

ABOVE: A view through the long bar area of the Ricordi Café with the multi-purpose space beyond. The room ends at a glowing light grid-wall, with horizontal lines of light drawing attention away from the low ceiling.

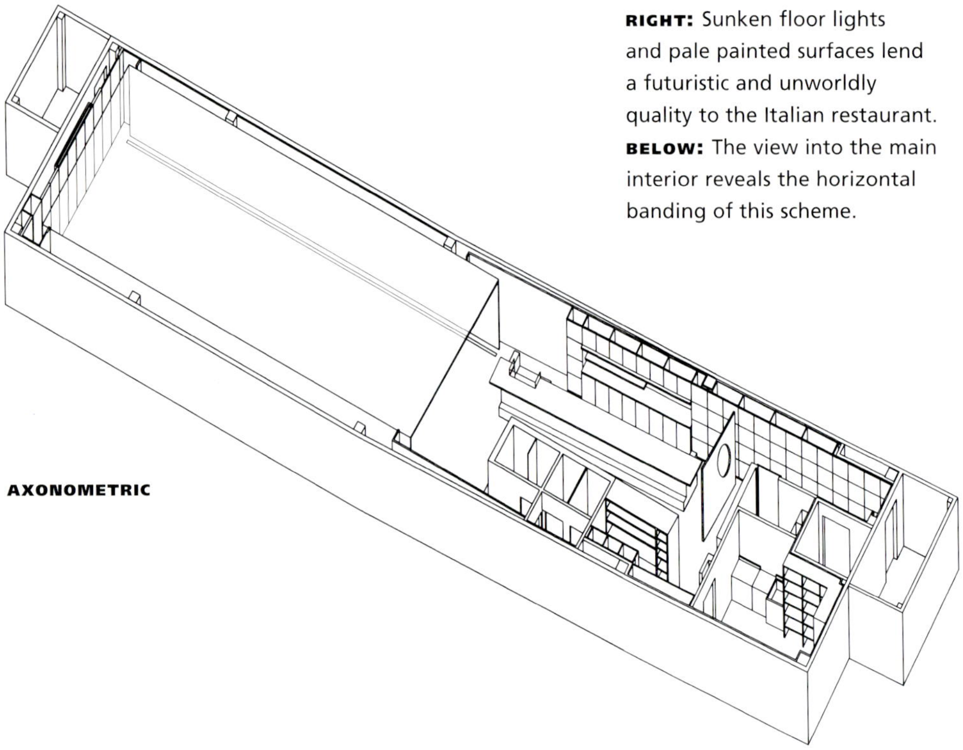

AXONOMETRIC

RIGHT: Sunken floor lights and pale painted surfaces lend a futuristic and unworldly quality to the Italian restaurant.
BELOW: The view into the main interior reveals the horizontal banding of this scheme.

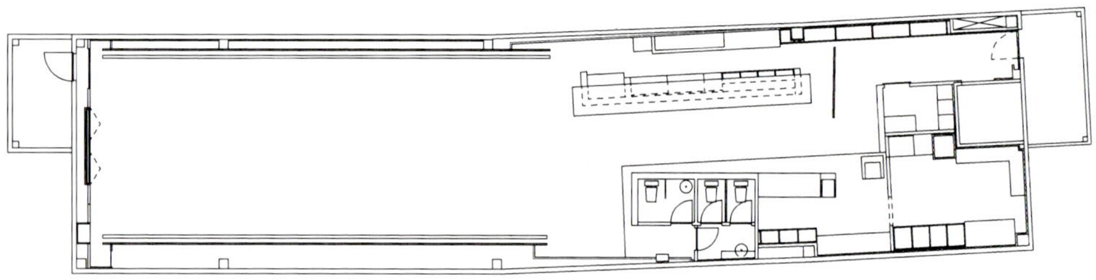

FLOOR PLAN

2.5 met studio
QE2 refit
global

The public interiors of one of the world's greatest ocean liners are redesigned in a contemporary style, which evokes the classic pre-war days of luxury cruising without resorting to pastiche

THE QE2 is perhaps the world's most famous cruise liner. Since its launch in 1969 with interiors designed by James Gardner and Dennis Lennon, however, it has been subjected to piecemeal alterations with little attention paid to any overall design logic or integrity. MET Studio's appointment as master planners for the QE2's public interior spaces, in the early 1990s, heralded a creative renaissance for this floating luxury palace, rescuing it from being a faded period piece and restoring a sense of order, harmony and openness.

MET's first major refit, completed in 1994, aimed to win over younger, more active cruise customers without alienating the blue-rinse brigade. It introduced improved horizontal and vertical circulation routes, better lighting, more distinctive interior landmarks and showpiece environments. Above all, it managed to suggest the great pre-war days of luxury liners while avoiding mere imitation, using contemporary design and materials to evoke an era when only the seriously wealthy took to the seas.

The 1996 refit builds on the previous work in its treatment of the ship's public spaces as part of a mini-city inhabited by strolling players, acting out roles on a giant multi-level stage, which alters at different times of the day and night. Into the newly created circulation framework are fitted interiors, upgraded since the first phase of the master plan. Features range from a sweeping new platform for diners entering the Mauretania Restaurant to new hard flooring, bar stools and artworks in the Crystal Bar. The essential quality of the new-look Queens Grill & Bar has been accentuated by prudent refurbishment. The total effect is of a series of linked fantasy environments through which passengers can promenade and people-watch: the ultimate social activity on any cruise.

COMPLETED **December 1996**

COMMISSIONING CLIENT **Cunard Line, New York**

TOTAL FLOOR SPACE **6,180 square metres**

NUMBER OF DECKS **7**

TOTAL CONTRACT COST **£12 million (including £3.2 million for furnishings)**

ABOVE: New look midship's lobby, a focal point of the first MET Studio refit, which aimed to introduce a more contemporary flavour to the luxury interiors of the QE2.

RIGHT: The world's most famous cruise liner is also a floating ambassador for British design.

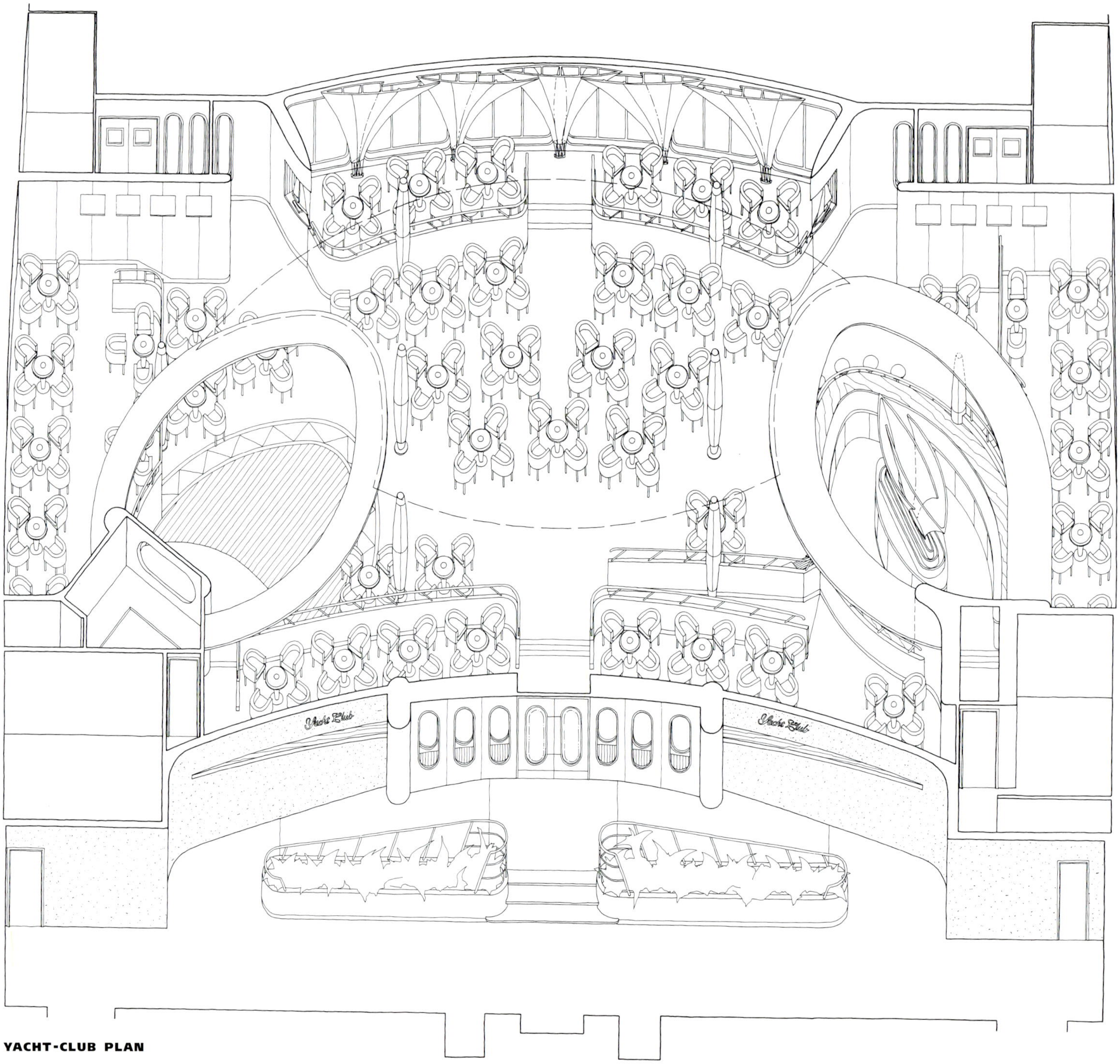

YACHT-CLUB PLAN

LEFT: The Yacht Club interior, a key feature of the 1996 QE2 refit. Design of this facility involved fabricating a new section of the superstructure and open deck. **RIGHT:** The refurbishment of the Crystal Bar, part of the 1996 programme, features new hard flooring (a marbled linoleum cut to a bespoke design), bar stools and artworks.

2.6 rockwell group
tapika restaurant
new york, usa

David Rockwell fashioned the Planet Hollywood chain on received media images of Tinseltown. Now, he has themed a Manhattan eaterie on cinematic reflections of the Texan ranch

THE theme restaurants by the American architect David Rockwell are never literal in content. They are sophisticated exercises refracted through the lens of popular culture, particularly cinematic and theatrical imagery. Tapika deploys the branding irons, rising corn and horseback motifs of a Texan ranch, but the mood is darker and more knowing than the little house on the prairie.

The restaurant, remodelled on the site of the Symphony Café at the corner of Eighth Avenue and West 56th Street, is shielded from the garish, flashing neon outside by an exterior perimeter fence, which incorporates handpainted draperies. The wood panelling, on the internal walls of the former eaterie, is plastered in the shades of desert clay and a wainscot is installed complete with patterns made by a genuine Texan branding iron. Back-lit golden wheat gazes out from behind cool blue glass as the Midwest meets Manhattan, which is enhanced by Paul Gregory's subtle lighting.

The main dining hall is divided into thirds by a raised platform, which creates more intimate and manageable seating areas through the change of level. In keeping with Rockwell's philosophy of 'architecture as theatre' – he once lit a Broadway production of *Dracula* – nearly all of the kitchen is exposed so that the chef's expertise becomes a performance piece at the centre of the restaurant. A chef's table carved out of the raised-seating platform allows aspiring gourmands and gourmets to talk to the chef while he is working.

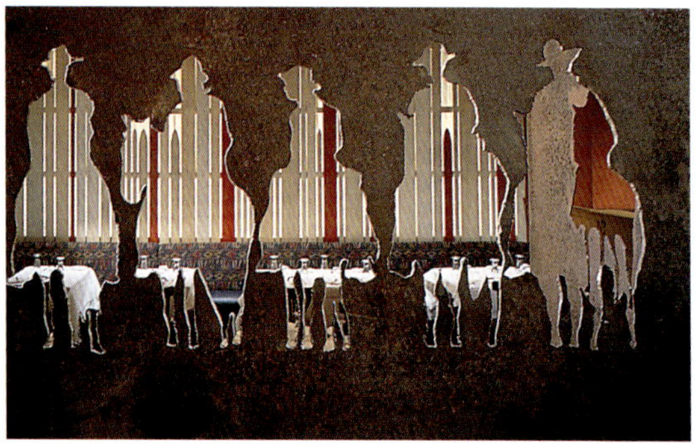

ABOVE: Internal wall plastered in shades of desert clay has cutout patterns made by a Texan branding iron.
RIGHT: View through the restaurant dining area towards the collage of lit wheat. Giant, saucer-like metal luminaires dominate the interior.

COMPLETED **Autumn 1995**
COMMISSIONING CLIENT **Peter and Penny Glazier**
TOTAL FLOOR SPACE **2,400 square feet**
NUMBER OF FLOORS **1**
SEATS **140**

LEFT: The bar area of the Tapika Restaurant, looking towards the interior panelling that shields diners from the garish neon on the street outside.
ABOVE: Rockwell's 'Wheat Wall', created by Surfacing Arts with blue art glass from F. J. Gray Glass and lighting by Paul Gregory of Focus Lighting.
BELOW: The floor plan shows the division of the dining area into three spaces. The central unit is a raised platform.

FLOOR PLAN

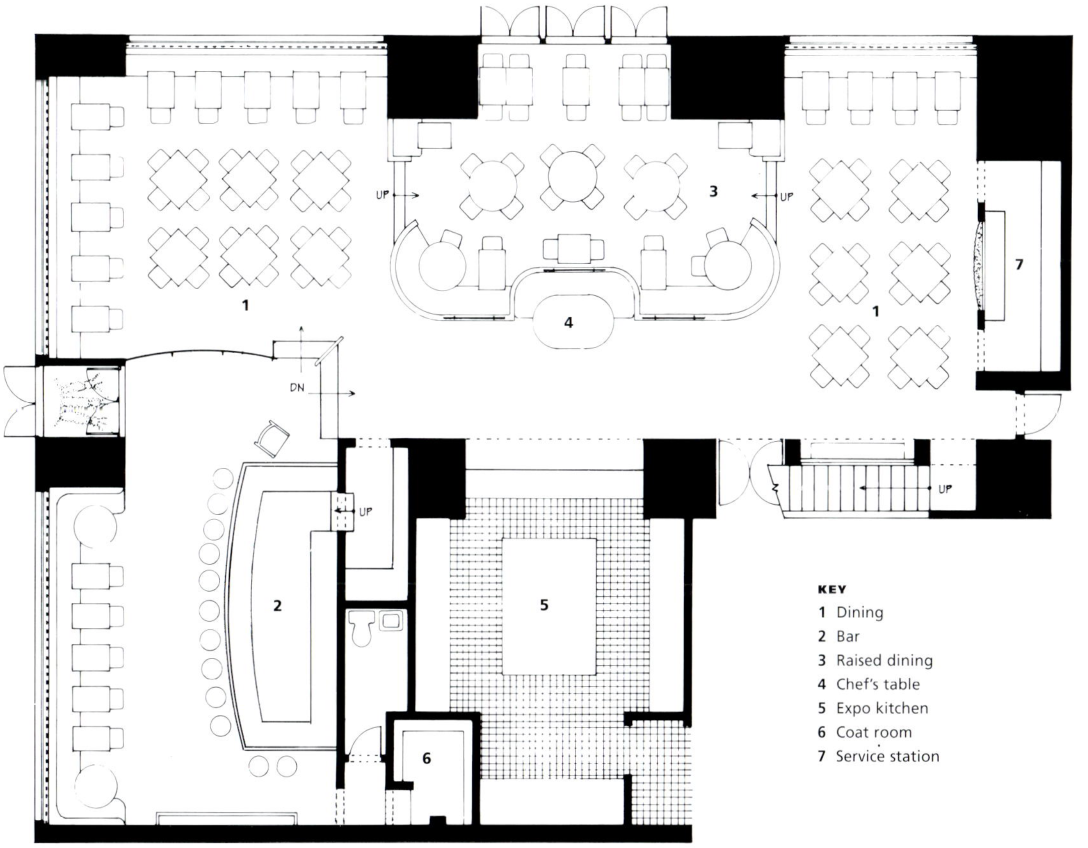

KEY
1 Dining
2 Bar
3 Raised dining
4 Chef's table
5 Expo kitchen
6 Coat room
7 Service station

2.7 branson coates architecture
bargo
glasgow, uk

The triple-height space of Glasgow's Cheesemarket has been turned into a contemporary bar that reflects the city's shipping heritage in its surreal evocation of a dockside at night

GLASGOW'S reputation as a hard-drinking city – all rough pubs with head-butting clientele – is being slowly transformed by a new generation of style-led contemporary bars. Bargo, on Albion Street, is the result of an unusual collaboration between a mainstream brewer, Tennent, and the avant-garde architectural practice Branson Coates, better known for its surreal exercises in leisure environments in the Far East.

One Branson Coates project in Japan, Caffe Bongo, strapped an aircraft wing to the building. Bargo is altogether more grounded. It takes its tone from Glasgow's gritty industrial heritage, although some surrealistic undertones remain in its evocative use of dockside metaphors. On entering the chief element of surprise is not a crash-landing stunt, but the sheer volume of the massive triple-height space. Behind the red-sandstone façade of the former Cheesemarket building, the venue has been modelled in timber, red-oxide steel, metalized fabric and resin.

A glazed screen slides open to the street, turning the bar into a street café by day. At night, the lighting transforms from strong top and sidedirected daylight to what its designers describe as 'the underwater glimmer of reflected dockside factory light at night'. The nocturnal narrative does not end there: a suspended canopy is hoisted out, and the effects of greenish light seeping through portholes, glimmering copper and steel plates are reflected back in angled fragments from a huge suspended mirror. The raw overscaling of the space is further accentuated by a triple-height light wall in opalescent resin. Seating is on two levels, including a well-crafted mezzanine. All the furniture is designed by Nigel Coates, with a tough-minded angular aesthetic, which reinforces the idea that the seating is shipping crates casually left on the dockside.

COMPLETED **September 1996**

COMMISSIONING CLIENT
Bass Taverns/Tennent's

TOTAL FLOOR SPACE
214 square metres

NUMBER OF FLOORS **2**

TOTAL CONTRACT COST **£550,000**

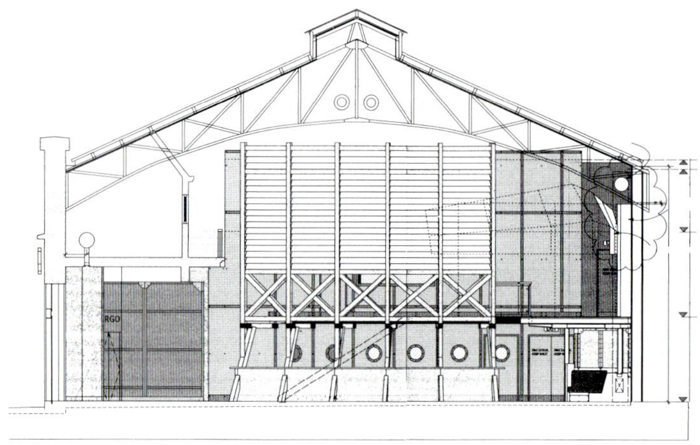

ABOVE: Long section towards bar.
RIGHT: The scheme exploits the triple-height space of the former Cheesemarket to create an interior evocative of the dockside warehouse.

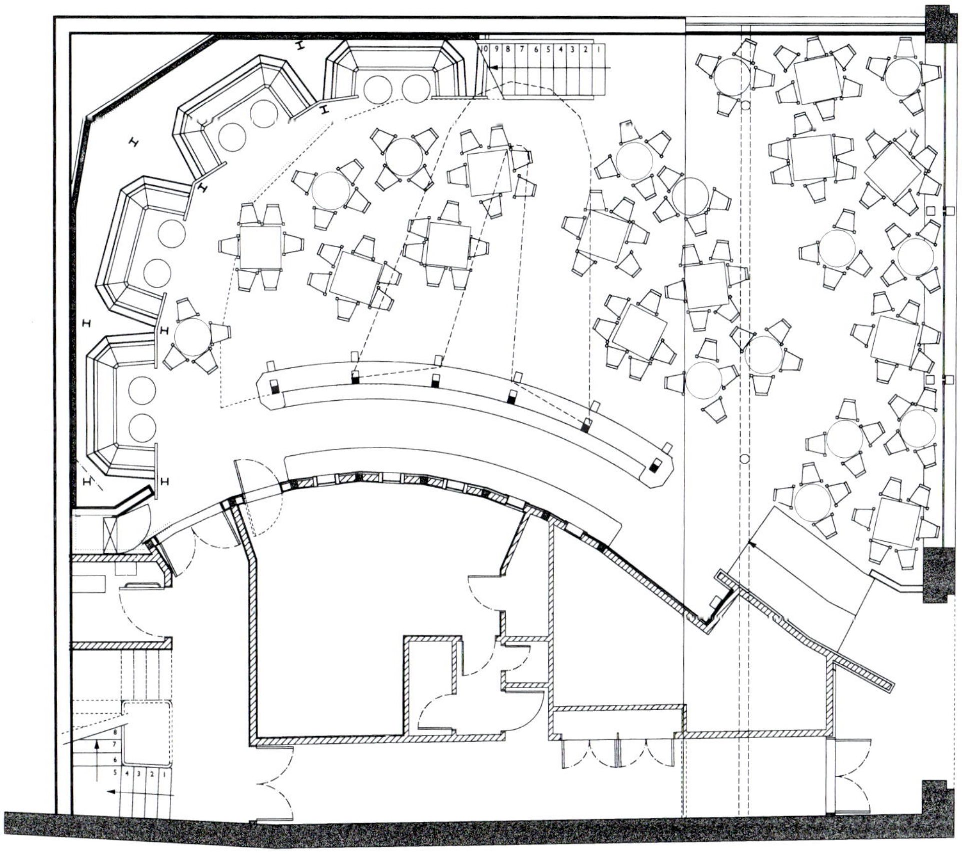

FLOOR PLAN SHOWING CONFIGURATION OF FURNITURE

LEFT: View into the pub through the glazed screen façade, which can slide open to create a street café by day.
RIGHT: Bargo's beechwood chairs and tables are described as taking 'a coltish stance' by their designer Nigel Coates. The metallic upholstery of the chairs and the zinc table tops are equally suited to sunshine or the greenish night-time glow within Bargo.

2.8 gensler

sony theatres lincoln square

new york, usa

The golden age of the American movie palace provides the inspiration for this opulent and highly entertaining film-theatre complex, in which Hollywood traditions are translated into public interior spaces

SONY'S powerful diversification into the American film industry has not been without controversy. Accused of being an alien invader, the corporate giant is particularly keen to connect with Hollywood's historical roots. Fittingly, the interior theme for this vast new, flag-ship Sony entertainment complex, near the Lincoln Center in New York, is the evocative heritage of the American movie palace. The Los Angeles office of Gensler was commissioned to design a giant venue in which the spaces would be as entertaining as the movies people were going to see.

The result is a scheme full of spectacle and stunts, which integrates a 900-seat auditorium for premieres, a 600-seat Sony IMAX theatre, four medium-sized 450-seat theatres and seven smaller auditoria which house between 200 and 250 seats. The famous traditions of Loews Theaters, now owned by Sony, are captured in such features as a 75-foot-high mural and an escalator that appears as a roll of film. Entrances to individual film theatres have names and design motifs derived from old Loews venues.

The concessions' area is ringed by a frieze of famous actors and actresses who visitors can match to their best-known roles. Its entrance is a replica of the gate at Sony's main studio lot at Culver City. Monitors hang from gilded palm trees and trail forthcoming movies. Counters designed in Deco style shift the popcorn. This facility may be situated in the Manhattan of the nineties, but the authentic echoes are of Tinseltown in the twenties and thirties. Through a bold orchestration of both decoration and movement Gensler always manages to keep it just the right side of kitsch.

COMPLETED **End of 1994**

COMMISSIONING CLIENT **Sony Theatres**

TOTAL FLOOR SPACE **130,000 square feet**

NUMBER OF FLOORS **8**

LEFT: An exterior view of the film-theatre complex reveals the drama of the giant mural inside.
RIGHT: Inside the 600-seat Sony IMAX theatre. The screen is 80-feet high. Showgoers wear 3-D headsets.

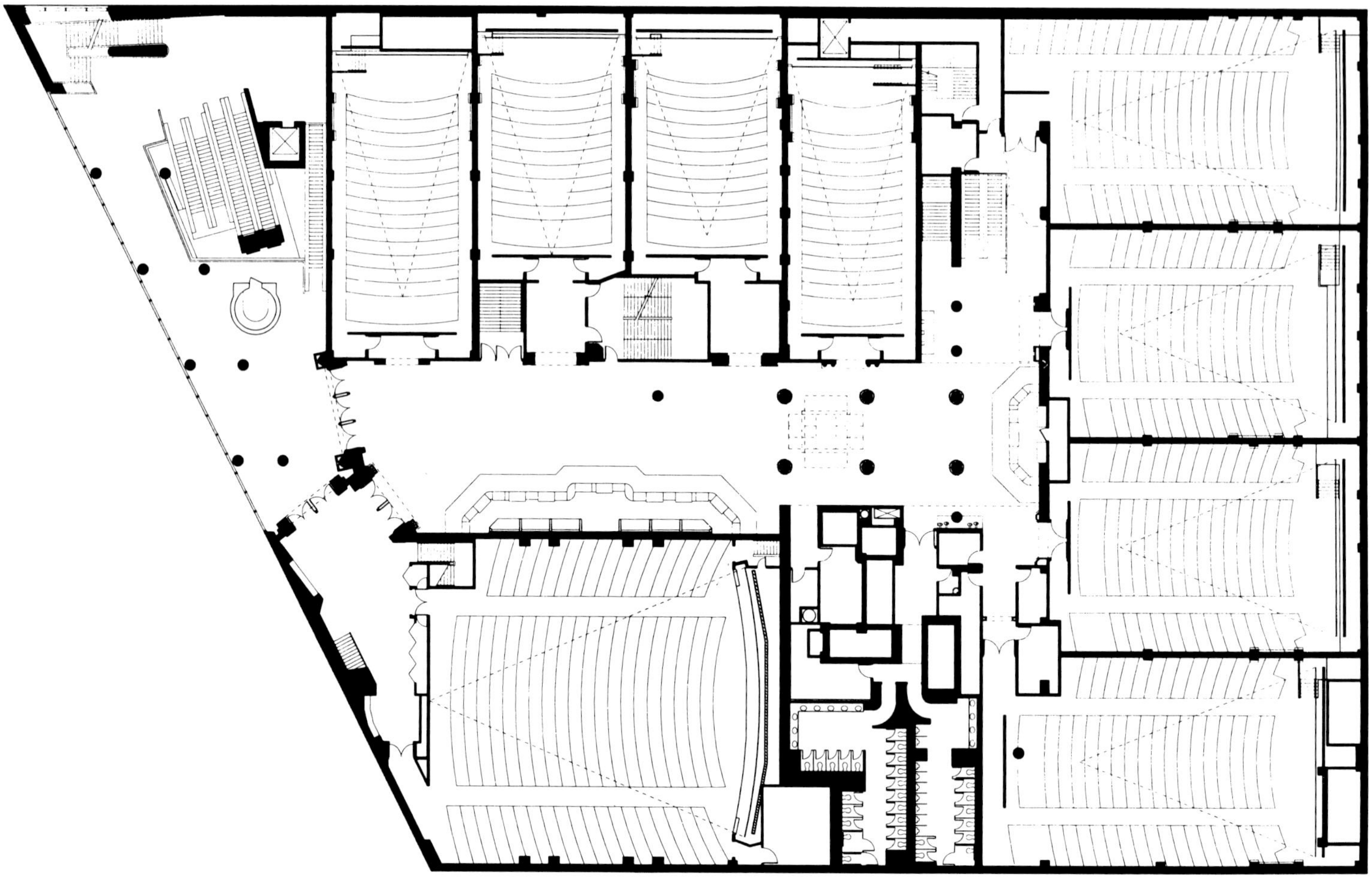

SECOND-FLOOR PLAN

MAJESTIC THEATRE ENTRANCE

ABOVE: The second-floor plan of Sony Theatres' Lincoln Square shows 8 of the scheme's 11 individual movie theatres clustered around an atrium.
LEFT: Exotic theatre entrance design, derived from one of the most famous of the old Loews Theaters.
RIGHT: The main concessions' hall is a grove of black and gold palm trees. High-resolution film monitors animate the space, while concession counters are detailed in black granite, stainless steel and brass.

Paramount Pictures Presents
In Association with Capella International
A Scott Rudin/Cinehaus Production
Paul Newman
Michael Hausman
Richard Russo
Robert Benton
REFRESHMENTS

BOX OFFICE
WILL CALL

LEFT: A view of the lobby area and box office evokes the Art Deco heydays of the thirties. **ABOVE:** The mural close-up celebrates the history of motion picture palaces and the place of Loews Theaters within that heritage. Gensler's designers worked with the Evergreen Painting Studio of New York to produce the artwork, which is 75 feet high and half a city block long.

2.9 design system
niseko higashiyama prince hotel
niseko, japan

A ski centre in winter and a golfer's paradise in summer, this Japanese hotel scheme takes its cue from its natural surroundings for its themes and its form – determined by extreme weather conditions

IN AN overcrowded country where practically every new golf course entails flattening a mountain range, tourism is inevitably on a collision course with nature. Nevertheless operators are at pains to express some kind of harmony between holiday developments and their natural settings. This giant hotel at Niseko, one of Japan's leading ski resorts, is typical of the trend. Spectacularly sited in a national park next to Mounts Yotei and Annuburi, it offers panoramic views of the changing natural environment from interiors designed to promote an interaction with what is happening outside.

The scheme is no cocoon against the elements but a window on the natural world. This is apparent in the shape of the guest rooms which open to their widest point at the outer windows and the banqueting halls angled within the U-shaped floor plan to give a diversity of exterior views. Soft, natural interior woods and fabrics support this theme. The main internal space is a gigantic, irregularly formed atrium in which suspended chandeliers patrol like spacecraft below a trussed, three-dimensional ceiling structure. Activities in this social theatre for visitors can be viewed from corridors above.

The Prince Hotel has a ski-gondola station sited at the front of the building and its basement level is given over to a golf-cart lot. It doubles as a ski attraction in winter and a golf facility in summer, and has been designed to withstand the extremes of temperatures of both seasons. This explains the use of sombre white resin panels on the exterior of the building which repel heavy snowfall. Inside, however, there is a diverse range of colour as varying shades of mud-brown, green and grey seek – not always convincingly – to emulate the hues and patinas of nature.

ABOVE: The hotel in its dramatic mountain setting.
RIGHT: The main irregularly formed atrium space.

COMPLETED **November 1994**
COMMISSIONING CLIENT **Seibu Golf Corporation**
TOTAL FLOOR SPACE **36,367 square metres**
NUMBER OF FLOORS **16 (plus basement level)**

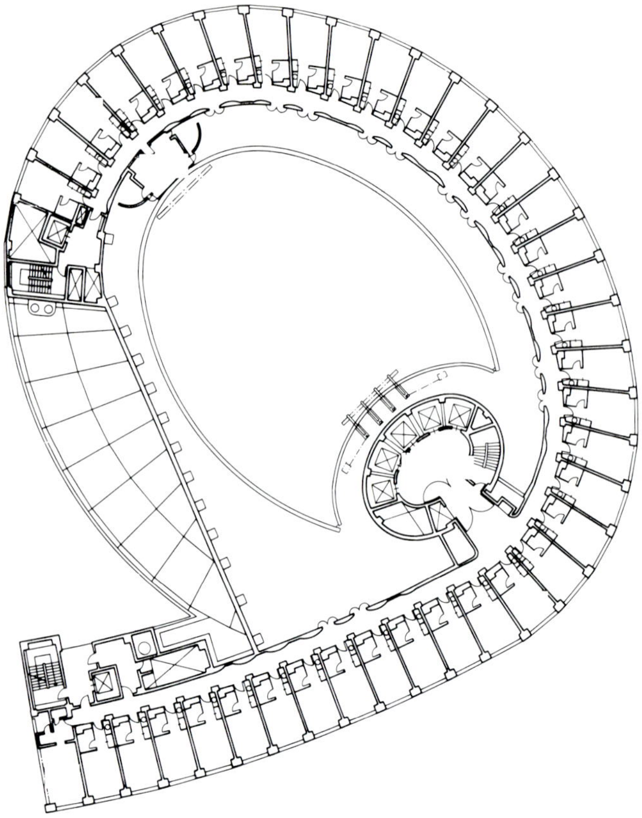

ABOVE: The U-shaped floor plan, designed to group guest rooms around the perimeter to give visitors dramatic views of the natural environment outside.
BELOW: The section reveals the funnel structure that penetrates the gigantic interior atrium.

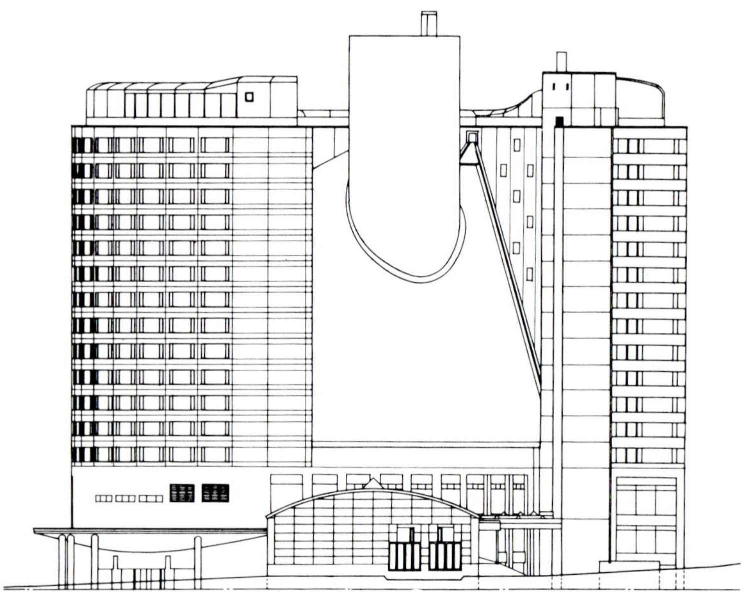

SECTION

ABOVE: The view through the guest lounge shows sinuous chandeliers suspended like glaciers and seating composed like a series of small grassy knolls. The natural inspiration is everywhere.

2.10 wickham & associates architects
bank restaurant
london, uk

Vibrant colours, custom seating, Hopperesque murals and a continuous glass chandelier, like the shimmering underside of a glacier, make this large-scale eaterie a success despite its difficult shape

THE 220-seater Bank is not simply distinguished among the breaking wave of big new central London restaurants by its offbeat location on the outer fringes of theatreland at the Aldwych. It is marked out by the confident, colourful tones of architect Julyan Wickham's signature interior and the way the site's awkward hourglass shape and extreme depth is overcome with a single, inspired lighting intervention that is at once full of bravado and sensitivity.

A continuous, horizontal chandelier leads diners to the rear of the restaurant and unifies the space. Composed of a polar landscape of 2,800 individually shaped and numbered, greenish-glass fins, it weighs more than 20 tons. Likened to the shimmering underside of a slowly melting glacier, it competes for attention in a space where two vast murals by Wickham's daughter Pola evoke a Hopperesque spirit of America for reasons that are not immediately apparent.

Restaurants today, however, are not required to explain, only to excite. Bank's buzz is in the juxtaposition of a sophisticated plan with almost cartoon-like colours and forms. A linear kitchen screened by a glass wall runs down the middle of the restaurant uniting the two widest points of the hourglass. One end presents a semicircular bar through full-height glazing to the street; the other becomes the food service station. Vibrant shades of blue, red, yellow and orange on walls and columns combine with Wickham's own trademark custom-seating designs to suggest a big-noise venue that is lively, diverse and quirky – qualities that no amount of sleek, undiluted, white Modernism can deliver.

RIGHT: Inside a 1914 steel-framed building, the restaurant interior is defined by the continuous chandelier of greenish-glass fins, which leads diners to the rear of the awkwardly shaped space.

COMPLETED **October 1996**

COMMISSIONING CLIENT **Marchthistle Ltd**

TOTAL FLOOR SPACE **940 square metres**

NUMBER OF FLOORS **2**

SEATS **220**

TOTAL INTERIOR COST **£1.8 million**

MARTINI

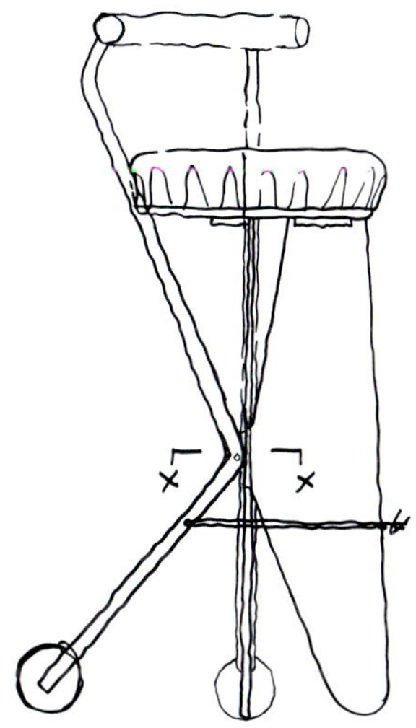

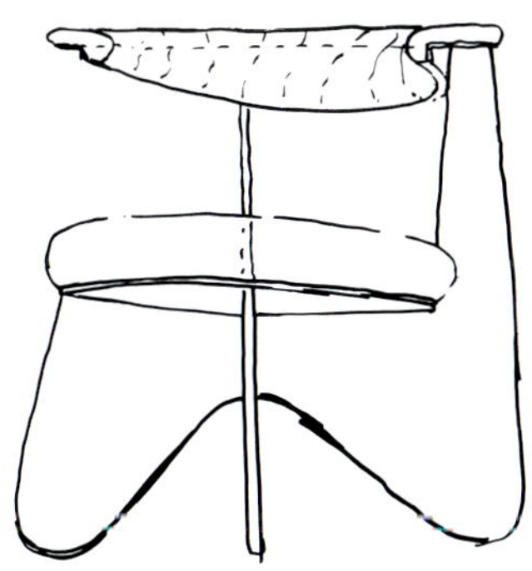

LEFT: View of the bar area. The bar stools are Julyan Wickham's own design, with a stainless-steel frame, aluminium fin legs and red-leather upholstery.
ABOVE: Wickham's sketches for the bar stool and dining chair.

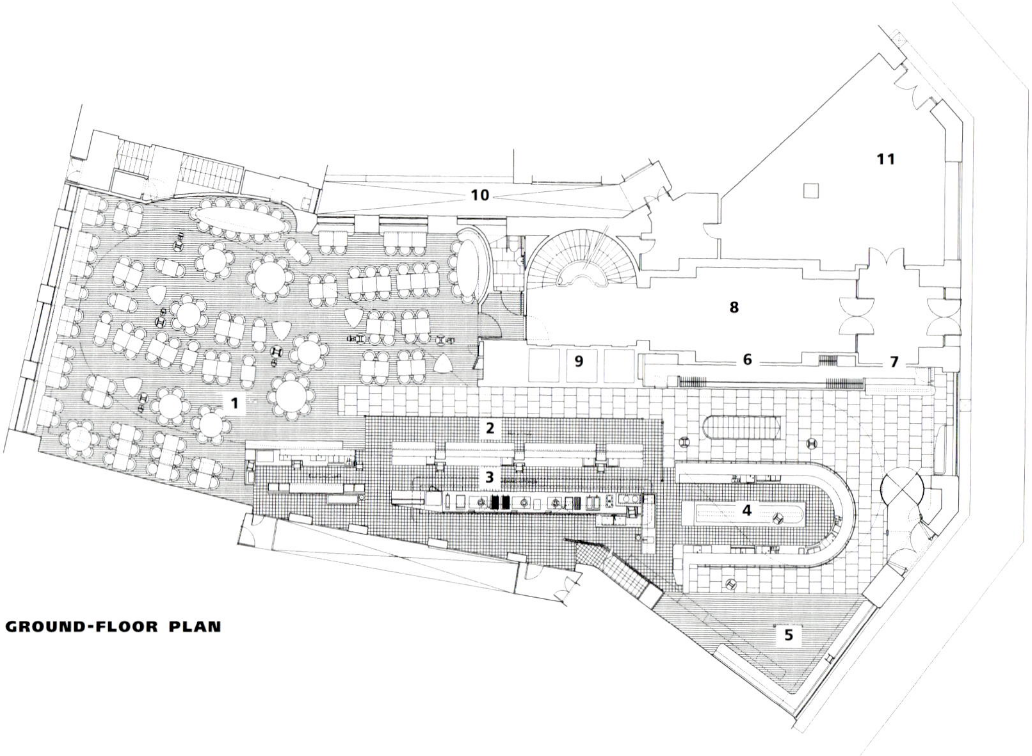

GROUND-FLOOR PLAN

KEY
1 Dining room
2 Main pass
3 Finishing kitchen
4 Bar
5 Bar seating
6 Cloaks
7 Reception
8 Common parts
9 Lifts
10 Lightwell
11 Office/retail unit

ABOVE: The plan shows the restaurant's difficult hourglass shape, which is given a sense of unity by a screened linear kitchen running through the space; this presents the semicircular bar to the street at one end and the serving station at the other.
LEFT: Bold graphic forms and finishes are a feature of the project.
RIGHT: Horizontal louvre elements shield diners from external view on the upper-level dining area, and frame glimpses of the Pola Wickham mural.

2.11 philippe starck
theatron
mexico city, mexico

Starck-watchers have learnt to expect the unexpected: this cavernous underground disco-nightclub reflects the darker side of the Mexican spirit in its portrayal of descent to the edge of madness

THEATRON is an imaginatively compelling and even disturbing restaurant, discotheque and nightclub. Situated in the concrete basement of Mexico City's National Auditorium, it was conceived by Philippe Starck as a labyrinthine descent 'to the edge of madness'. As a master of interior fantasy, Starck has few equals. Here, on a site of national significance, he reveals a darker side to his design through his interpretation of the Mexican spirit. As he explains: 'I detected real Mexican character on the site, the force of dead souls and spirits, and felt the need to channel, provoke and open up ....'

Entry to the three-level venue is through a small bunker-like structure, which gives a sense of archaeological discovery and denies any hint of the extravagant space below. Plunging underground, the visitor is confronted by a giant print of Richard Avedon's 1961 photograph 'Killing Joe Piro'. At 9 x 12 metres it dominates the interior. There is no escape. Starck dazzles with the sheer wealth of materials – polished mahogany, white leather, grey velvet, purple silk, marble and carved and gilded wood – and disorientates with odd juxtapositions and perspectives that lead the eye astray.

The soft curves of a fabric ceiling on the upper level, for example, melt away into a maze of transparent screens. A staircase without banisters takes you up to an illuminated bar, but the steps become steeper the closer you get to your destination. The main narrative route is, of course, all downhill – from heaven to hell, says Starck – to a 'crazy box' where vinyl-covered foam masquerades as great blocks of stone. This is a most surreal leisure landscape, where the visitor is all but engulfed by an environment, staring metaphorically into the abyss of insanity. Like any house of horror, it is also great fun.

COMPLETED **September 1995**
COMMISSIONING CLIENT **Grupo Hostemex**
TOTAL FLOOR SPACE **1,500 square metres**
NUMBER OF FLOORS **3**

ABOVE: Oversized elements in a stage-set scheme, which is the result of Starck's outlandish imagination. The Avedon photographic blow-up faces a giant staircase leading up to an illuminated bar.

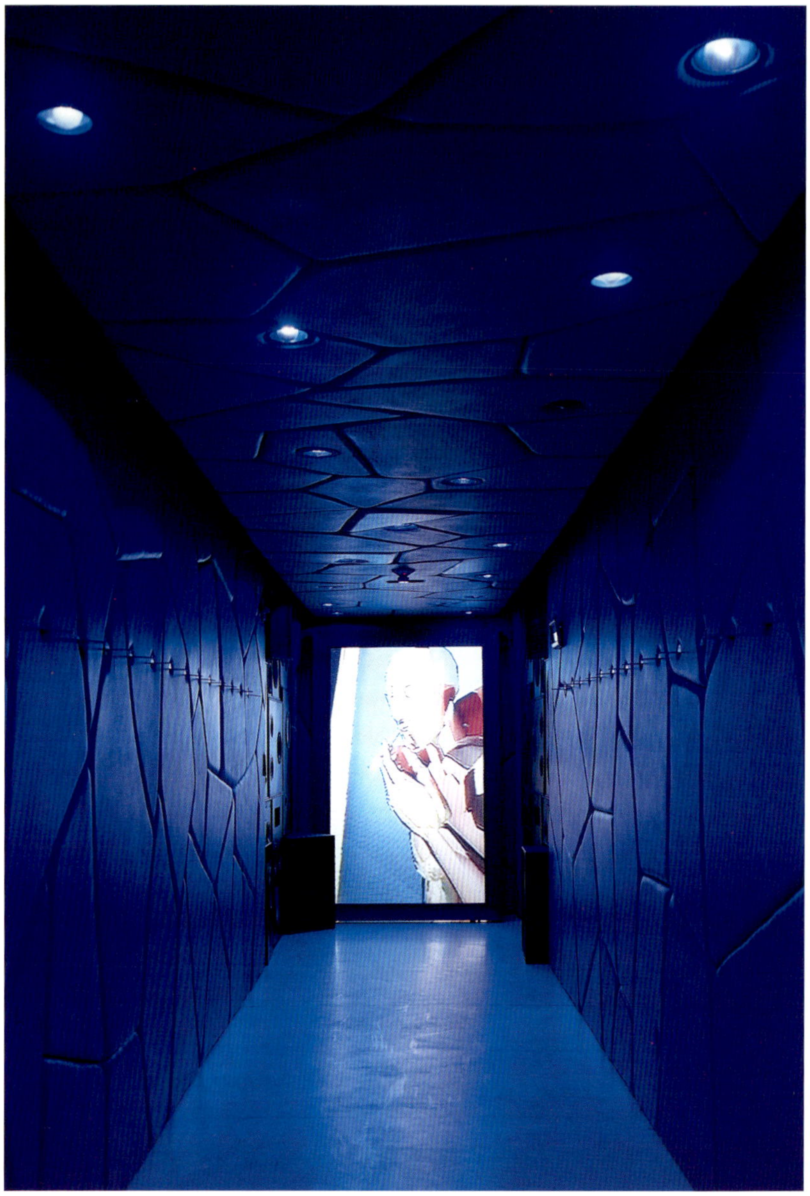

BELOW: Everywhere you go in Theatron, there is no escape from the manic image of Avedon's 'Killing Jo Piro'. The dining room reflects Starck's fascination with different shades of white. **RIGHT:** Inside Starck's 'crazy box' vinyl-covered foam imitates stone blocks as part of a landscape of madness.

OPPOSITE: Avedon's riveting 1961 portrait is casually leaned against a wall.

2.12 daryl jackson international

cannons sports clubs

london, uk

Two smart sports clubs have been created out of a couple of inhospitable nooks and crannies in urban London: one under six railway arches, and the other in the concrete basement of a printworks

ABOVE: Entrance to the Cannon Street club, which is housed in a series of railway arches.
RIGHT: View of the Covent Garden swimming pool, which has a ceiling of tensile fabric on to which images can be projected.

CREATING large spaces for sporting activities within the dense urban fabric of London is a difficult and expensive business. A phased programme by design firm Daryl Jackson International has created two sports club interiors in unlikely environments. The first has involved the conversion of six railway arches behind Cannon Street Station; the second occupies a former printing works in a two-storey concrete void below street level in Covent Garden. Both schemes share a robust and respectful treatment of original structure – Victorian brick vault in Cannon Street and concrete frame in Covent Garden – with new insertions kept to a minimum.

At Cannon Street, the architects combated the darkness, dampness and dust associated with railway arches to create a range of areas for the body beautiful. A limited palette of materials – steel, glass, oak and painted plasterboard – complements the brickwork. Glazing, mirrors and a special polished stainless-steel staircase enhance the sense of transparency and animation underneath the arches. All the facilities are accessed via a central circulation spine defined by the interconnection between the six main arches and smaller jack arches. The scheme, with two new mezzanine levels, increased the floor space by 45 per cent.

If improving circulation was a priority at Cannon Street, the brief at Covent Garden reflected the need to install new facilities and conceal ungainly services strung across ceilings. Accordingly, the aerobics studio has a suspended ceiling of aluminium tubes while the swimming pool is covered by a tensile fabric ceiling. On both sites, work was carried out while the keep-fit continued, further complicating the programme. It is to the credit of the designers who have fashioned intelligent and good-looking solutions in such unlikely urban recesses.

COMPLETED **June 1996**

COMMISSIONING CLIENT **Cannons Sports Clubs (UK)**

TOTAL FLOOR SPACE **10,000 square metres (Cannon Street), 3,250 square metres (Covent Garden)**

NUMBER OF LEVELS **3 in each venue**

TOTAL CONTRACT COST **£3.2 million (Cannon Street), £1.5 million (Covent Garden)**

STRICTLY NO DIVING
DEPTH
1·5m

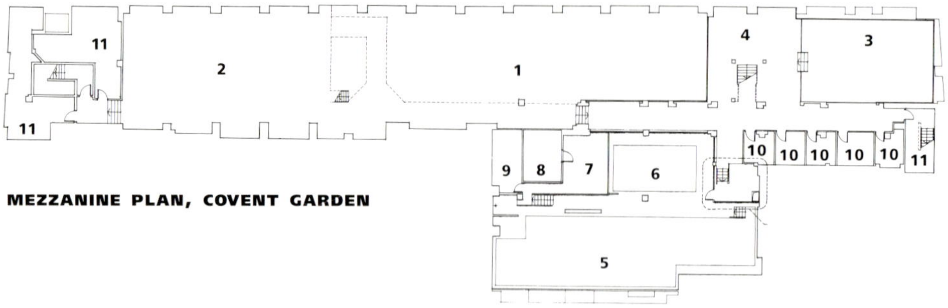

MEZZANINE PLAN, COVENT GARDEN

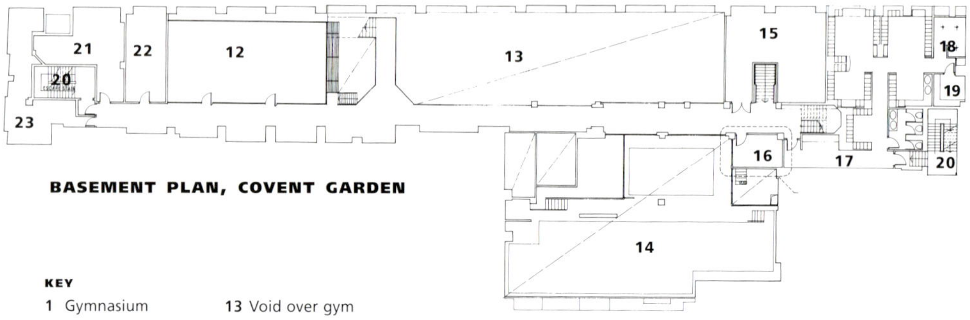

BASEMENT PLAN, COVENT GARDEN

KEY

1 Gymnasium
2 Aerobics studio A
3 Free-weights gym
4 Warm-up area
5 Swimming pool
6 Hydrid pool
7 Relaxation area
8 Steam room
9 Plant/store
10 Sunbed
11 Store
12 Aerobics studio B
13 Void over gym
14 Void over pool
15 Plant room
16 Therapy room
17 Ladies' changing room
18 Showers
19 Sauna
20 Escape stair
21 Plant/store
22 Plant
23 Plant/store

GROUND-FLOOR PLAN, CANNON STREET

RIGHT: The swimming pool deftly inserted into the arches at the Cannon Street venue.

ABOVE: The Cannon Street reception area leading to retail concessions. Suspended artworks offer wry commentary on the pursuit of the body beautiful.

LEFT: The Covent Garden aerobics studio. The wavy ceiling of aluminium tubing softens an environment fashioned from a printworks in a concrete void.

retail

3 stores/showrooms/retail centres

Brand warfare among the big manufacturers has pushed the retail interior to the front line and introduced a new language of flexible displays, interactive technologies and engaging materials

RETAIL interior designers now have every reason to feel better about themselves. After years of recessionary caution, the retail environment is becoming essential ammunition for brands planning offensive strategies in the global marketplace. A decade ago, the major competitors for customers were predominantly retail chains. Today, the big manufacturers and entertainment companies have joined the battle. Sony, Swatch, Disney, Reebok, Nike, Levi and Warner Brothers are just some of the household consumer names that are trading on their brand status as part of a phenomenon known as 'destination shopping'.

SonyPlaza, Nike Town and Planet Reebok, for example, are American stores which have all set new standards in how to turn manufacturers' brands into physical environments, offering a unique consumer experience based on recognizable brand values. The fact that the consumer is always changing is given tacit recognition in Fitch's scheme for Planet Reebok close to Lincoln Centre in New York, which has been designed

1

2

for total flexibility. Mobile merchandising, graphics and visuals can all be repositioned during the course of a day as the customer base fluctuates.

Planet Reebok also has some of the entertainment pizzazz in its use of videos and interactive information screens that one finds in the mainstream 'entertainment retail' venues such as the Disney Store or Warner Store. While most of the branded store action has originated in the United States, Europe can also lay claim to retail innovation. Studio Mendini's scheme for the Swatch Shop on Milan's prestigious Via Montenapoleone is a swirling exercise in material invention, which sprinkles the Swatch brand with a rich seasoning of mysterious sci-fi imagery.

It is interesting to compare Mendini's approach with that of Pentagram's Daniel Weil, who has designed prototype Swatch stores in Geneva and New York. In Geneva, Weil has developed a new display concept called 'Coastline' which replaces Swatch's shop-in-shop system and gives the manufacturer the ability to shed the skin of the shop interior and change its personality in line with changing market demands. In New York, Weil has worked with fellow Pentagram partner James Biber to create the 'Swatch Timeship', a vast three-floor environment that projects the 'machine with personality' idea behind the Swatch brand.

The level of retail activity surrounding Swatch is indicative of current trends, which are largely concerned with projecting

1/2 KOKUYO SHOWROOM, TOKYO, JAPAN
Designed by Studio Iosa Ghini
This futuristic design for the Tokyo showroom of a large Japanese office equipment company expresses the impact of new technology on the office of tomorrow through a sequence of fibreglass walls moulded to create triangular modules 40 centimetres deep into which are fitted liquid crystal screens and lights.

3 PLAZA RABONE COSMETICS SEMINAR ROOM, CHUO YAMATO-SHI KANAGAWA, JAPAN
Designed by Masayuki Chichii
This unusual showroom for a cosmetics sales agent uses a giant wire object spiralling upwards and a broad curved screen to divide the space for different functions. Cosmetic pigments are used to decorate the interior.

4 SWATCH STORE, GENEVA, SWITZERLAND
Designed by Pentagram Design
Designer Daniel Weil's Geneva prototype for Swatch uses frosted back-lit polycarbonate and metal foldings and extrusions as part of its flexible skin.

3

4

branded goods and services in a way which is modular, responsive to change, inclusive of interactive information technologies and guaranteed to maximize consumer impact.

Another emerging trend concerns materials. The early 1990s saw deliberate emphasis on 'poor' materials in retail and interiors – dubbed 'the new modesty' by commentators – as part of the austerity of the period. Today, as shoppers return in numbers to the high street and mall, retailers and their designers are choosing more durable and upmarket finishes.

This is especially evident in fashion retailing. John Pawson's Jigsaw outlet in London and Petzinka Pink & Partner's Eickhoff store in Düsseldorf both luxuriate in specifying thick materials that spatial interventions must slice through. In Jigsaw the floors, for example, are granite and large timber plank; in Eickhoff, they are a seamless sandstone. These projects suggest that retail displays within the architecture of shops can be as transient and adaptable as they like but that the architecture itself should have a timeless and durable neutrality.

Clearly, materials and finishes send key messages to consumers. One need only compare and contrast two very different hairdressing salons in our selection to see this is the case: Caulder Moore's Arts and Crafts-inspired Mahogany salon in London delights in playing gently with surfaces of purple plaster, amber and blue glass, and fret-cut metal; Anderson/Schwartz Architects' four-level Bumble & Bumble salon in New York speaks a much harder industrial language in its aggressive collage of poured-concrete, exposed-steel, aluminium, acrylic and stained-plywood details.

There is a similar richness of contrast in recent showroom projects around the world, as product companies follow the high-street retailers in their investment in design to win over customers. At one end of the spectrum, Studio Iosa Ghini's excitable stage set for the Tokyo showroom of a Japanese office equipment manufacturer expresses the impact that new technologies will have on the future workplace by creating a sequence of matt-painted fibreglass walls; these are moulded to create triangular modules into which are fitted liquid-crystal screens and lights. At the other extreme, Bolles-Wilson's lighting showroom for Zumtobel-Staff, in Lemgo, Germany, calmly translates a technical light diagram, outlined on the floor, into a controlled exhibition area wrapped around with a white plasterboard skin.

The only department store in our selection stands apart not only for its retail genre. Jean Nouvel's Galerie Lafayette in Berlin is uncompromisingly architectural in its use of two giant glass cones to create a mesmerizing interior space. Yet the reflections and images that bounce from its curved glass and mirrored surfaces are ideally suited to the glamour and movement of city-centre shopping. Just for once, the designer is hero, not the merchandise. The brand on display is Nouvel himself.

1

2

1 **BHS STORE, CAMBRIDGE, UK**
Designed by 20/20 Design Consultants
This new store concept for mainstream British retailer BHS, piloted at Cambridge, features a 10-metre high window display as part of the openness of the design.

2 **SPACE NK, LONDON, UK**
Designed by Hodgkinson & Co.
Propeller detail of interior designed for the first London Space NK apothecary store. This niche retail concept has been developed by entrepreneur Nicky Kinnaird and interpreted with finesse by designer Andrew Hodgkinson.

3 **D&G BOUTIQUE, MILAN, ITALY**
Designed by Claudio Nardi
Warmth, light and natural materials define this Milanese flagship, one of the first in the D&G chain. Black-and-white fabric designs and hand-decorated ceramic tiles create large floor patterns within the space.

4 **ARTFORM GLASS SHOP, SAN FRANCISCO, USA**
Designed by Lorcan O'Herlihy
The glass products are the stars of the show in this delicate scheme by the Bay-area architect who specializes in small-scale retail and domestic projects.

5 **SHIRTSMITH, LONDON, UK**
Designed by David Bentheim
This Westbourne Grove shop, in London, selling tailor-made clothes to order, creates a sensual, almost surreal atmosphere, through its unusual composition of amoebic form, strong colour and odd materials.

retail projects

3.1 jean nouvel et associés

galerie lafayette

berlin, germany

Jean Nouvel proves a master of architectural illusion with this geometric exercise, using inverted and mirrored cones to create a truly compelling retail environment

THERE are few retail images in Europe with the impact of French architect Jean Nouvel's dramatic mirror-like interior design for the Galerie Lafayette department store on the corner of Berlin's Friedrichstrasse and Französischestrasse. The project is an extraordinary exercise in inversion and distortion as Nouvel places a large glass cone on top of the up-ended base of a smaller glass cone at the centre of the block. The effect is mesmerizing, allowing visitors to take in all the different levels of the store in a kaleidoscope of reflected and distorted images achieved by curved mirrors and mirror surfaces.

In this fantastical composition, messages, themes and pictures from the bustle of the department store are filtered from surface to surface through the reflective void, until one begins to question what is real and what is not. Nouvel describes the two giant mirror cones as 'objects of fascination' and explains their role as 'giving everyone the means of seeing where one is and where one goes at any time'. He suggests that the reading of the different spatial levels is simple. However, the diffusion of artificial and natural light through this twilight cone zone at different times of the day and evening is anything but simple.

This, of course, is interior design formed entirely by architectural place-making. Nouvel, however, is no stranger to interior architectural illusion. Aspects of his Lyons Opera House similarly play games with light, transparency, emptiness and reflective surfaces. Throughout Galerie Lafayette, his expressive geometry is at work – from the giant screens on the façades and open glass frontage at street level, which is dematerialized by light to allow easy penetration, to the series of white, light cones that perforate the interiors of the office space enclosing the store, which sits at the heart of the scheme.

COMPLETED **March 1996**

COMMISSIONING CLIENT **Euro-Projekt Entwicklungs**

USABLE FLOOR SPACE **39,585 square metres**

NUMBER OF FLOORS **7**

TOTAL CONTRACT COST **DM 211 million**

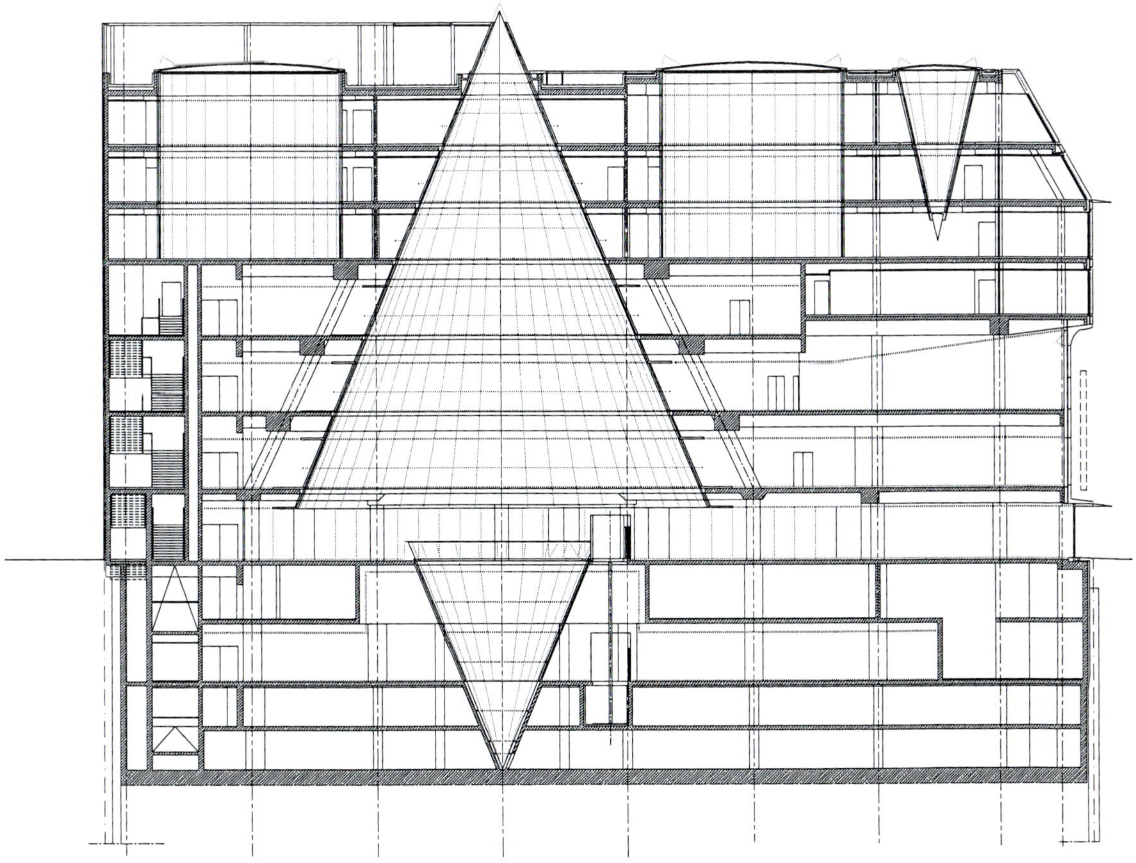

ABOVE AND OVERLEAF: Views into the up-ended base of the smaller glass cone reveal the transparency of this exceptional department-store scheme. Diffusion and reflection of light plays tricks with depth and perspective. **FAR LEFT:** Exterior view of the rounded contours of Galerie Lafayette on the corner of Friedrichstrasse in Berlin. Large inset screens advertise the building's presence.

SECTION

BELOW: The second-level plan of Galerie Lafayette describes the central, circular atrium void surrounded by four smaller lightwells.
RIGHT: View into the inverted lower pyramid, one of two mirrored shapes that provides the focus for this retail environment.

SECOND-LEVEL PLAN

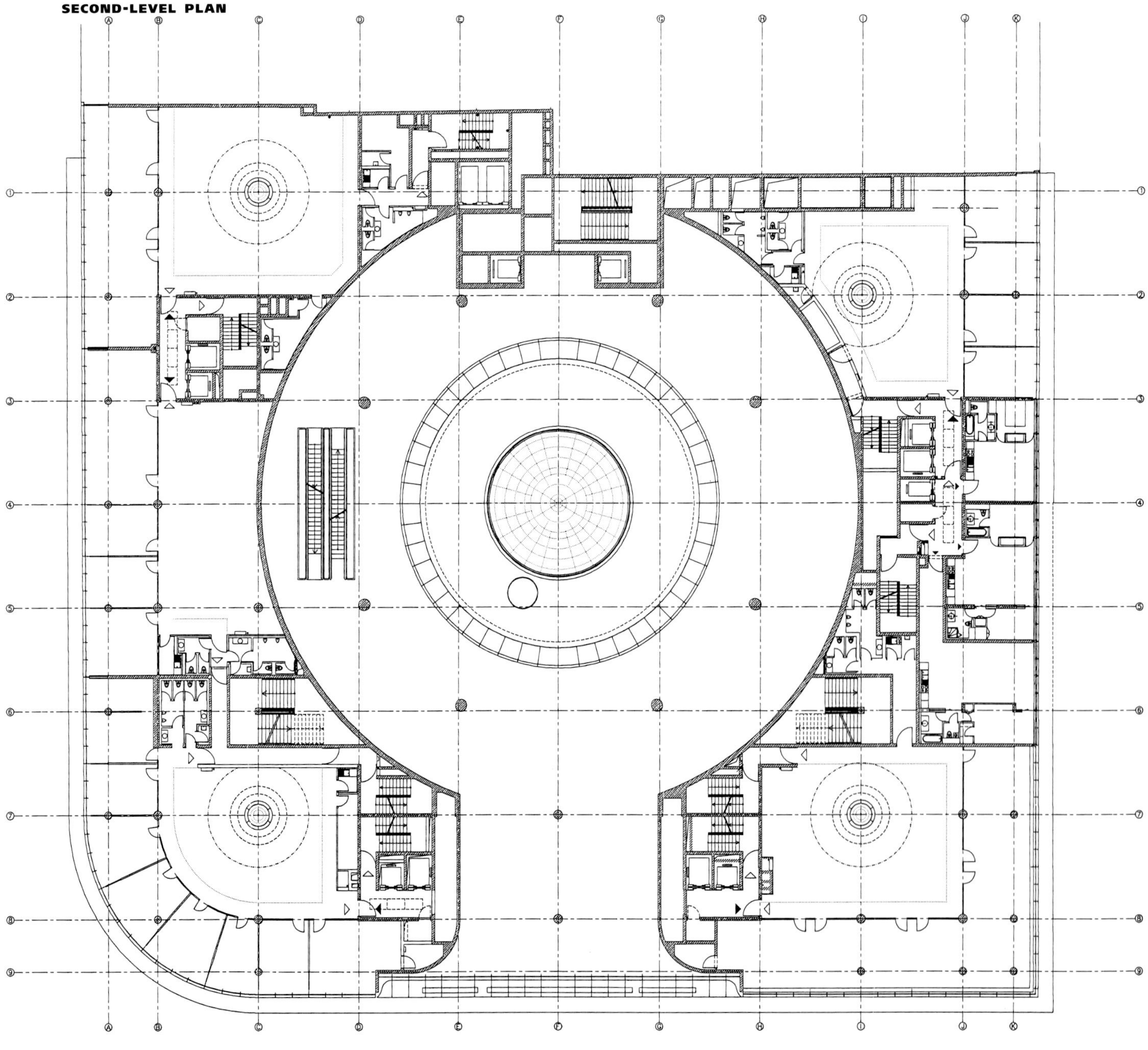

3.2 design shed
ricci store
liverpool, uk

Contrasting treatments of internal walls provide the key to this gallery-like clothing-store project, in which architectural, interior and graphic elements are integrated with finesse

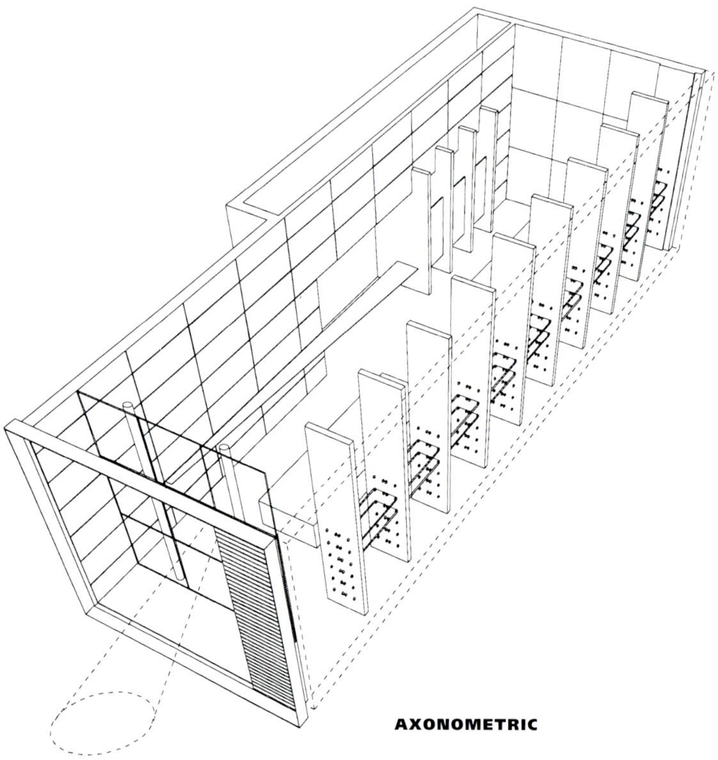

AXONOMETRIC

COMPLETED **November 1995**

COMMISSIONING CLIENT **Goodman International**

TOTAL FLOOR SPACE **75 square metres**

NUMBER OF FLOORS **1**

TOTAL CONTRACT COST **£70,000**

THIS retail outlet for an established clothing company, looking to develop a younger brand image, reflects a cross-disciplinary approach in which Liverpool practice Design Shed has treated architectural, interior and graphic elements of the scheme in a satisfyingly integrated way. The result is a vibrant, gallery environment delivered with rigour and control.

The architectural coherence of Ricci's long, thin interior stretching 15 metres in length is expressed in the contrasting treatment of the side walls. As you enter, the left-hand side is clad with yellow timber panels into which are inserted all service elements, tills and changing rooms. The right-hand wall is punctuated by a number of interior fins at right angles to the wall: these create a series of flexible display bays, allowing different shelving and rail configurations. The fins are extended to the store exterior where the first fin in the series – in grey metallic brick – enables a full-height, glazed entrance panel to be recessed from the street. A picket gate slides into the external fin for security. The large, glazed entrance, which has two existing cast-iron columns positioned centrally, allows unimpeded views into the internal volume of the store even at night.

Signage and point-of-sale communications are closely related to the spatial solutions of the total scheme. A lighting projector is used to cast signs through the shop and on to the pavement outside. So many retail environments have different elements set up in noisy competition with each other. This project demonstrates just how effective a mixture of disciplines can be when carefully orchestrated.

ABOVE: The glazed façade of the Ricci clothes store is inserted into the first in a series of fins which punctuate the right-hand wall of the interior. The left-hand wall is clad in yellow timber panels.
LEFT: The axonometric reveals the contrasting interior wall treatments.

ABOVE: A spare, industrial aesthetic creates a sense of space in a generously volumed interior.
RIGHT: Mobile merchandise trolleys and factory-style pendants enhance the understated mood of the scheme.

3.3 architekturbüro bolles-wilson
zumtobel-staff showroom
lemgo, germany

This flexible hall, designed to demonstrate the capabilities of a newly combined lighting company, uses a technical-light diagram and a white-plasterboard skin to define a suitable environment for exploration

CREATING a showroom for lighting equipment is an unusually difficult task because the interior must not only display the technical proficiency of the products but also demonstrate the quality of light. This customer-care centre for the German light manufacturers Zumtobel-Staff – a large-scale, flexible demonstration hall inside an existing industrial shed – succeeds in its direct and coherent exploration of the relationship between luminaires and light.

Designers Peter Wilson and Julia Bolles-Wilson, with project architect Jim Yohe, set out to provide a controlled framework and spatial hierarchy against which the newly combined company's large range of products could be viewed without turning the luminaires themselves into fetishistic objects. A marriage of architectural language and the technical-design qualities of the manufacturer produces a light distribution diagram printed on the showroom floor that translates directly into the form of an elegant conference room, with the appropriate title 'Built Light'. This enclosed space is clad in cherrywood and seats up to 80 people for conferences, seminars or lectures. The fixed point of the curve of the light diagram projects on to its walls.

The demonstration hall itself is wrapped by a white-plasterboard screen, which acts as a second skin with the building: free of any physical installations, it registers different light qualities. Sandwiched between this screen and the outer walls of the shed are smaller rooms, including the reception area, design office and meeting spaces, each with their own lighting ambience. A geometric constellation of lighting products hangs from blacked-out ceiling trusses, overlooking a calm exhibition landscape in which free-standing display walls and roving display furniture on castors further facilitate experiment and demonstration with light.

COMPLETED **May 1996**

COMMISSIONING CLIENT **Zumtobel-Staff**

TOTAL FLOOR SPACE **1,000 square metres**

NUMBER OF FLOORS **1**

TOTAL CONTRACT COST **£1 million**

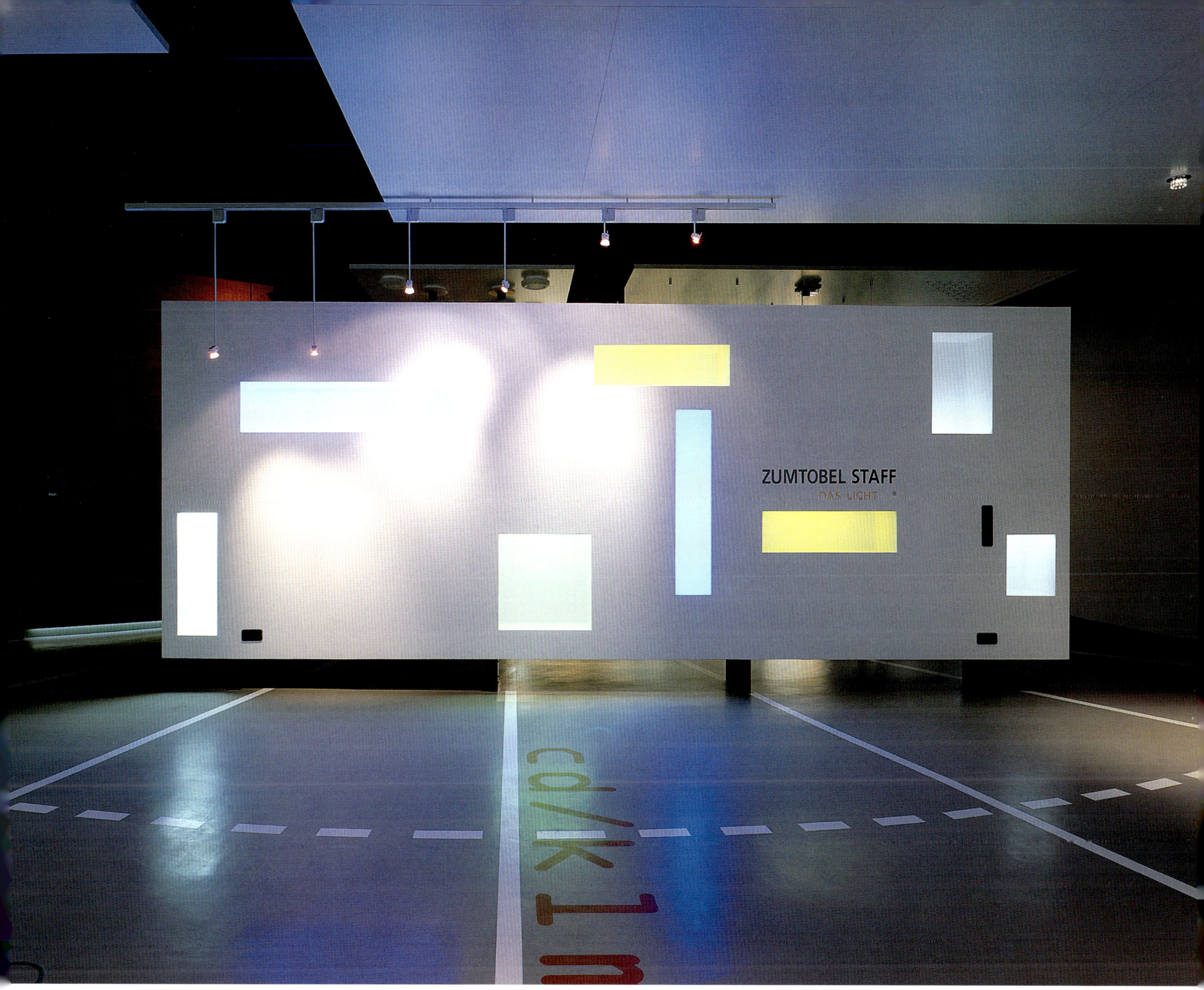

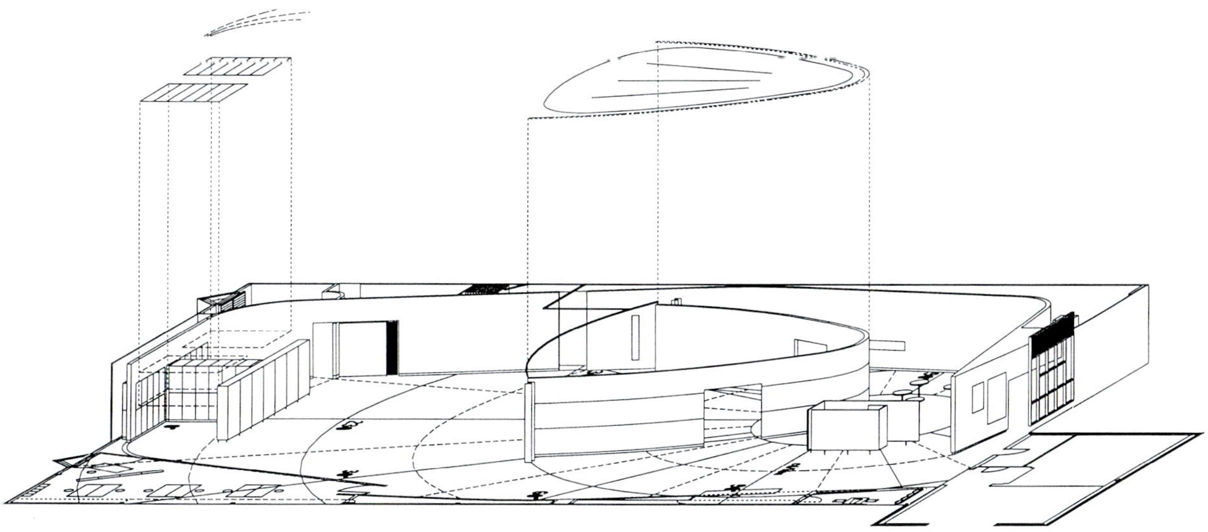

ABOVE: The light wall shows the quality of the manufacturer's luminaires in an environment interpreted literally from a technical light-distribution diagram. **LEFT:** The axonometric reveals how the arrangement of key 3-D elements, such as the conference room, is derived from the floor pattern of the technical diagram.

AXONOMETRIC

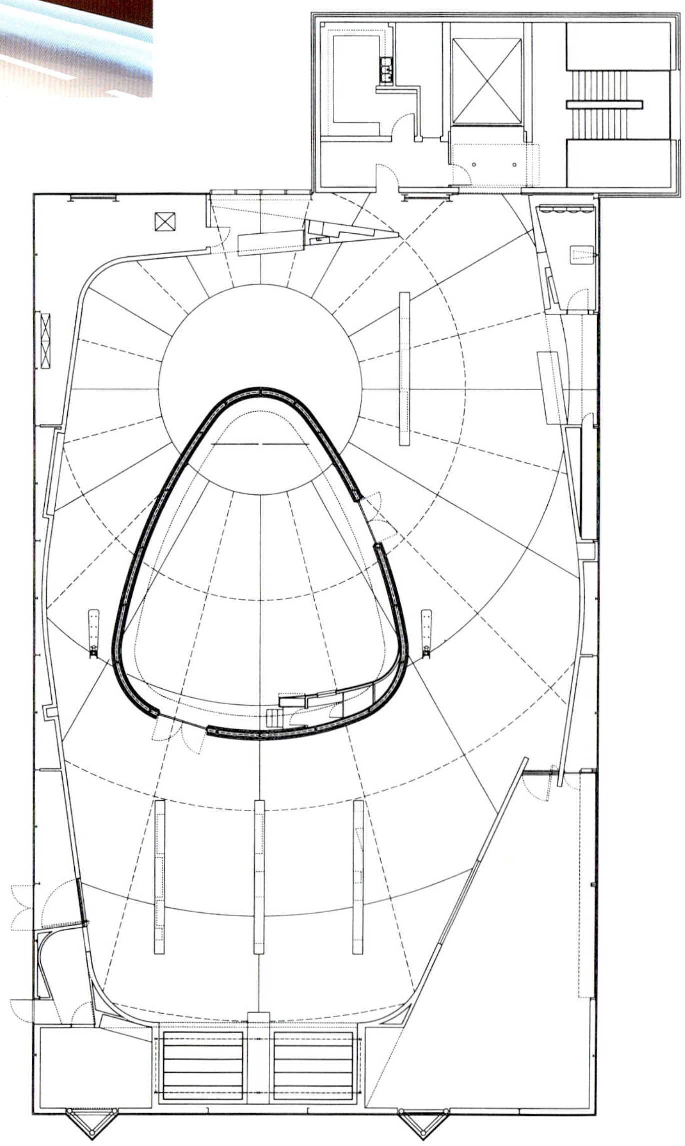

FLOOR PLAN

ABOVE LEFT: The flexible conference room is clad in cherrywood panels.
BELOW LEFT: The floor plan shows the radiating lines of the light diagram.
BELOW: Lighting displays are hung from existing blacked-out ceiling trusses in a scheme which creates a white plasterboard inner-skin within a light-industrial building.

3.4 atelier mendini
swatch store
milan, italy

Mendini's orchestration of spiral forms, steel curves and exaggerated perspectives turn this jewel-like Milanese shop for the watch company Swatch into a sophisticated play on both time and space

SWATCH'S myriad lines of wrist-watches, some of them in limited editions, have won both mass-market appeal and cult status. Alessandro Mendini and his studio are long-term collaborators with the company and have used this perspective to interpret the aesthetic of the timepieces in an intriguing Italian retail store described by Mendini as a 'sci-fi gathering space'.

Even before entering the Via Montenapoleone store, the glazed shop front reveals a bank of brushed stainless-steel undulations in semi-darkness forming the back and side walls. These sections hold display cases with back-lit panels and deep-blue sides that lift the watch colours from the surrounding steel curves. The perpendicular emphasis of the steel curves is stretched almost out of view by a mirrored ceiling, in the middle of which swim the reflections of customers on the finely detailed, coloured-mosaic floor. The ascendant theme reaches its pinnacle in the corner behind the sales desk where a column with a spiral design, painted by Massimo Iosa Ghini, hints at the millennial architectural inspiration behind the display.

Just as the surface patterns and colours of the watches are drawn out into the retail environment, so the mix of metal and plastic creates its own narrative. Serried lines of brushed-steel screws are exposed in a playful imitation of Swatch's new metal watch-straps. Closely detailed materials – reflective and textured – combine to futuristic effect. The swirling forms, the exaggeration of perspective and the combination of colours create a kaleidoscopic experience where, even if time stands still, the space will keep on moving.

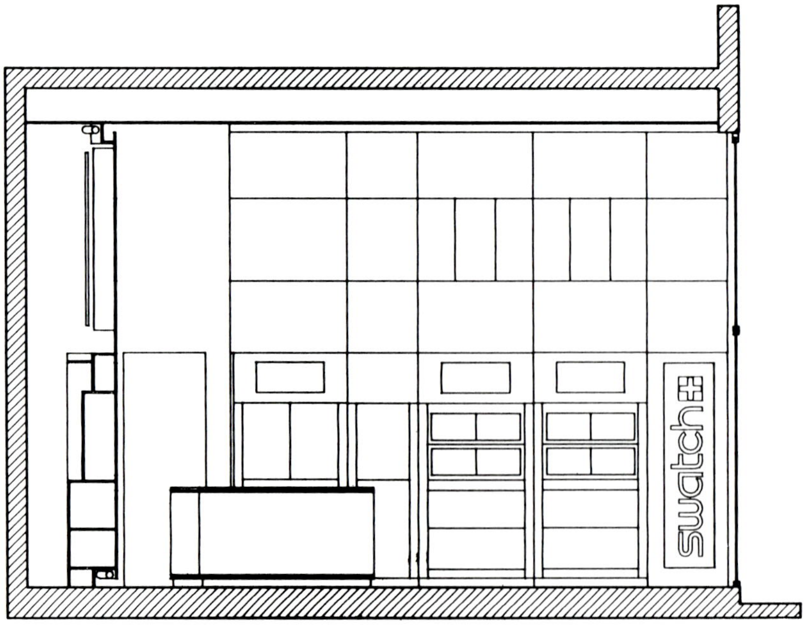

SECTION

COMPLETED **November 1994**

COMMISSIONING CLIENT **Swatch AG**

TOTAL FLOOR SPACE **30 square metres**

NUMBER OF FLOORS **1**

LEFT: The undulating curves of display panels combine with a mosaic floor and spiral column design to create a kaleidoscopic effect, as Swatch plays up to its cult-style status in this Milanese flagship store.

BELOW: View towards frontage from rear of store. Controlled decoration gives a small space a visual identity.

LEFT: Massimo Iosa Ghini's spiral column emerges from the deliberate gloom within the depths of the store, which is given a mysterious sci-fi flavour.

FAR RIGHT: Curved display panels open to reveal merchandise inside.

BELOW RIGHT: The floor plan reveals an arrangement of back-lit display cages.

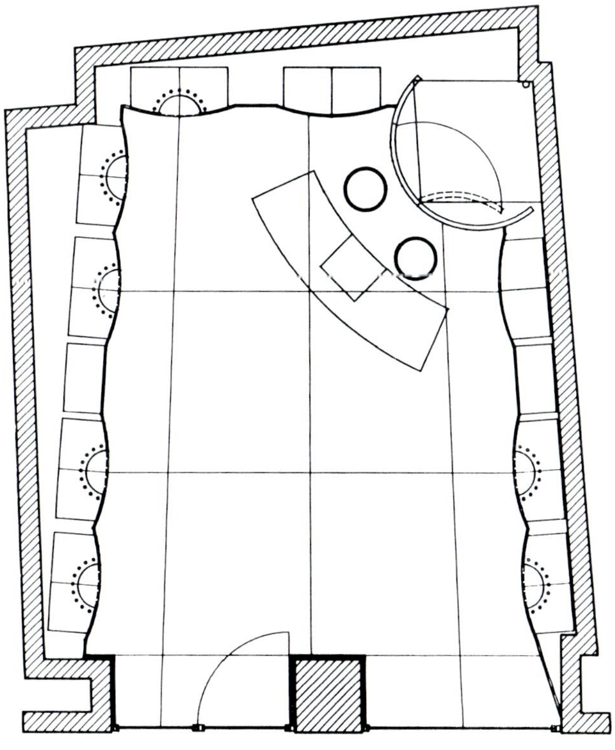

FLOOR PLAN

3.5 john pawson
jigsaw
london, uk

Set on a canvas of pure white plaster, John Pawson's Jigsaw clothing store transcends the fickleness of the fashion industry in the timelessness of its materials and the generosity of its proportions

THE architectural minimalism of John Pawson has become so much part of popular culture that it has received the ultimate accolade: satirical treatment in a TV commercial for a bar of soap. London's New Bond Street, meanwhile, has become a kind of gladiatorial shopping arena for the international fashion-retail giants to compete against one another. What would New Bond Street make of Pawson, and vice versa? The answer is that Pawson has respected both the grain of the famous shopping avenue and the personality of the Jigsaw merchandise in this carefully composed flagship scheme, without ever losing sight of his own mission to explore the fundamentals of space, light and materials.

ABOVE: The double-height window exhibits the interior space.
RIGHT: The staircase to the lower level reveals the purity of the concept, the thickness of the materials and the generosity of the interior volumes.

Jigsaw is based in a pair of domestically scaled nineteenth-century buildings previously used as an electronics shop. Pawson has stripped the façade of any additions and carried this pared-down visual simplicity right back beyond the bronze-clad frontage through the full 30-metre depth of the store. He has hidden all services behind smooth white planes, using light to create space by 'floating' the walls free of the ceiling. The palette of materials is restrained and expansive at one and the same time: white bush-hammered granite and large timber plank floors to create continuous, generous surfaces; semi-translucent etched-acrylic screens, walnut furniture and timber-shelving units to adorn the canvas.

From the upper sales floor, which has a soaring double-height space of six metres, a pair of staircases penetrate the wall down to the lower level, really cutting through the thickness of the material. Within this setting, Jigsaw's stylish clothes stand out without any effort. That minimalist-mocking TV commercial features an urban couple living with nothing but stark concrete forms and planes of light, one of whom cannot resist retaining one secret luxury – a bar of foamy soap. Pawson's Jigsaw, however, is not about denial. The effect is one of quiet, understated luxury.

COMPLETED **March 1996**

COMMISSIONING CLIENT **Jigsaw (Robinson Webster Holdings)**

TOTAL FLOOR SPACE **660 square metres**

NUMBER OF FLOORS **2**

TOTAL CONTRACT COST **£1 million**

ELEVATION OF SHOPFRONT

ABOVE LEFT: The shopfront respects the grain of the street. The store is inserted into two Victorian buildings, taking on their essential proportions.

ABOVE: Behind the corridor-like partitioned sections at the front of the shop is a luminous space furnished with sofas.

FAR LEFT: Jigsaw's clothes are given prominence in a scheme which uses light to 'float' walls from ceilings.

3.6 pep zazurca
ronda store
barcelona, spain

A historic brick-lined vault is transformed into a stylish and practical clothing store in this Spanish project, which uses an economy of means to produce pleasing results

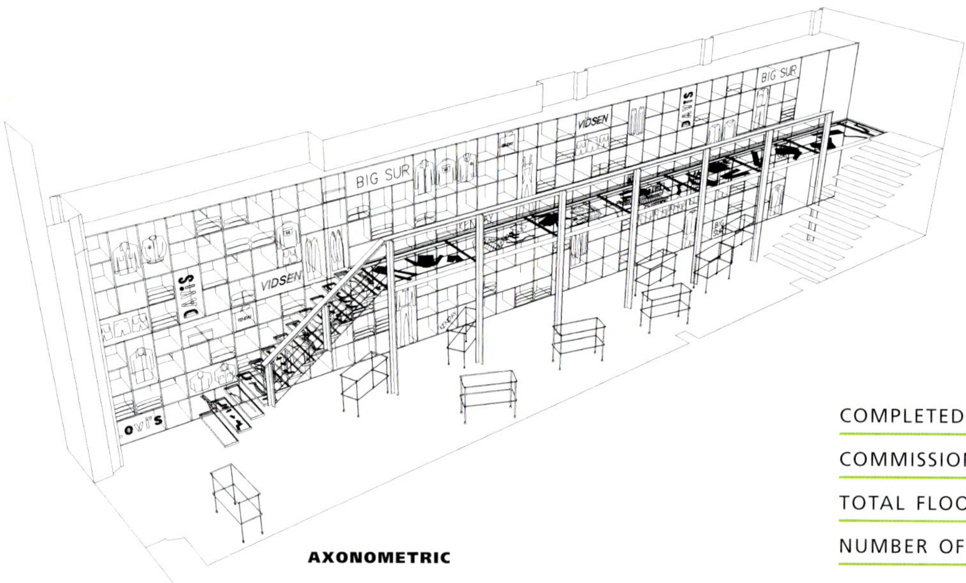

AXONOMETRIC

COMPLETED **January 1996**

COMMISSIONING CLIENT **Ronda SA**

TOTAL FLOOR SPACE **90 square metres**

NUMBER OF LEVELS **2**

THE Ronda fashion store in Barcelona is anything but round. This stylishly utilitarian clothing outlet has been fashioned by architect Pep Zazurca within a long, narrow, brick-lined tube in a listed historic building. The recently restored walls of this vault are under a protection order so Zazurca created an autonomous shopfitting structure, with a wooden shelving system running the full 20 metres length and 4.5 metres height of the store. This smooth-fronted shelving was specially designed with different depths to correct the uneven texture, defects and inclines of the brick wall.

Stairs to a lightweight, glass footbridge take customers up on to a mezzanine level so that they can view merchandise on the upper tiers of the flexible shelving unit. This footbridge creates a fluent circulation path around the store and is subtly under-lit with fluorescent tubes so that the lines of perspective are accentuated. At the back of the store a mirror gives the illusion of space, while three rows of ceiling-mounted television monitors screen commercials through the interior. The brick wall opposite the shelving unit has been left bare apart from painted graffiti-style trademarks of the designer gear on sale.

At ground-floor level, merchandise is casually piled on glass and metal carts: these represent a series of miniature, mobile refrains of the glass footbridge. This is a simple, but highly effective scheme, in which Zazurca's collaboration with interior designer Mar Ruiz has created a selling environment that respects the fabric of the vault without being overawed by it.

ABOVE: View from the glass footbridge along the wooden shelving system which is separate from the historic brick vault. Three rows of ceiling-mounted TV monitors punctuate the space.

LEFT: The interior expresses a clearly delineated circulation flow. Glass and metal merchandise carts complement the large, horizontal footbridge structure. **RIGHT:** The shelving system was custom-designed with different depths to fit flush with uneven brick walls. **BELOW:** The drawing shows the capacity and versatility of the shelving unit.

SHELVING UNIT

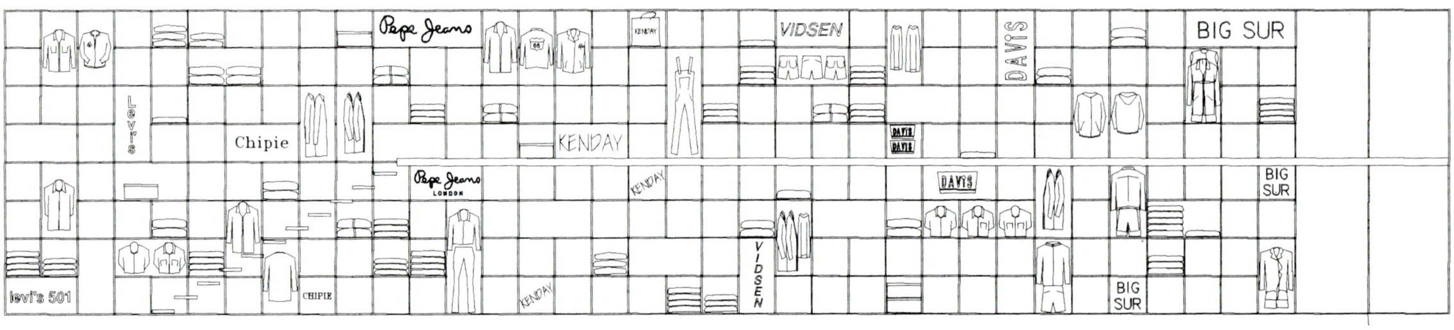

3.7 petzinka pink & partner
eickhoff store
düsseldorf, germany

Relaxed and understated, this flagship fashion store combines the quality detailing and furnishings of Europe with the scale and space of the New York loft

THIS project to rebuild and extend Eickhoff's clothing showrooms at 30 Königsallee, in the fashion-conscious city of Düsseldorf, relies on understatement and simplicity to create a relaxed and approachable minimalist interior. Although the scheme is German in the scrupulous quality of its execution and detailing, the key influences on the retail design are from further afield.

COMPLETED **1996**

COMMISSIONING CLIENT **Eickhoff-Königsallee GmbH & Co**

TOTAL FLOOR SPACE **720 square metres**

NUMBER OF FLOORS **3**

TOTAL CONTRACT COST **DM 4.2 million**

The designers have used the impressive scale of the space as you look up from the ground-floor level to evoke the feeling of a New York loft. All three main retail spaces are knitted together by the calm, pale French sandstone of the floors, which are echoed in the surfaces of counters and cash desks, and by the greenish glow of sand-blasted glass panels. Only on the stairs and upper floor is Japanese ash introduced to add a third soothing tone. The sole detailing on the empty walls is a large embossed Eickhoff logo, in the same colour as the walls themselves, and a line of three video screens. In such a pared-down space, individual elements take on an amplified role: metal handles, clothes racks and mirrors describe tall elegant shapes in the pools of light thrown down from the track lighting recessed in the high ceilings.

The display surfaces and clothes rails remain true to the rectilinear Modernist proportions of the overall scheme. Within this restrained stage set, the clarity of the clothing immediately catches the eye, as do furniture pieces by Marcel Breuer, Philippe Starck and Peter Preller. Most striking of all is Preller's ellipsoidal pear-wood display table, covered in 24-carat gold leaf. This is an extravagant flourish in an otherwise modest and muted project that handsomely achieves its aims with an economy of means.

LEFT: The shopfront sets the tone of understated finesse on a Düsseldorf street.
ABOVE: Lofty ideals are expressed in this view through the double-height space of the Eickhoff store.

LEFT: The staircase to the lower level reveals a calm oasis studded with Philippe Starck chairs. The pale French sandstone floor and the sandblasted glass panels are the project's unifying elements.
BELOW: Against the immaculate detail of the muted interior palette, the clothing immediately draws the eye.

3.8 caulder moore

mahogany hair salon

london, uk

Rich, subtle and exotic in colour, form and material, this hairdressing salon extends the craft tradition on a London site intimately associated with William Morris

COMPLETED **May 1995**

COMMISSIONING CLIENT **Mahogany**

TOTAL FLOOR SPACE **2,500 square feet**

NUMBER OF FLOORS **2**

TOTAL CONTRACT COST **£250,000**

DESIGNED on the site of the original showroom and workshop of the father figure of the Arts and Crafts Movement, William Morris, this London hairdressing salon extends more than a cursory contemporary nod in the direction of the craft tradition. It is a rich and subtly eclectic space in colour, shape and material. The accent on luxury, permanence and longevity befits a client aiming to open new salons in other international cities using the same design blueprint.

There is a hint of the exotic about an organic interior which combines stone and timber flooring, wall sections in purple plaster, amber and blue glass, and fret-cut metal in a cool, calm and measured way. The ground floor is devoted to haircutting and finishing. The staircase down to a colour/perm and conditioning service in the basement is given an atmospheric textural interest, which would overcome any reluctance customers may have in descending to the bowels of the listed building. This staircase was moved from the front to the rear of the space to improve circulation, in what was the scheme's major structural alteration.

Hairdressing salons need to meet many physical and psychological requirements. Materials must be durable, hard-wearing and non-porous so that dyes, colourants and chemicals will not be absorbed. Equally, customers must feel relaxed enough to escape into a daydream while the scissors are taken to their precious locks. Mahogany meets both sets of criteria with a visually stimulating environment which never strains for unnatural effects.

LEFT: The treatment of the salon's exterior hints at its Arts and Crafts roots.
ABOVE: The brightly lit basement salon has durable, hard-wearing finishes. Colourful pendants and tiling add an unusual flourish to the environment.

LEFT: The staircase down to the basement level at the rear of the showroom was designed to make the journey to the depths of the building a tactile and aesthetic pleasure.
RIGHT: Ground-floor view towards the front of the salon. The timber flooring in the scheme is called Jarrah. It comes from a sustainable source and resembles mahogany, which is a threatened resource.

BASEMENT PLAN

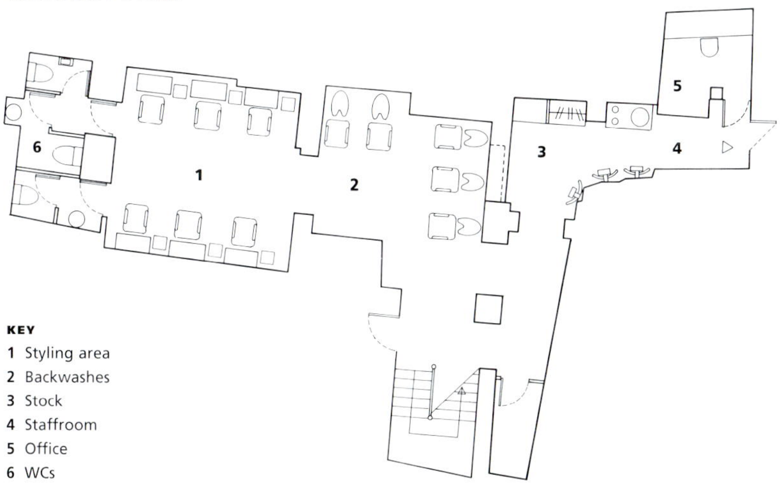

KEY

1 Styling area
2 Backwashes
3 Stock
4 Staffroom
5 Office
6 WCs

GROUND-FLOOR PLAN

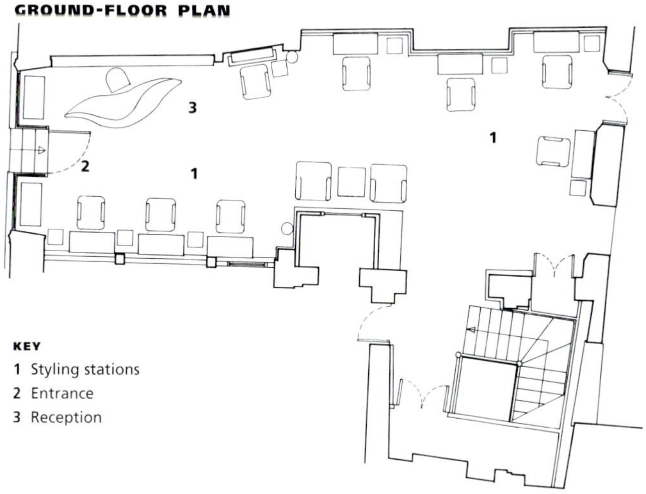

KEY

1 Styling stations
2 Entrance
3 Reception

3.9 anderson/schwartz architects

bumble & bumble hair salon

new york, usa

Part-factory and part-marine underworld, this vast New York City hair salon adopts an industrial aesthetic which fuses together four levels in an inventive collage of colour, material and detail

BELOW: The section reveals the entire four-storey hair factory.
RIGHT: The view of the third-floor salon reflects the playful combinations of industrial materials and finishes.

MOST hairdressing salons assume a coherent domestic scale, which reflects the intimacy of their service. This innovative New York project is an entire four-storey hair factory, expressing the uncompromisingly industrial language of its interiors in its choice of materials and spatial relationships. The mood for visitors is immediately set by a robotic device in reception – an animated construction of rubber tubing, suction cups, metal feet and video monitors – and carried through spaces of invention and ambiguity that play games with the transparent, translucent and opaque.

The scheme's background sets this adventurous interior programme in context. A fire on 1 April 1995 completely gutted the nineteenth-century former carriage house, which housed the old Bumble & Bumble salon. Its owner opted to take over all four storeys of the building and give it the unity of a 'single enterprise'. The response by designer Ross Anderson was to give each floor a distinct identity, while maintaining throughout common architectural features, often in unexpected assemblages, with greenish-plaster surfaces and exposed steel finishes to create an 'aquatic' feel.

The basement is a support and storage space; the ground floor consists of the main entry, cutting salon and café; the offices are on the second floor, with executive offices on the mezzanine; and the third floor between the two office layers contains the colour salon with its reception and make-up studio. Fibreglass and acrylic screens, aluminium brackets, poured-concrete cutting stations and stained-plywood flooring are all part of the dynamic material mix. The floors are linked by a stairwell, which contains a two-storey tower of angular steel and metal grating, and displays some of the 20 different industrial and marine lighting fixtures that illuminate this imaginative and often disconcerting scheme.

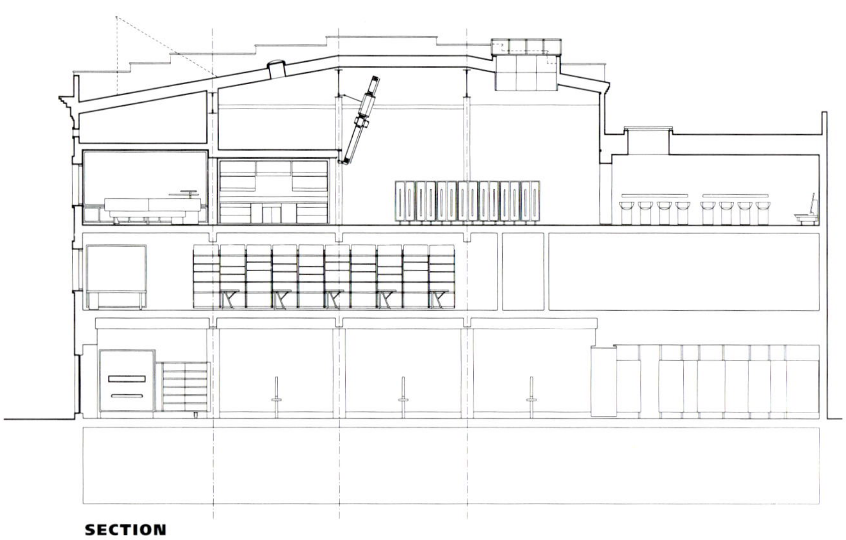

SECTION

COMPLETED **January 1996**
COMMISSIONING CLIENT **Bumble + Bumble**
TOTAL FLOOR SPACE **16,800 square feet**
NUMBER OF FLOORS **4**
TOTAL CONTRACT COST **$1.4 million**

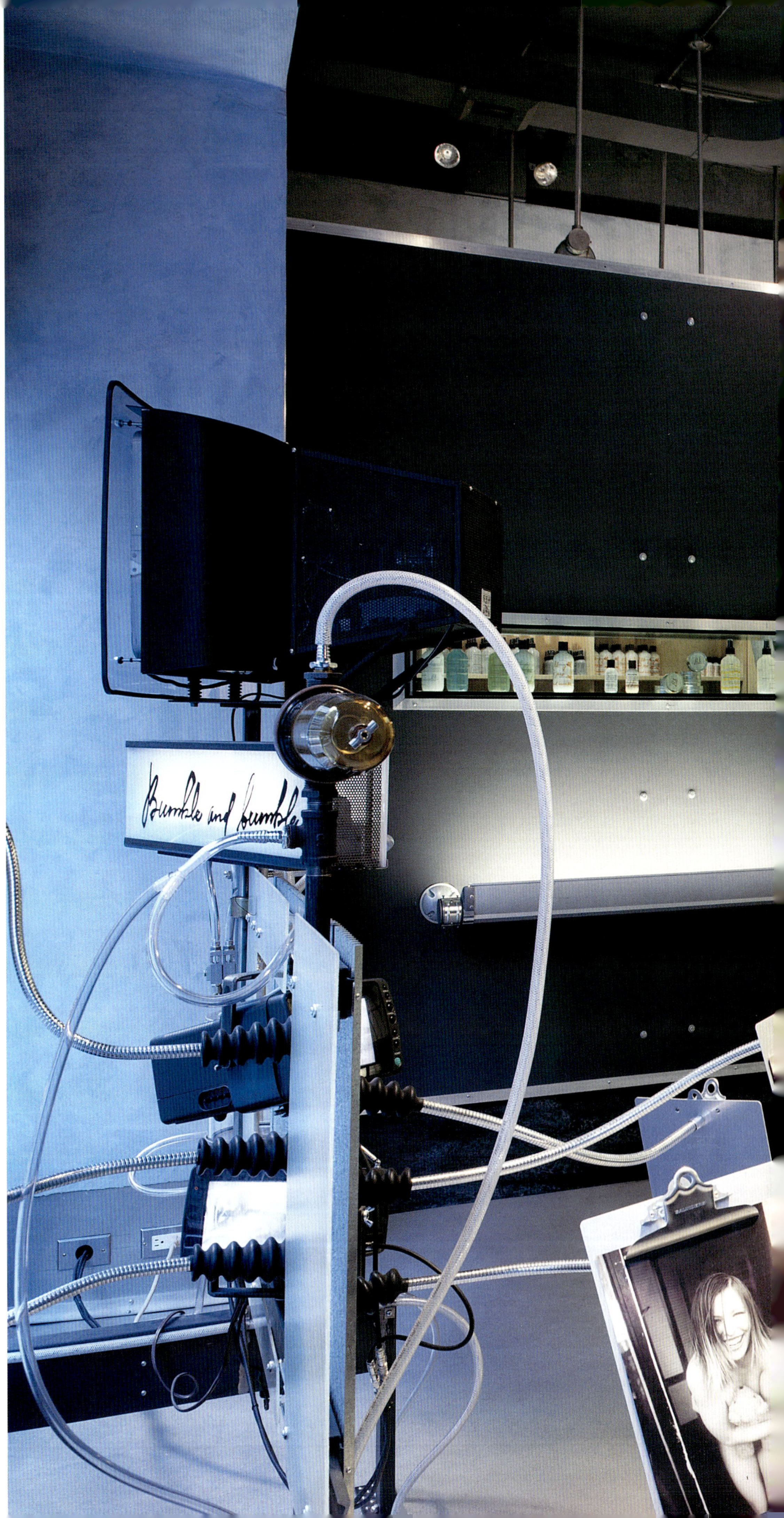

RIGHT: The ground-floor reception features a robotic assemblage of rubber tubing, suction cups and video monitors, which is visible in front of a window on to Manhattan East 56th Street. The main salon reception is a translucent structure sheathed with light-green acrylic and fibreglass panels to create a sense of anticipation and curiosity. The entire scheme plays games with transparency and openness.

ABOVE: Whitewashed plywood flooring is painted with black dye, in a design based on Brice Marten's 'First Blotting Drawing'. The idea is for additional stains to complete the painting over time. **ABOVE CENTRE:** View of third-floor salon. Box-like colour workstations, as shown on right, are mobile. **ABOVE RIGHT:** Ground-floor cutting stations are a hive of industry, with tough, durable finishes.

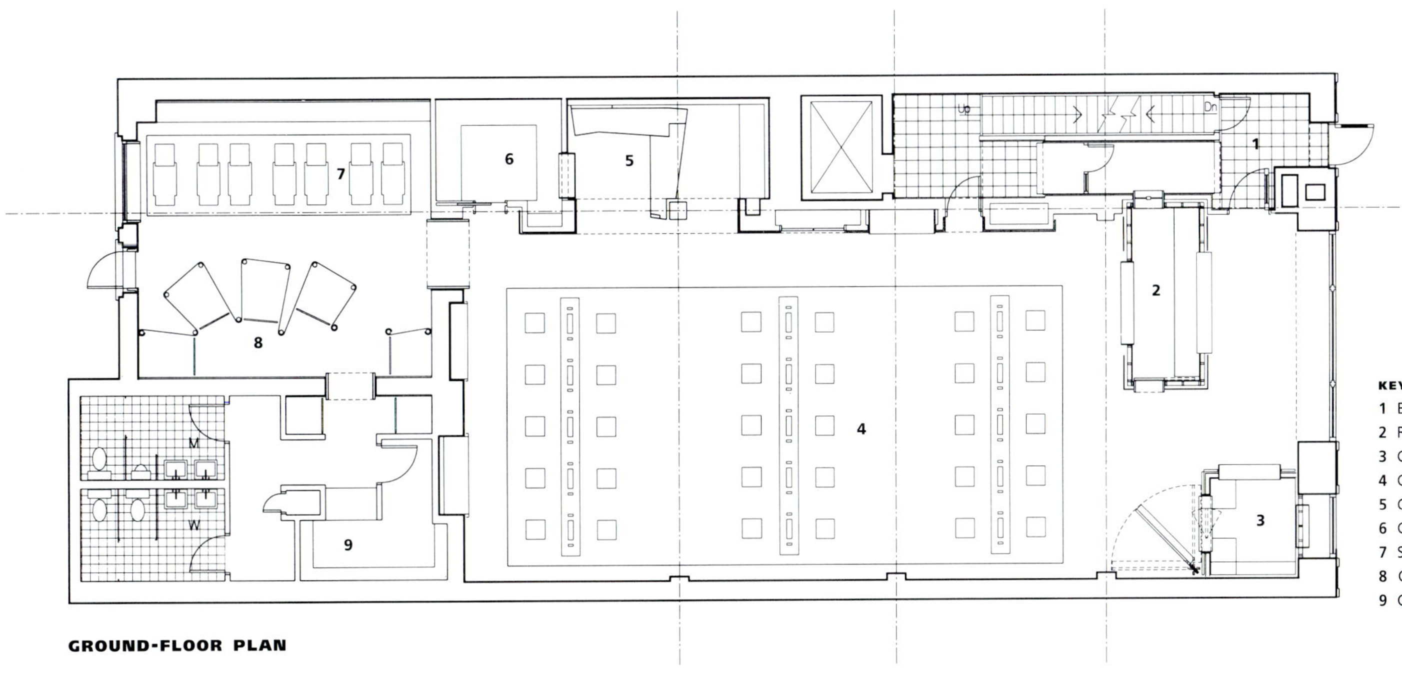

KEY

1 Entry
2 Reception
3 Cashier
4 Cutting stations
5 Café
6 Café preparation
7 Shampoo
8 Changing area
9 Coats

GROUND-FLOOR PLAN

3.10 makoto koizumi
toppan network lounge
tokyo, japan

A shrine to the spirit of software, this Japanese Internet showroom provides an intriguing access point to the super-information highway in its composition of ready-made materials, space and light

THIS showroom for Internet users is an imaginative and unusual response to the task of expressing the virtuality of the worldwide web within the physicality of a small space. Designer Makoto Koizumi has exploited the compactness of the interior to create a spatial ambiguity in which large objects are made to appear and disappear, depending on where you are standing, in a careful orchestration of colour, light and material effects. This attempt to reduce the impact or dissolve physical artefacts reflects the dematerializing process of the Internet.

The showroom is dominated by two shapes: a brown-diagonal bar, behind which computer terminals await the user, and a blue-rotunda form, in which a screen is set towards the glazed entrance. One interior view within this converted warehouse building presents the artefacts as pure forms in an abstract composition, concealing the high-tech equipment beyond and behind. The mood is of a clean-lined shrine dedicated to the spirit of software, with no visually distracting hardware.

An additional factor is the designer's decision to use only ready-made materials: the yellow walls in the workstation area are aluminium spandrels usually found in Japanese underground stations' ceilings. The total effect is of an object-interior singular in intent and strangely calming to the eye, with its linoleum floor and painted-acrylic surfaces.

COMPLETED **May 1996**

COMMISSIONING CLIENT **Toppan Printing Co.**

TOTAL FLOOR SPACE **70 square metres**

NUMBER OF FLOORS **1**

RIGHT: View along the bar that faces on to the glazed frontage. A studious calmness is presented by the composition of abstract shapes.

LEFT: View to the rear of the showroom is a collage of shape, line and light, with all hardware and wires hidden from view. The emphasis is on the dematerializing process of new technology, but there is also an ecological theme in the reuse of newly mades: the yellow walls are aluminium spandrels usually found in Japanese underground stations.
RIGHT: The glazed showroom frontage beckons Net surfers inside.

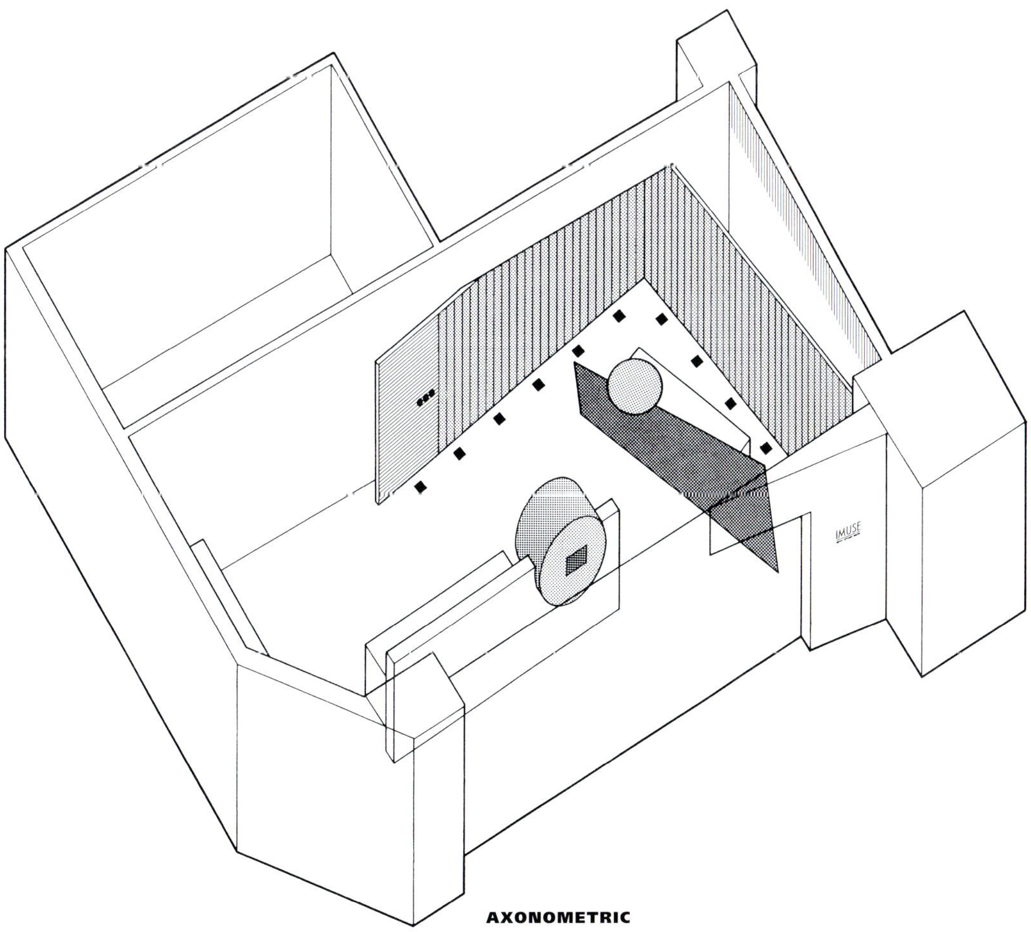

AXONOMETRIC

3.11 fitch inc.
planet reebok
new york, usa

Interactive information sources, website links, mobile display units and sport-specific video monitors turn Reebok's product line into a dynamic, transmutable merchandising 'laboratory' for the brand

NOWHERE is the phenomenon of brand manufacturers moving into the retail arena more vividly expressed than in the American sporting goods industry, where Planet Reebok is now head to head with Nike Town in the battle of the running shoe. The aim in each case has been to translate the philosophy of the product brand into a dynamic retail environment. Fitch's work on Planet Reebok is aimed at consumers who want to be 'fit for life': it is a flexible, fast-paced scheme on a single floor with the accent on information, service and celebrity endorsement of the Reebok range.

A key theme of the project, which is sited in the heart of Manhattan next door to the Reebok Sports Club and near the Lincoln Center, is the large-scale introduction of interactive touch-screen information kiosks to help customers get to grips with the wide choice of footwear, apparel and accessories. A 'sports concierge' is on hand to answer questions and provide access through an Internet link to Reebok's website. Sport-specific video monitors for tennis, basketball, aerobics and other sporting activities help customers to navigate the large floor space, in which a series of dynamic display arcs, overlaid on the building's box-like interior shape, create a strong sense of movement.

Fitch has designed the store as a flexible set: merchandising, graphics and visuals are all easily movable. This wheels-on-everything approach allows reshaping of the retail space for events in-store and also allows physical repositioning of merchandise throughout the day as the customer base fluctuates. The floor plan creates separate 'worlds' for the display of men's and women's clothing, each with their own dressing-room areas. This is part of a modular concept designed to enable Reebok to constantly experiment with and amend its trading format in response to changing customer needs. Little wonder that Fitch describes Planet Reebok as a 'merchandising laboratory'.

RIGHT: A concept board shows a section through the merchandise display. **FAR RIGHT:** View of the main trading floor at Planet Reebok. The accent is on total flexibility of movement.

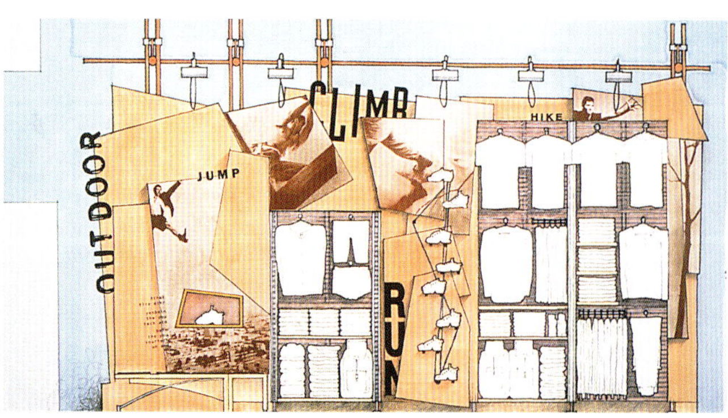

COMPLETED **August 1995**
COMMISSIONING CLIENT **Reebok International**
TOTAL FLOOR SPACE **4,500 square feet**
NUMBER OF FLOORS **1**

NO MERCY
NO LIMITS

FLOOR PLAN

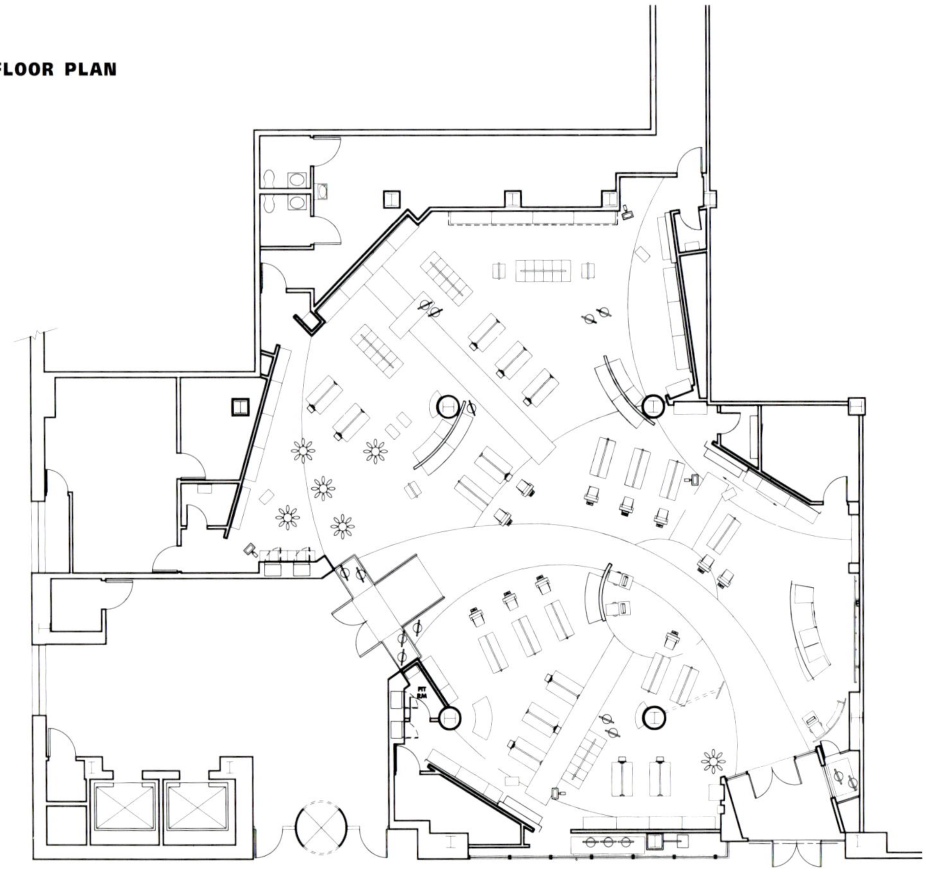

ABOVE LEFT: Women's clothing area. Research revealed that each sex wanted their own 'worlds'.
ABOVE CENTRE: Planet Reebok store front. The dynamic curve of the logo is given rhythmic expression in the store interior, especially in the floor plans.
ABOVE RIGHT: Curved merchandising unit with built-in video information monitor reflects a high-tech, dynamic approach to shifting the merchandise.

4 cultural and public amenity buildings

public

Public patronage of the civic interior continues to flourish as signature schemes brimming with inventive forms and materials are regarded as prime vehicles to communicate local and national aspirations

MUCH has been written about how the growing competition between cities and regions around the world has fuelled a boom in landmark public buildings and interiors. Civic commissions, designed and built to act as a catalyst for economic and cultural regeneration, kept many architects and designers afloat in the early 1990s at a time when private-sector clients were shelving their plans amid loss of business confidence.

Today interior design continues to flourish on a scale that is constantly being revised upwards as regional and national authorities, especially those in the Asia Pacific region, up the ante. We have already witnessed Cesar Pelli's Petronas Twin Towers in Kuala Lumpur, Malaysia, being officially designated as the world's tallest buildings, at more than 450 metres high. Ironically, however, the largest and most ambitious public complex of all, the $1.5 billion Tokyo International Forum, owes its development not to the civic competition of the 1990s, but to the economic expansionism of the late 1980s.

1

At the end of the last decade, Tokyo's mayor, Shunichi Suzuki, decided to capitalize on Japan's financial bubble with a Mitterrand-style *grand projet* to remodel Tokyo's rundown financial district. Kenzo Tange's 1957 City Hall was demolished, the Tokyo Metropolitan Government was relocated to the outskirts of the city, and an international competition was held to find a scheme to give Tokyo a new commercial and cultural heart. The New York-based Argentinian designer Rafael Viñoly beat a field of 395 entries from 68 different countries to gain the commission; the result is a design that sets new standards in the scale of public interiors.

The Forum extends across a seven-acre site and has four major theatres. At its centre is a Glass Hall, a structure so dramatic that the *New York Times* was moved to declare: 'Hagia Sophia, the Guggenheim Museum and Grand Central Terminal have a new cousin.' The thrilling vision of the Tokyo International Forum may be inexorably linked to the powerful patronage of one exceptional public official, Suzuki. Other signature schemes around the world owe their realization not just to persuasive individuals but also to persistent committees and councils, whose collective approach has shown equal commitment to using design to express the future of their cities.

In Leipzig, for example, the city fathers have built a giant new Messe complex at speed on the site of a former airport, aided by post-reunification federal funds poured into the East

1 BARCELONA MUSEUM OF MODERN ART, BARCELONA, SPAIN
Designed by Richard Meier
Meier's trademark whiteness, used to sharpen perception of visual form, is applied with customary Modernist rigour in this scheme, which creates flexible daylit galleries within a complex urban medieval setting.

2 MYCAL CULTURAL AND ATHLETIC CENTER, SHIN-SANDA, JAPAN
Designed by Emilio Ambasz & Associates
Conceived as an L-shaped wall that braces a hillside garden, the immense 450,000 square-foot massing of this complex has been reduced by sympathetically covering facilities with earth and turfing through which water flows from one reflecting pool to the next. Skylights within these pools allow natural light to filter down to public areas below.

3/4 TECHNIQUEST SCIENCE DISCOVERY CENTRE, CARDIFF, WALES
Designed by Ahrends Burton & Koralek
A derelict marine engineering repair shed, built on the Cardiff waterfront in 1898, has been converted into a new science centre. The original fine cast and wrought-iron structure remains integral to the light and airy new building. The centrepiece of the scheme is the main exhibition hall which soars 11 metres high into the vaulted roof.

by the German government. Designed by Von Gerkan Marg & Partner, this too has an inspirational glass hall as its focal point. There is an irony that the Victorian spirit of Joseph Paxton's Crystal Palace clearly lives on in public environments produced for the new millennium.

Leipzig's Neue Messe is typically German in its planning and grid, its generous volumes and anticipation of future growth. Indeed many of the projects in our selection reflect a strong sense of place. While a global design style can be seen in many offices, stores and leisure chains, architects and designers appear to regard the public interior as a prime vehicle to communicate national identity. Nowhere is this better demonstrated than on the far-flung shores of Iceland where Studio Granda's Supreme Court at Reykjavik, facing directly on to the Atlantic, incorporates ocean hues in the fluent contours of its locally crafted interiors.

The American vernacular, in design, can be seen at work in the use by Michael Graves of reclaimed Oregon timbers to create a derrick structure in one of the main reading rooms of his much enlarged Denver Central Library. The city of Weimar in Germany, meanwhile, evokes its Modernist legacy as the first home of the Bauhaus with a new music school designed by Thomas van den Valentyn along Corbusian lines. National identity of a different order can be discerned in the colourfully eclectic interiors of John Outram's Judge Institute at Cambridge, which appear to follow the noble tradition of the English eccentric.

Outram invented a colourful new material for the Judge Institute project: Doodlecrete, an inlaid concrete made with rubber moulds. Material invention is indeed a theme of our selection. The Banyoles Municipal Theatre in Spain, for example, does amazing things with high-density plywood; Dubus & Lott's expressive Palace of Justice at Evreux, in France, demonstrates the plasticity of concrete; while The Basement designed by Ben Kelly for the Science Museum is a tactile, technicolour experience which introduces youngsters to the different properties of materials – from tiles and bricks to linoleum and exposed steel.

One tends to think of the public environment as a solemn design statement for adults, typified by the civic library, university campus and town hall. A number of the projects shown here, nevertheless, were designed specifically for children. Just like The Basement, the Techniquest Science Discovery Centre – a Welsh scheme by Ahrends Burton Koralek in Cardiff's docklands – is all about giving children a vibrant introduction to the wonders of science. In Japan, the spiralling forms of the Environment Design Institute and Mitsuru Senda's fantastical Children's castle at Aichi demonstrates Senda's belief in the benefits of circular play. The current motto in public interiors is clearly: catch them young.

1

2

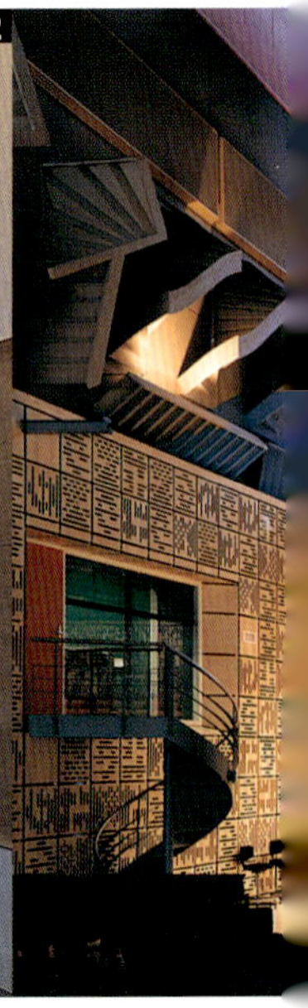

public projects

1 NAKAMADICHAI COMMUNITY CENTER, YOKOHAMA, JAPAN
Designed by Hiroshi and Akiko Takahashi
The dramatic curve of a glazed forecourt is the public face of a scheme that unites a range of facilities for local residents in one building.

2 WHITWORTH ART GALLERY, MANCHESTER, UK
Designed by Ahrends Burton & Koralek
This impressive restoration scheme for a famous Edwardian art gallery includes a new sculpture court which incorporates the building's original rear façade and is topped by an elegant, curved white ceiling.

3/4 BROADCASTING AUTHORITIES MUSIC CENTRE, HILVERSUM, THE NETHERLANDS
Designed by De Architekten Cie
Patterned acoustic panelling in this Dutch concert hall scheme is both practical and decorative.

5 SCIENCE INDUSTRY AND BUSINESS LIBRARY, NEW YORK PUBLIC LIBRARY, NEW YORK, USA
Designed by Gwathmey Siegel & Associates Architects
A 250,000-square-foot scheme housed on seven floors of the historic B. Altman Building in New York creates an important new facility tailored to house the latest information technologies.

3

4

5

4.1 rafael viñoly architects

tokyo international forum glass hall

tokyo, japan

One of the largest civic architectural projects of the late twentieth century remodels Tokyo's business district with a new cultural complex, featuring a Glass Hall of exceptional design and engineering virtuosity

RIGHT: Pedestrian bridges connect conference rooms across the void beneath the magnificent shiplike, 56 steel-rib structure, which comprises the centrepiece of Rafael Viñoly's Glass Hall.

IT HAS been described as Tokyo's Crystal Palace. The awe-inspiring Glass Hall which forms the centrepiece of Argentinian Rafael Viñoly's massive 1.5-million-square-foot Tokyo International Forum project, is in the best architectural-engineering traditions of the great light-filled nineteenth-century civic hall. This beguiling enclosure, however, actually says a lot more about the city of the future than of the past. Its daring skeletal roof structure, rib-shaped like a ship's hull with a clear-span 750-foot truss balanced on top of two monumental steel-pipe columns, is the entire scheme's structural tour de force, as well as its transparent social heart.

The Tokyo International Forum is a public regeneration project that almost defies belief in its ambition and proportions. When the Tokyo Metropolitan Government decided to relocate its city hall from the main business district to the city's periphery, it held an international competition to develop a new complex to restore cultural and civic functions to the area. Viñoly's winning scheme extends across a staggering seven acres and includes four major performance halls for dance, music and theatre; these are arranged in a series of diminishing volumes that follow the convex curve of the epic Glass Hall.

Add commercial exhibition, conference, retail, library-mediatech and café spaces – all connected by a series of dramatic walkways, bridges and ramps, and linked to an underground train terminal – then you have an urban nexus of immense scale and complexity. The abiding memory, however, is of the Glass Hall which is open to the public 24 hours a day and is a powerful statement about civic openness and responsibility. In an earthquake-prone city where any glass construct is very much an act of faith, its glass curtain wall – 187 feet high – reaches up to where restaurants and art galleries offer views of a Tokyo forever changed by Viñoly's stunning intervention.

COMPLETED **June 1996**

COMMISSIONING CLIENT **Tokyo Metropolitan Government**

TOTAL FLOOR SPACE **47,000 square feet**

NUMBER OF STOREYS **3**

TOTAL CONTRACT COST **US $1.5 billion (entire Tokyo International Forum scheme)**

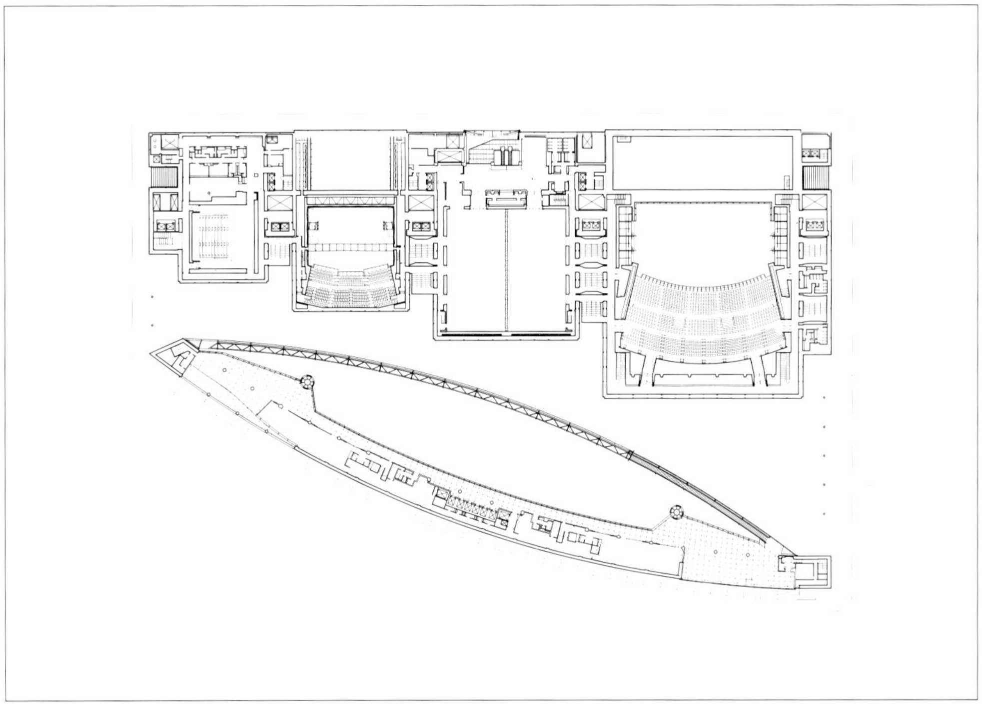

THEATRE-LEVEL PLAN

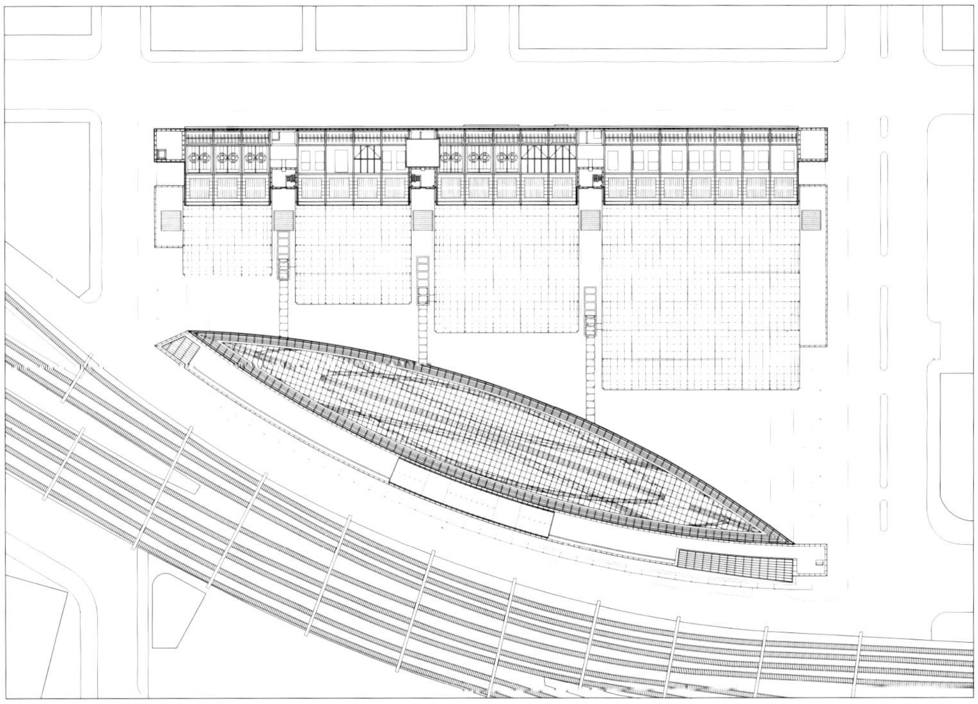

ROOF PLAN

LEFT: The exterior view of the Glass Hall of the Tokyo International Forum reveals the sheer audacity of constructing a glass curtain wall 187 feet high in an earthquake-prone city.
ABOVE: The plans show how the four main performing arts theatres are differently scaled to fit into all the convex curves of the Glass Hall on a constrained urban site.

4.2 studio granda

the supreme court of iceland

reykjavik, iceland

A unique position overlooking the Atlantic Ocean sets the local colour, materials and craftsmanship of this intelligent courtroom scheme in its own special context

ABOVE: Exterior of the court with upper levels of façade clad in patinated copper sheet. **RIGHT:** View of the main courtroom which uses local craft skills and a sombre and dignified palette of colours. The cool-blue band of glazing reflects the building's location overlooking the Atlantic Ocean.

SITED ON a low hill in the centre of Reykjavik, which is open on its west side to the Atlantic Ocean, the Supreme Court of Iceland makes the most of its sea aspect in its interior design. Not only are there commanding views of the sea from the judges' quarters – a series of exceptionally high rooms on the top floor – but a palette of cool blues and greens used on the walls and in the glazing reflects a calm, sombre ocean.

Colour, natural materials and local craft skills knit this dignified scheme together: the oak, plaster, polished concrete and steel of the interior echo the mainly rectilinear shapes of the building's exterior form, with its upper street façades of patinated-copper sheet above a hewn-basalt plinth. The internal functions are organized around a stair and lift core which lead up to the judges' rooms and are surrounded by meeting rooms, a library and secretarial areas.

So concerned were the designers with separating the public from the judiciary that there is the sense of two complete, independent environments within a single enveloping skin. On the public side of the court, a ramp runs the length of the building from the ground-floor reception at the south façade and back again on a higher level; different courtrooms and reception rooms are posted along this ramp with diminishing volumes in relation to their scale, as daylight penetrates through narrow slots. This is a finely tuned project which manages to convey a measured authority without ever losing the natural vitality its ocean-facing location deserves.

COMPLETED **September 1996**

COMMISSIONING CLIENT **The Icelandic State**

TOTAL FLOOR SPACE **2,613 square metres**

NUMBER OF FLOORS **4**

TOTAL CONTRACT COST **4 million Icelandic Kroner (approx. £3,225,806)**

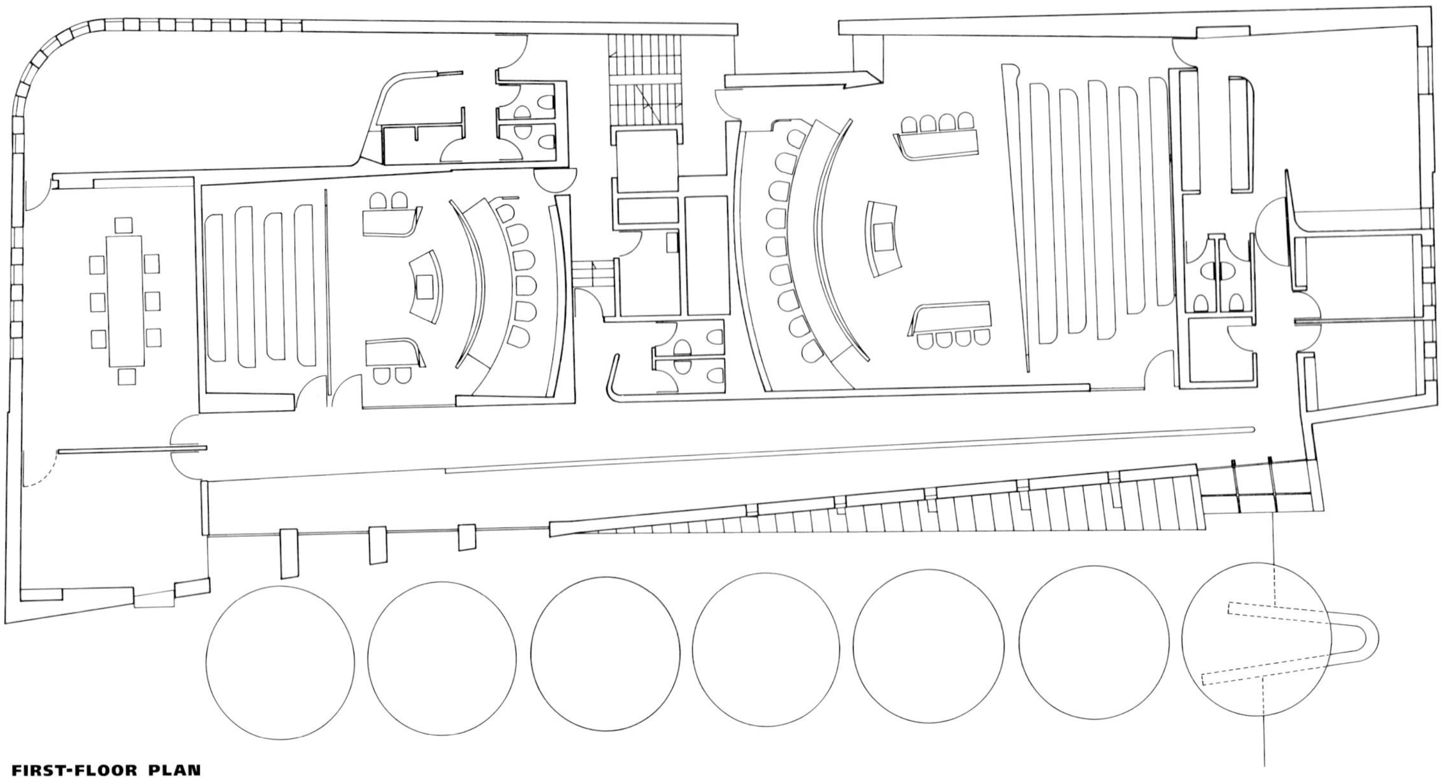

FIRST-FLOOR PLAN

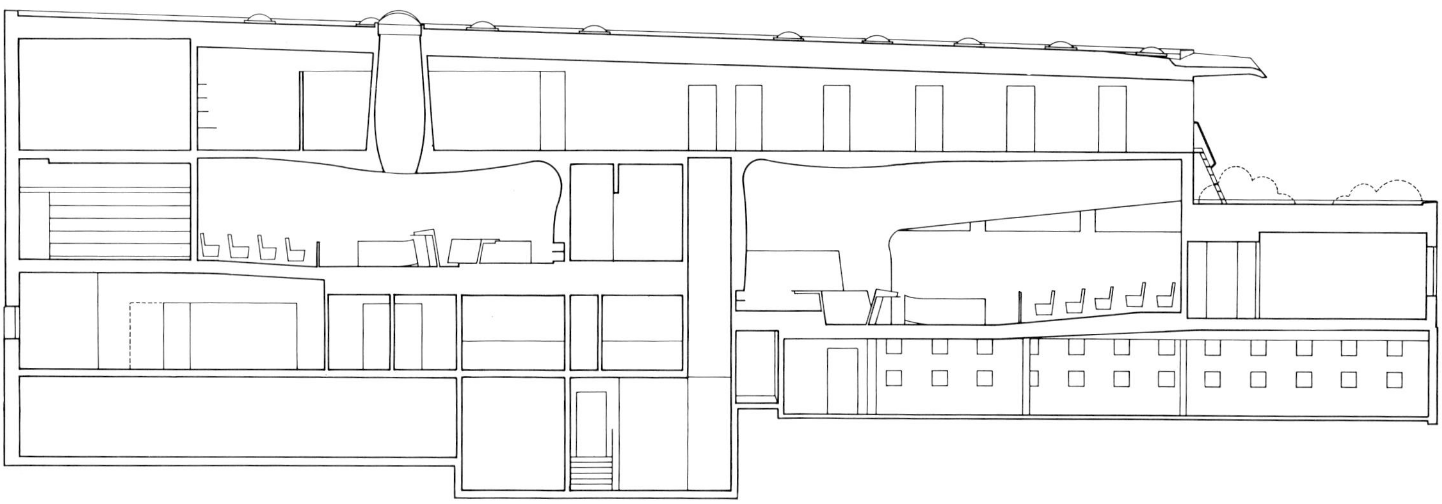

SECTION

RIGHT: The public area on the ground floor designed as a continuous ramp along the edge of the building. The scheme was concerned with keeping the judiciary and public separate. Note the distant view of blue light, reflecting ocean views outside the building. The ramp, which gives access to the courtroom, can be seen on the first-floor plan above.

4.3 environment design institute/mitsuru senda
aichi children's centre
aichi, japan

The Children's Castle is a large-scale play and discovery centre which brings the influential 'circular play system' theories of Japanese designer Mitsuru Senda vividly to life

THIS innovative children's centre – an all-weather atrium for play covered by an umbrella-shaped teflon membrane – reflects the ideas of designer Mitsuru Senda, whose background in developing play and discovery environments for children spans 30 years. Senda is the architect of the 'circular play system' theory, which suggests that the best play centres conform to several conditions: they should have a clear circulation pattern and flow of movement; they should be rich in variety, with lots of short cuts and bypasses; they should offer symbolic high points, and places where children can feel dizzy; they should have large and small gathering places; and they should be open with a number of access routes.

Working with the Environment Design Institute and Fujikawa Hara Architects, Senda has put these ideas into vivid practice at Aichi in a scheme known as Kodomo no Shiro, or Children's Castle. A central leaning tower, egg-shaped in plan, supports the canopy and houses a double helix ramp. From this focal point, a myriad of play structures and bridges spiral outwards in bright colours and a range of materials – steel, wood, rubber, brick, tile – enhance the tactile experience.

At the top of the 'challenge tower' there is an inspiring view of distant cities. Adjacent to the main play space is a children's museum. Outside, in the woods, there is more children's play equipment. A restaurant, water plaza, miniature-town zone, robot theatre, and handicraft and sound studios are also elements of a project which is a dream-come-true environment for children and a powerful reflection of Senda's circular motion ideas.

COMPLETED **July 1996**

COMMISSIONING CLIENT **Aichi Prefecture**

TOTAL FLOOR SPACE **7,600 square metres**

NUMBER OF FLOORS **3**

TOTAL CONTRACT COST **US $52.4 million**

SOUTH ELEVATION

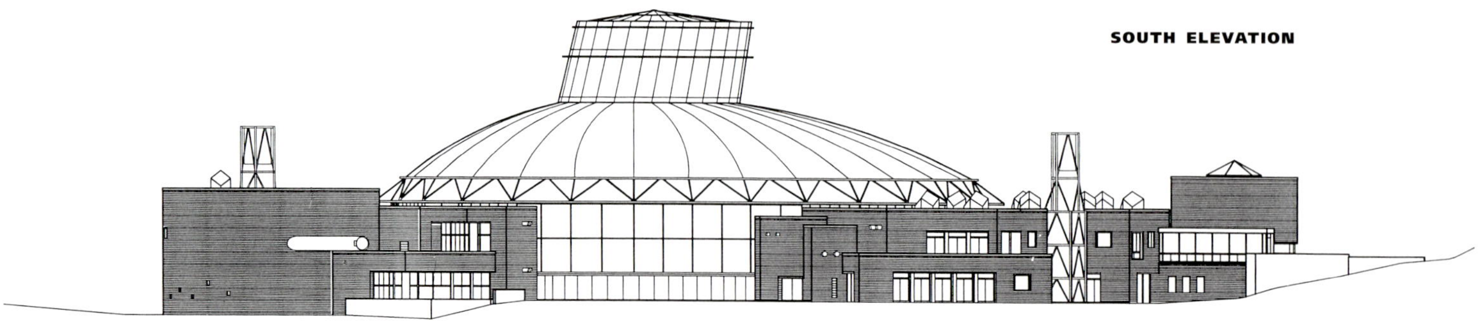

ABOVE: The tensile umbrella roof of Mitsuru Senda's play centre is supported by an egg-shaped tower.
BELOW: Japanese children scramble along a walkway in a scheme which reflects the architect's theories on a circular play system. Creating clear circulation patterns and flows of movement are essential.

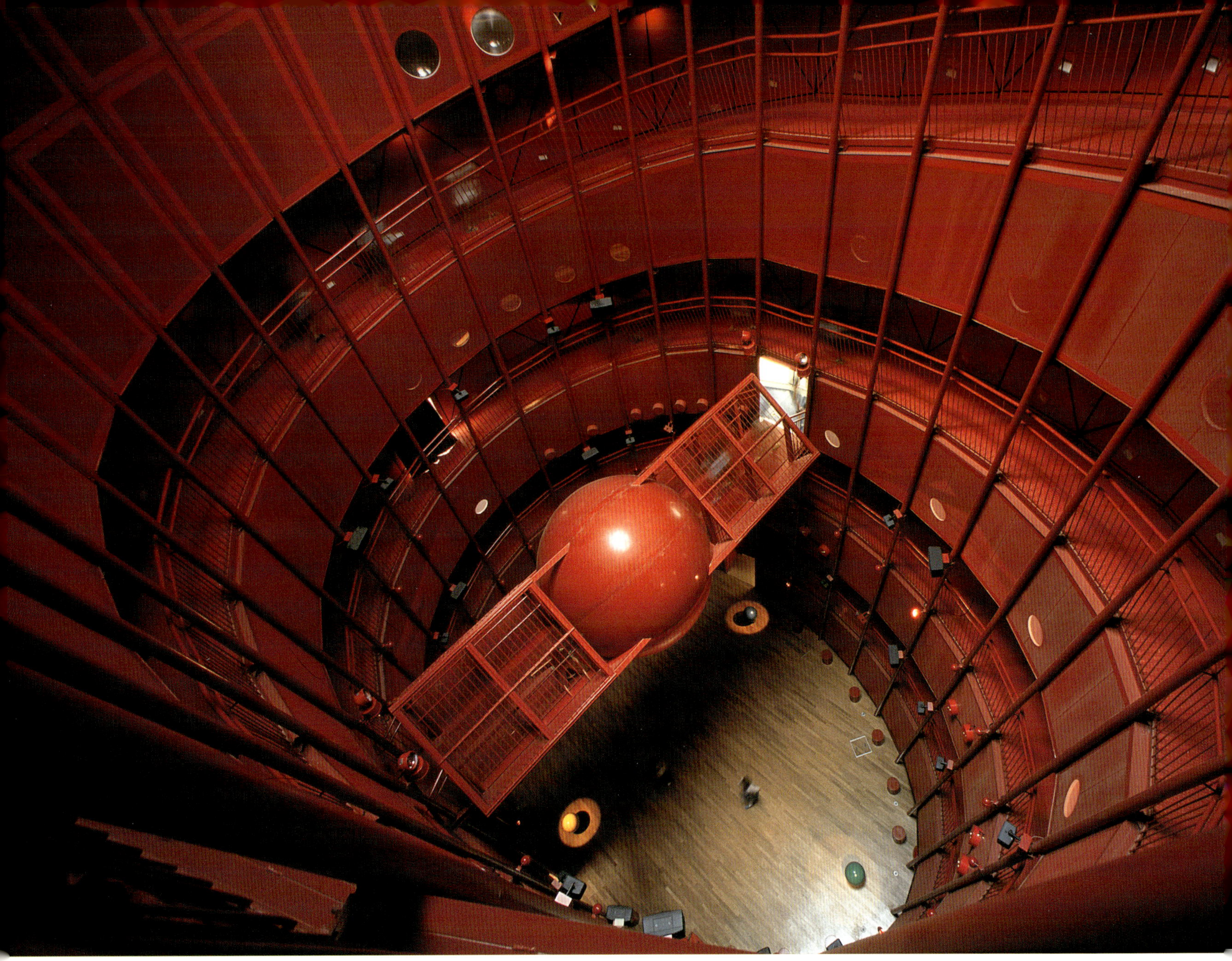

ABOVE: Inside the tower, children can look down from a dizzying height.

GROUND-FLOOR PLAN

KEY

1 Challenge Tower
2 Infants' corner
3 Discovery zones of forests
4 Discovery zones sounds
5 Power room
6 Machine room
7 Robots' theatre
8 Visitor's walk
9 Exhibition corner
10 Water square
11 Handicrafts studio

4.4 john outram associates
judge institute
cambridge, uk

John Outram's complex and colourful scheme for a new management studies centre on the site of a civic hospital combines the rich language of synthetic medieval masonry with a landscape narrative

ABOVE: The exterior of the Judge Institute shows classical restraint compared to the fantastic invention inside. **RIGHT:** The Institute's main hall, evoking earlier great civilizations in its rich and complex patterning. It is clad in brick and acid-etched polychrome concrete, including Blitzcrete (concrete made from crushed brick) and Doodlecrete (inlaid concrete made from rubber moulds).

THERE is something quite fantastical about the richly ornamental interiors John Outram has designed as part of this scheme for Cambridge University. The Adenbrookes City Hospital has been entirely remodelled and rebuilt as a centre for management studies, but this is no high-tech homage to modern business. Outram conceived the project as sitting at the heart of the medieval city and has introduced what he describes as new coloured and inlaid 'synthetic masonry' into his interiors, which 'inscribe a script'.

Working with listed ward blocks and arcades, Outram has turned the hospital's central block into the main hall of the Judge Institute, with library, seminar rooms and other facilities attached. He has also added three new buildings to the complex: the Ark, which houses the academics and administration; the Castle, containing an auditorium, debating room and other spaces; and the Gallery, which connects to the main hall, and has multi-level circulation routes and seminar boxes.

Into this complex structure, Outram has woven a complete landscape narrative: an 'endless forest' of hollowed-out columns and beams, carrying all the building's technical services; 'caves' where researchers work in private; and a 'river valley', the Institute's social space. The intense colouring and patterning of the public interiors creates a magical place, described by one critic as the 'headquarters, perhaps, of some exotic hallucinatory order of monks'. This, however, is also a project of considerable technical virtuosity. Outram even developed a new material – Doodlecrete – to clad his new work.

COMPLETED **September 1995**

COMMISSIONING CLIENT **Faculty of Management Studies, Cambridge University**

TOTAL FLOOR SPACE **9,000 square feet**

NUMBER OF LEVELS **6**

TOTAL CONTRACT COST **£11 million**

LEFT: Lecture room colour and detail.
ABOVE: Hollowed columns which house the technology of this modern management studies centre are central to Outram's scheme. He describes these robot-columns as belonging to a new classical order – the Ordine Robotico or Working Order – to add to the Doric, Ionic and Corinthian Orders.

ABOVE: Rooms, especially in the listed ward blocks, are lit by daylight wherever possible as Outram creates a new community based on the idea of the undulations of natural landscape.

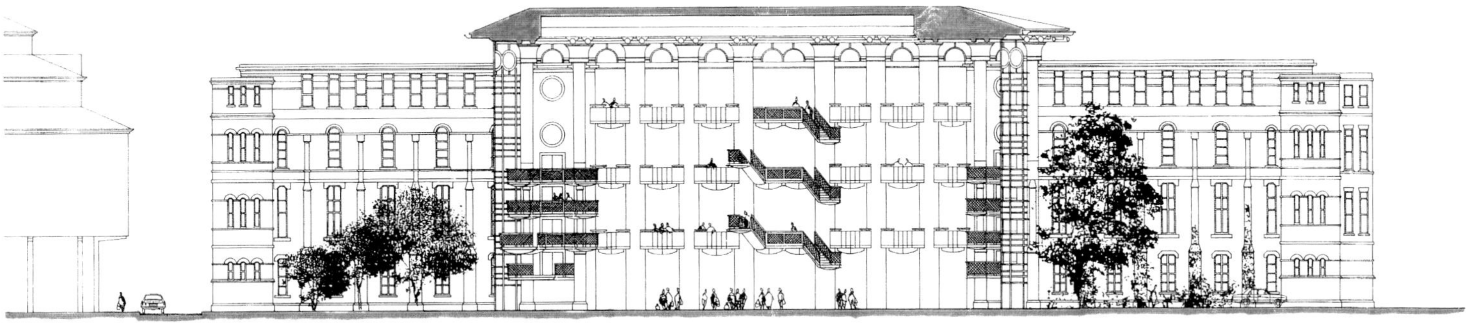

NORTH-SOUTH SECTION THROUGH GALLERY

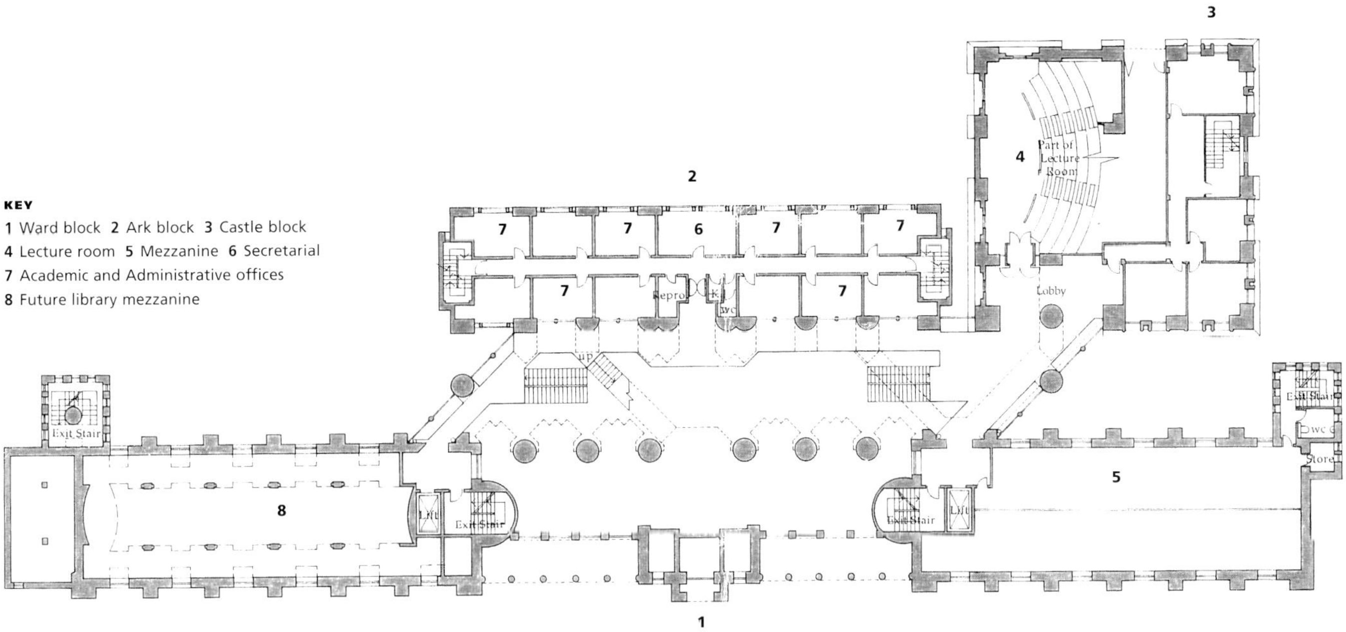

KEY

1 Ward block 2 Ark block 3 Castle block
4 Lecture room 5 Mezzanine 6 Secretarial
7 Academic and Administrative offices
8 Future library mezzanine

FIRST-FLOOR PLAN

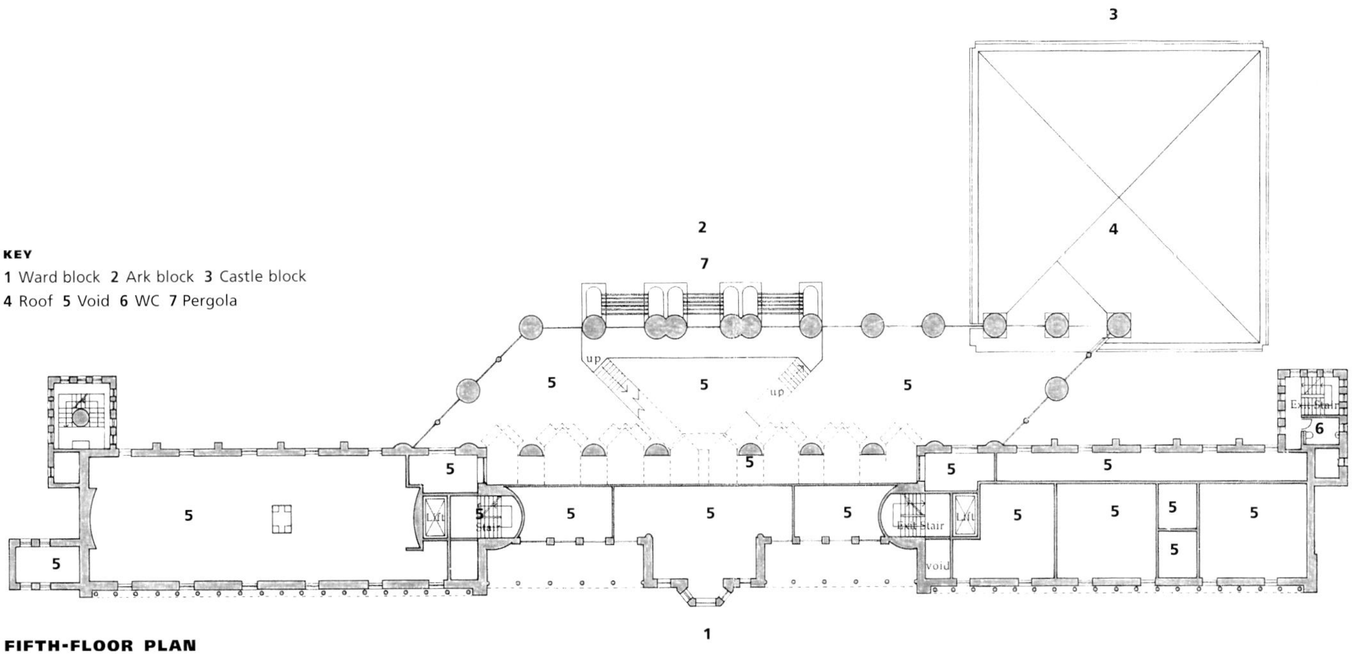

KEY

1 Ward block 2 Ark block 3 Castle block
4 Roof 5 Void 6 WC 7 Pergola

FIFTH-FLOOR PLAN

4.5 m.b.m. arquitectes s.a.
banyoles municipal theatre
banyoles, spain

A singular approach to lighting and materials dissolves the divide between stage and audience in this theatre-auditorium scheme which finds new expressive uses for plywood

IN THIS Spanish municipal theatre, the design emphasis is on creating a dialogue between the performers and the audience. A large proscenium stage of more than 60 square metres flows out into the audience and gradually dissolves into the sides of the auditorium. Seating for 250 is ranged in three blocks in front of the stage occupying the full width of the relatively shallow space; the arc of the architectural configuration, however, ensures optimum views for all the seats.

What makes the scheme unusual is the way in which its interior designers Lluis Pau, Josep Martorell, Oriol Bohigas, David Mackay and Jeroni Moner have resolved all the acoustic and architectural issues by using a single material and lighting system. High-density plywood is used in a variety of thicknesses, textures, positions and finishes. In the audience area, the ply is visibly textured, but is dark matt in the stage areas. Meanwhile unconcealed mono-directional lines of small halogen lamps composed in an irregular weave and a trail of optical-fibre points directly focus attention on the performance in an abstract interpretation of the 'flow' between stage and seating.

The cohesive volume, created by such concentrated means, invites the audience and performers to share the same ambience, drawing the onlooker into the complicity of dialogue before the performance has even begun. Beyond the auditorium, the foyer provides access to all the back-stage areas and the public spaces immediately adjacent, its lighting, colours and materials acting as a bridge between the street and the performance space. The theatre auditorium occupies the ground floor of a carefully considered building in which art lives with commerce: there are offices above and basement levels for underground parking below.

COMPLETED **1995**

COMMISSIONING CLIENT **Town Council of Banyoles**

TOTAL FLOOR SPACE **715 square metres**

NUMBER OF FLOORS **4**

SEATS **250**

SECTION

ABOVE: The view of the auditorium reveals how a unified material and lighting strategy draws stage and audience closer together. High-density plywood panels range from the visibly textured in the seating area to dark matt on stage.

FLOOR PLAN

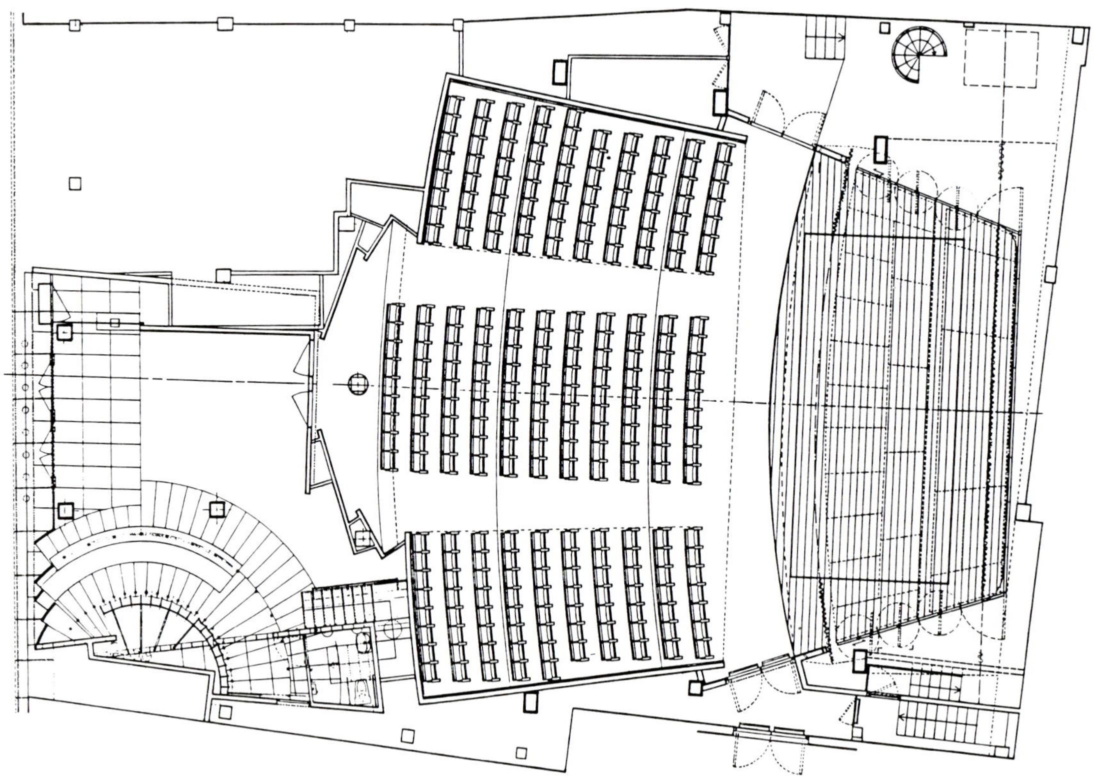

ABOVE LEFT: The foyer is designed as an intermediary space between the outside world and the ambience of the theatre. Certain elements prefigure the material textures that are found in the auditorium.
RIGHT: The high-density textured plywood wall is both sculptural and functional in terms of acoustics. Lines of halogen lamps accentuate the texture.

4.6 von gerkan marg & partner

neue messe

leipzig, germany

In the post-Communist era, Leipzig is seeking to recapture former glories in trade and commerce with a new business exhibition complex that adds art to industry to create visitor-friendly interiors

NOTHING symbolizes the massive investment in the economic infrastructure of the former East Germany, following reunification, more than this large-scale scheme to create a new trade-fair complex in Leipzig. The Neue Messe has been built in just three years with federal funds on the northern outskirts of the city, on the site of a former airport. It is a coherent and expansive facility comprising five exhibition halls, seven conference auditoria, 12 seminar rooms, extensive catering facilities, plus a 30,000-square-metre, open-air exhibition space.

The Neue Messe is organized as a series of low pavilions around a central glass hall to allow for future growth. Its distinctive focal glass structure was designed, according to its architects, in the spirit of both Joseph Paxton's Crystal Palace of 1851 and the steel-vault Leipzig Zeppelin Hall of 1913–14. The composition is rational and orderly – based on the planning rhythm of a micro-grid of 1.25 metres – and the interiors have a muted palette: exposed grey-steel structures, white-painted walls, stone floors, silvery-ceiling cladding and warm wood for counters, cloakrooms and internal doors.

What saves this vast scheme from the grid-like orthodoxy of soulless functionalism is the inspirational span of the glass hall (for which designers Von Gerkan Marg were responsible) and the programme of work by international artists (for which they were not). Twenty-five art installations from such names as Sol Lewitt and Jenny Holzer enliven the large interior spaces. If, however, you thought that this project would immediately propel Leipzig into the German Messe big league, think again. This new complex only ranks Leipzig seventh among the likes of Hanover, Düsseldorf, Frankfurt and Munich.

COMPLETED **April 1996**

COMMISSIONING CLIENT **City of Leipzig**

TOTAL EXHIBITION SPACE **102,500 square metres**

NUMBER OF HALLS **5**

TOTAL CONTRACT COST **DM 1.3 billion**

LEFT: The exterior view presents a cross section of the glass hall of the congress centre, the focal point of the scheme. **RIGHT:** The spiral staircase gives a twist to the grid-like orthodoxy of the congress centre interior.

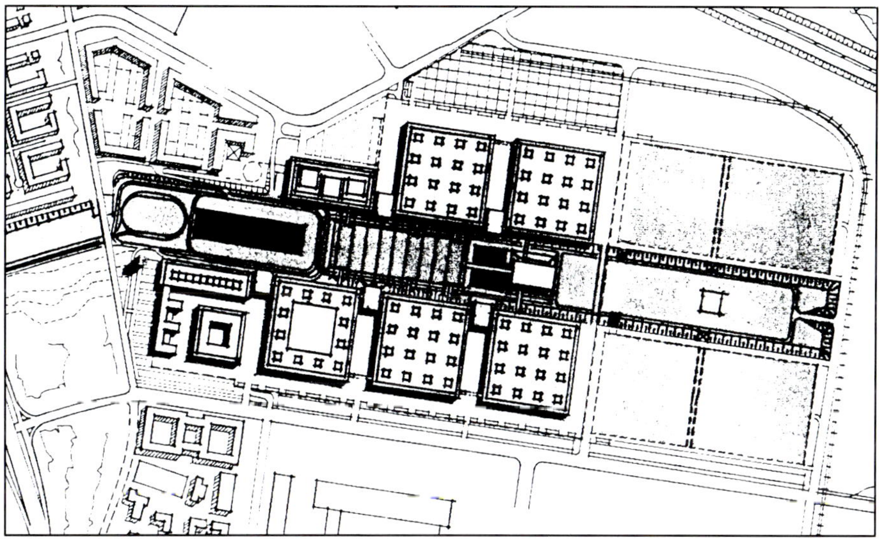

SITE PLAN

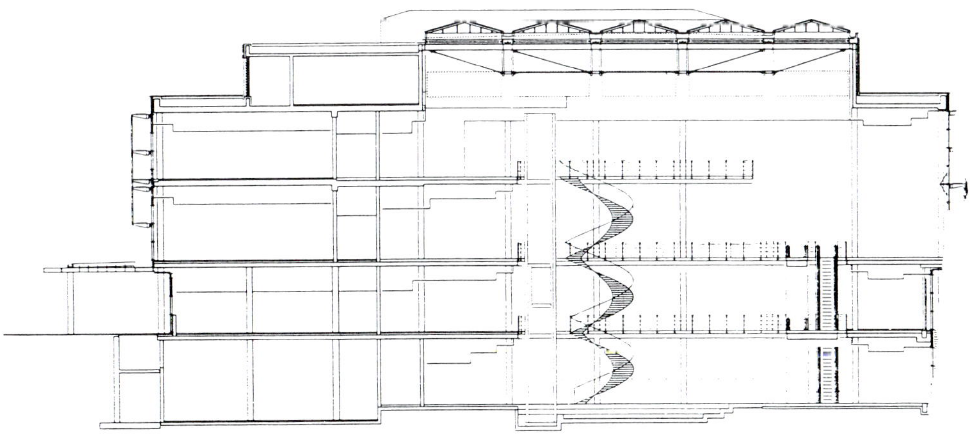

SECTION THROUGH ENTRANCE HALL

LEFT: Access tunnel to the Leipzig Messe's glass hall which, as site plan above shows, sits at the centre of the complex surrounded by low exhibition pavilions. An important consideration of the scheme was space to expand in the future. An outdoor exhibition area sits behind the glass hall.

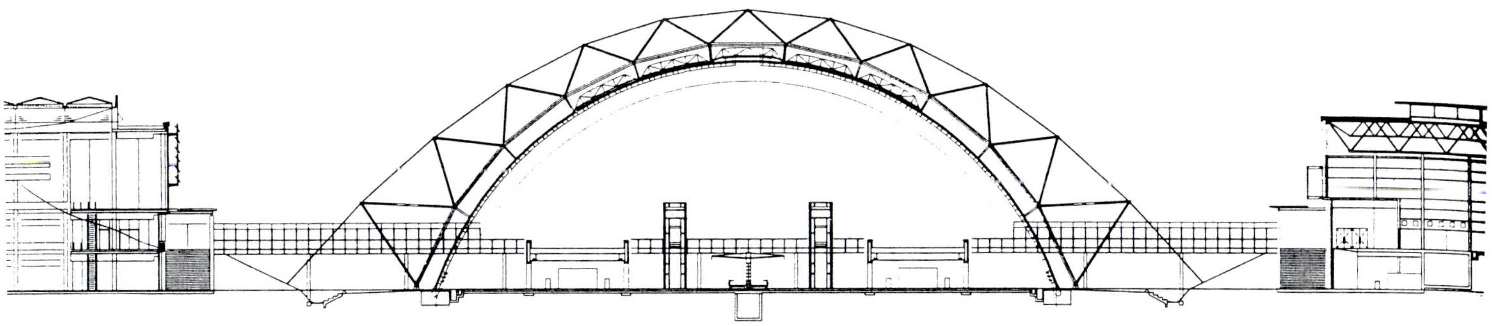

SECTION

LEFT: The inviting cafeteria in the eastern wing of the glass hall has furniture designed by Frank Gehry.
TOP: The congress centre's public areas feature giant artworks by Sol Lewitt, as part of the scheme's programme of art installations.
ABOVE: Cross section through the congress centre, glass hall and high hall.

4.7 shin takamatsu
meteor plaza
shimane prefecture, japan

Ferry terminal, city hall, health therapy pool and museum are combined in one distinctive project, which commemorates the falling of a meteor from outer space on to a Japanese town in 1992

ABOVE: The Meteor Plaza exterior shows the random assembly of elements, with the giant boulder of the museum sitting on top like a rock fallen from outer space.
RIGHT: The Meteor Entrance to Meteor Hall, the main civic auditorium. The scheme creates buffer spaces between its disparate functions.

COMPLETED **December 1995**

COMMISSIONING CLIENT **City of Mihonoseki and Shimane Prefectural Government**

TOTAL EXHIBITION SPACE **5,558 square metres**

NUMBER OF HALLS **4**

TOTAL CONTRACT COST **£11 million**

SHIN TAKAMATSU'S Meteor Plaza in Shimane Prefecture combines four very different public functions on one site within a single architectural concept, which needed to be very powerful to hold such disparate elements together. The project includes a ferry terminal for routes to and from Oki Island, a health facility which makes use of sea water, a 500-seat city hall and the Meteor Museum, which commemorates an event of great local significance. In December 1992, a meteor which had apparently been travelling around outer space for 60 million years dropped on to the town of Mihonoseki-Cho in Shimane. The civic authorities embarked on an architectural competition to build a public facility to mark this momentous event.

Takamatsu's signature scheme beat rival projects which respected the waterside setting with calm landscaping and traditional roof tiles, by creating a building complex that has the same impact on the townscape as a falling meteor. The architect decided not to try to fuse the different functions but to create spaces between them. He conceived the plan as a seemingly accidental composition. In section, the health-spa pool sits above the ferry passenger terminal, while the city hall, named the Meteor Hall, sits off a central entrance area. The Meteor Museum, shaped like a giant boulder, sits on top of this assembly, and is reached from the entrance plaza.

The scheme's most outstanding interior space is that of the Meteor Museum: the fragment of rock from outer space is given a womb-like setting, evoking a sense of awe for the approaching visitor.

← メテオホール入口
1~15
化粧室
メテオホール入口 →
16~50
METEOR HALL

RIGHT: Inside the Meteor Museum. The womb-like curved walls and flow of light are designed to inspire a sense of awe as you approach the unit which holds the fragment of rock that fell from outer space on to this Japanese town in 1992.

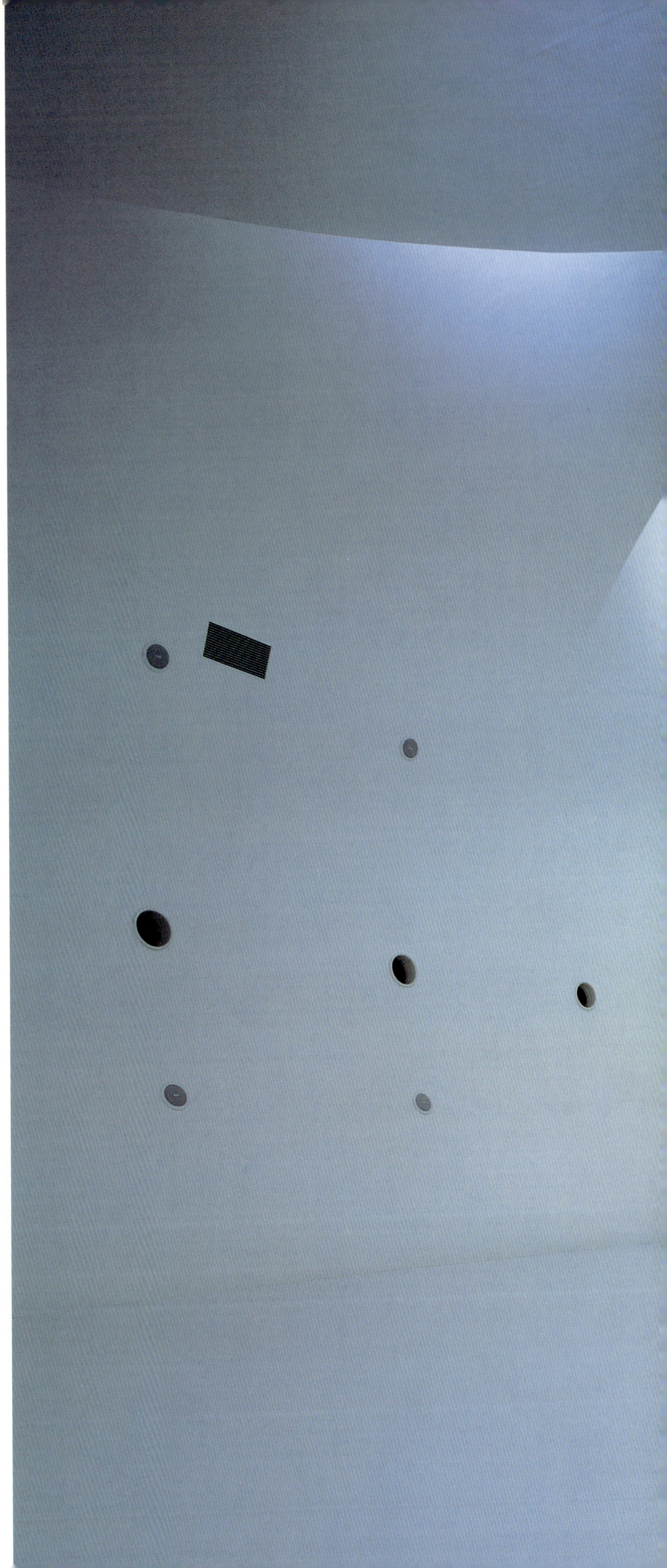

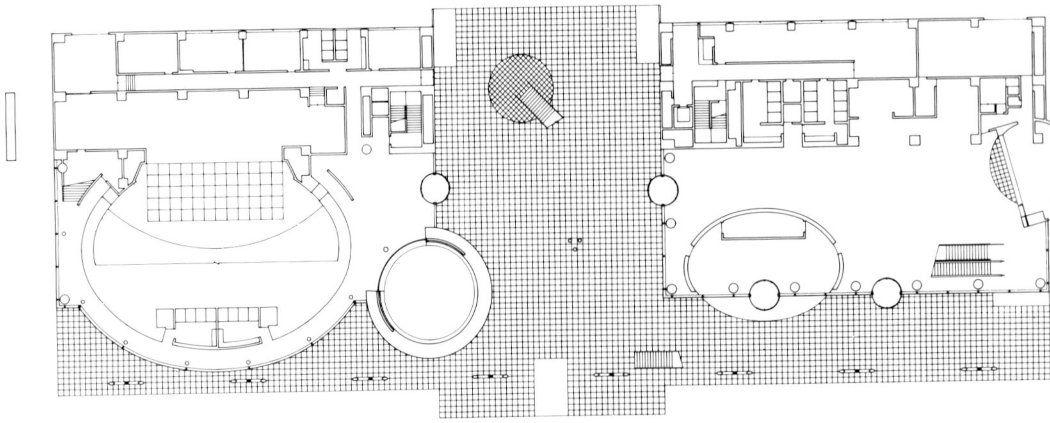

GROUND-FLOOR PLAN

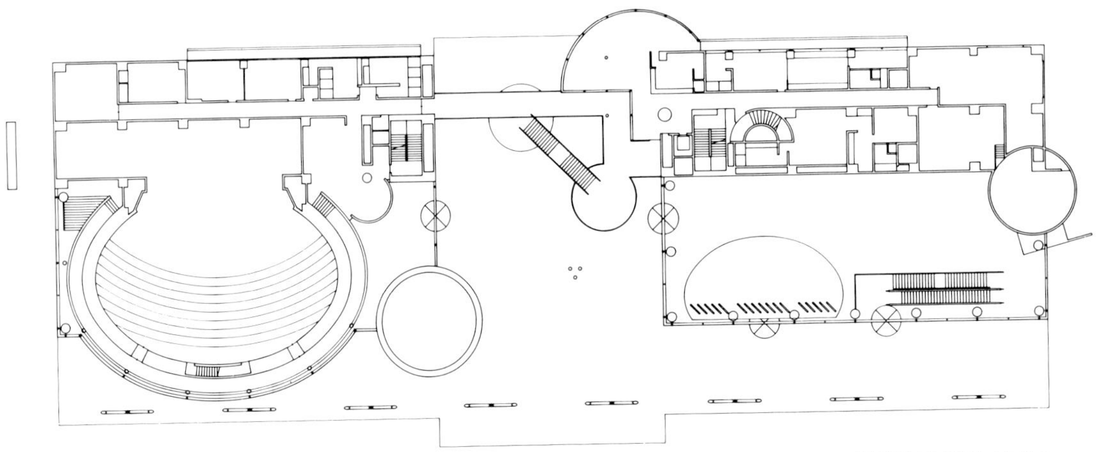

FIRST-FLOOR PLAN

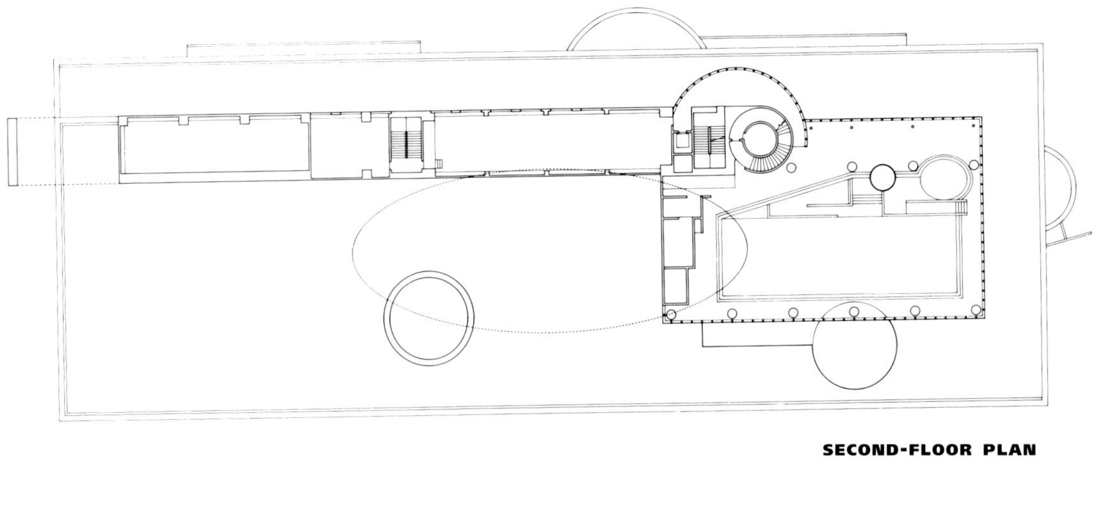

SECOND-FLOOR PLAN

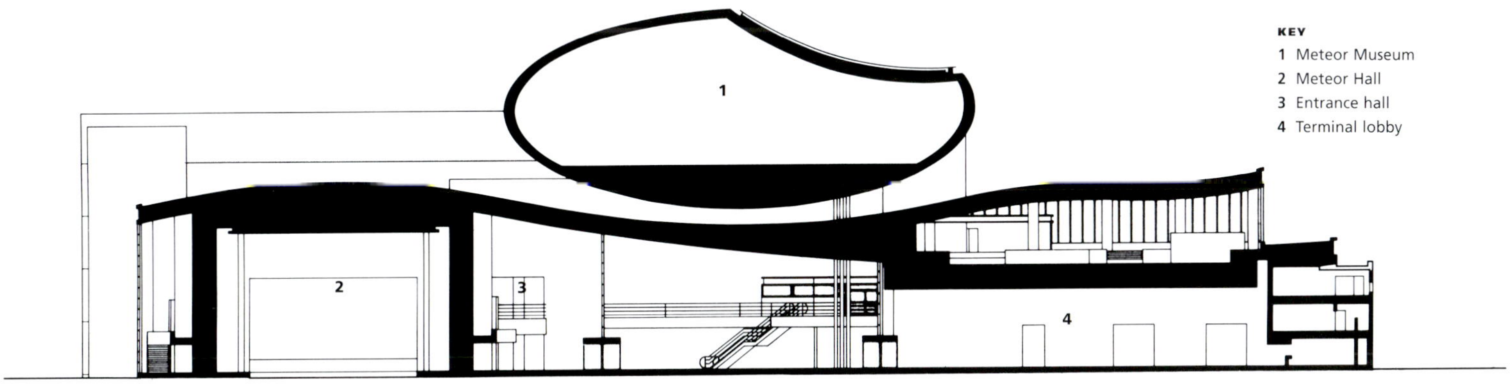

EAST-WEST SECTION

TOP: View of the Meteor Hall auditorium, which has 300 fixed seats and 200 movable seats.
ABOVE: The section shows the arrangement of different functions topped by the museum itself.

4.8 michael graves

denver central library

denver, usa

An adept use of changes in scale enables a major enlargement of Denver's main library to avoid cold monumentality, creating in its place warm, intimate reading rooms suffused with natural light and materials

THERE is a single interior point at which the governing themes of Michael Graves's bold and imaginative enlargement of Burnham Hoy's 1956 Denver Central Library dynamically converge. It is under a 'derrick' structure made of reclaimed honey-brown Oregon timbers in the library's Western History Reading Room, where scholars can sit in an attractive space flooded with natural light, scored with strong geometries and surrounded by warm, natural materials. This interior is the culmination of a strategy which balances the need to make a powerful civic statement against a concern not to create a building that lacks the human scale of the surrounding historic district.

In extending Denver's main library to provide more space for the eighth largest library collection in the US, Graves has added a massive 390,000 square feet to the previously cramped original area of 150,000 square feet. But he manages to avoid monumentality by creating spaces of varying scale: large circulation channels often lead to surprisingly intimate rooms. Two major public entrances within the best US civic traditions of Carnegie establish an east-west axis through the building, linked by the scheme's grandest gesture – the Great Hall. This is a vaulted three-storey space which enables visitors to orient themselves to facilities on all levels.

Externally, Graves's library is a striking addition to the skyline, with its copper-trussed square crown sitting on a coloured stone rotunda. The true spirit of the project, though, is reflected in the soft, warm patterning of the interior where custom-designed carpeting and a combination of warm-temperature lighting in reading rooms enhances the mood. Flexibility to adjust to advances in information technology, durability and ease of maintenance were key elements of the brief. Graves has met these challenges very much on his own aesthetic terms.

RIGHT: The new landmark on Denver's skyline – the library's copper-trussed crown. **FAR RIGHT:** Inside the Western History Reading Room, a space suffused with light, which creates quiet areas for scholars beneath the structure of rectilinear timbers. The carpet is custom designed by Graves.

COMPLETED **Autumn 1995**

COMMISSIONING CLIENT **City and County of Denver Department of Public Works**

TOTAL FLOOR SPACE **540,000 square feet**

NUMBER OF FLOORS **8**

TOTAL CONTRACT COST **US $48 million**

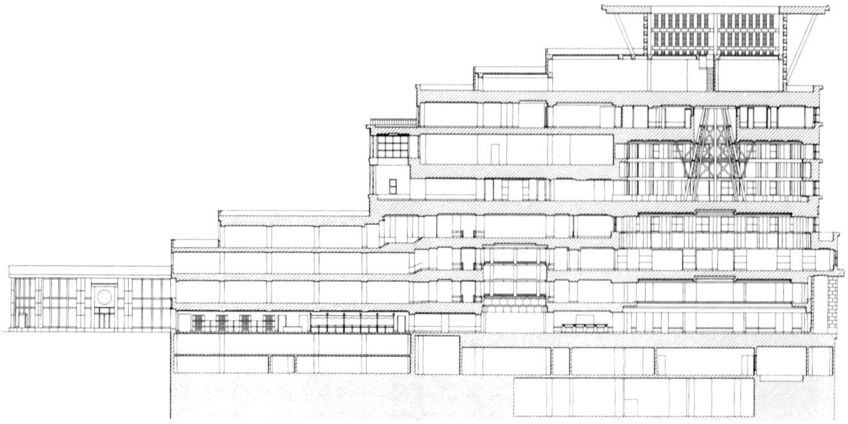

NORTH-SOUTH SECTION THROUGH EXISTING BUILDING, GREAT HALL AND ROTUNDA

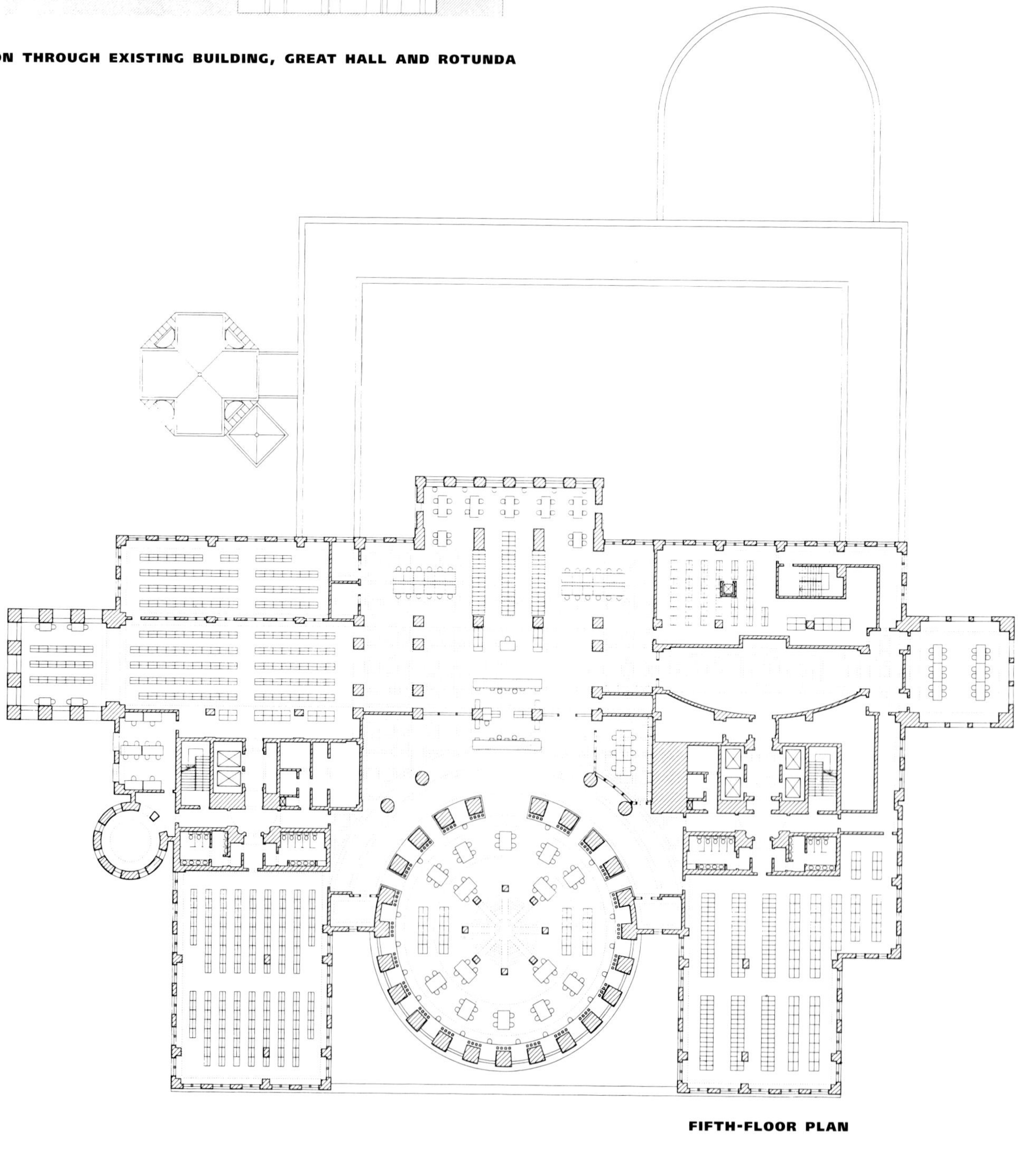

FIFTH-FLOOR PLAN

ABOVE: Despite the monumental scale of Graves's enlargement of the Denver Central Library, the reading rooms are surprisingly intimate and human in their character. This double-height area for reading and bookstacks is inside the scheme's new rotunda block and has an 80-foot diameter.

4.9 ben kelly design
the basement
london, uk

Deep in the bowels of the Science Museum, this tactile and technicolour environment knits together a range of attractions for youngsters, its raked form providing a picnic area with a difference

BEN KELLY'S master plan for The Basement at the Science Museum in London has transformed a dull, difficult space into a kind of tactile, technicolour airport lounge designed to 'switch children on to science'. Ranged with shallow steps, screens, ramps and walkways in a vivid array of oranges, purples and lime green, the scheme fulfils a wide range of requirements through its colours, graphics and spatial arrangements. Robust materials reflect the need to withstand the movement of more than 2,500 children a day through the space.

Structural alterations have brought natural light to an interior which not only directs its audience efficiently on to surrounding galleries and performance spaces but also provides incident and information along the way. There are coloured tiles and glass bricks, linoleum and terrazzo, girders and concrete cutaways to expose the steel structure and services of the building to view. Adjacent exhibits such as 'The Garden' for three-to-six year olds (designed by Casson Mann) and the 'Secret Life of the Home' (by inventor Tim Hunkin) are united within The Basement's offbeat town square dynamic.

The facility is accessed dramatically by glass lifts from the ground-floor entrance. The steps of the terrace have been designed as an alternative to tables and chairs for the picnic area, which provides a panoramic view of a facing information wall that runs down the centre of the space. Once the Science Museum had all the allure of a mausoleum. Today this national institution is a vibrant attraction, its creative energy symbolized by The Basement's playful use of colour, light and form.

RIGHT: The Basement has concrete cutaways to reveal the steel structure beneath, bold graphics and an unusual collage of materials to attract young people to the workings of science in the physical world.

COMPLETED **October 1995**

COMMISSIONING CLIENT **The National Museum of Science and Industry (UK)**

TOTAL FLOOR SPACE **1,300 square metres**

NUMBER OF FLOORS **2**

TOTAL CONTRACT COST **£1.2 million**

4
the terrace
3

LEFT: A scheme, described by its designer Ben Kelly as 'about transition, about movement of people', creates a picnic area with a difference for school parties. The terrace steps are in terrazzo and reclaimed Burmese teak. Signage reflects the item at The Basement as a 'tactile, technicolour airport lounge'.

4.10 van berkel & bos

rijksmuseum extension

enschede, holland

A continuous thread of new and restored galleries at a public museum in Enschede creates a tension between the vertical accent of the original halls and the horizontal emphasis of the extension

THIS NEW EXTENSION to the Rijksmuseum Twente, in Enschede, is a delicately managed encounter between old and new. The original halls of this national museum were built in Dutch vernacular style in 1928 in the form of a pentangle around a sculpture garden and expanded over the years with a second courtyard. The latest bold insertion to the site by architects Van Berkel & Bos introduces 900 square metres of new exhibition space to the 2,600-square-metre building in a project which also involved putting in new services in the modern art wing and replacing a restaurant with a multifunctional space within the previously restored interior.

The point of departure between the original architecture and the modernity of the new galleries is expressed in the switch from vertical to horizontal emphasis. The elements of the extension were conceived as a single ongoing line connecting the new exhibition area, restored modern art wing and multifunctional space. The two ends of this line burrow above ground in the sculpture garden and the courtyard as horizontal bands of concrete, glass and steel. To accommodate the new insertion, the sculpture garden has been redesigned.

While the configuration of the construction is both pragmatic and imaginative, the scheme's focus on creating a visual tension in the transition from the existing halls to the new galleries presents interiors which are an art form in themselves. From the spacious high rooms lit from above in the modern art wing, we proceed to smaller, lower rooms lit from the side, so embracing the horizontal accent of the scheme. Slanting steel girders, light-wells, frosted glass and concrete elements are arranged to create exhibition spaces that are both flexible and finely detailed.

COMPLETED **March 1996**

COMMISSIONING CLIENT **Ministry of Housing and Construction, The Hague**

TOTAL FLOOR SPACE **900 square metres**

TOTAL CONTRACT COST **US $7.4 million**

ABOVE: A fin-shaped exhibition wall in a new gallery space suspended partially above the ground on a concrete pedestal. The emphasis of the new side-lit space is horizontal.

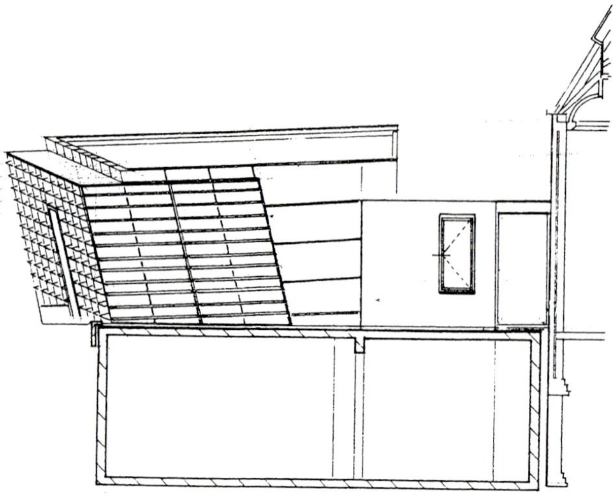

AXONOMETRIC SECTION

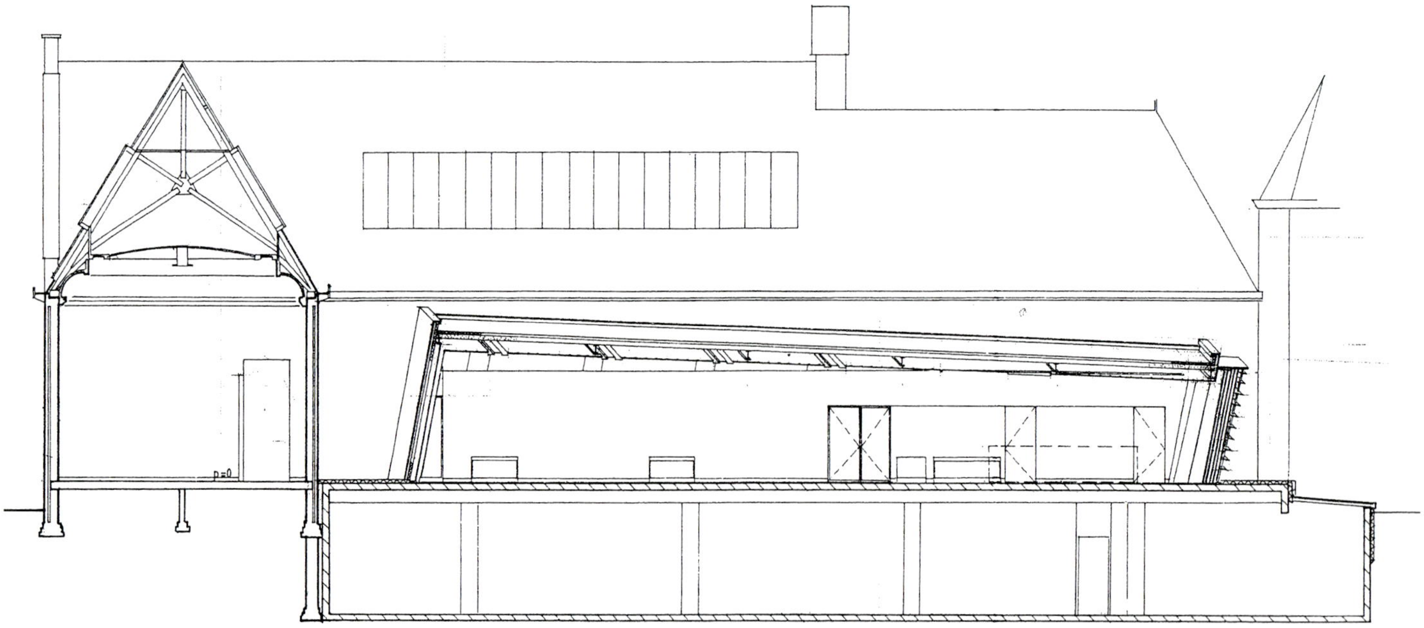

SECTION

FAR LEFT AND LEFT: The two courtyards of the Rijksmuseum Twente, built in 1928 in a Dutch vernacular style, have modern glass and steel additions with a pronounced horizontal accent.

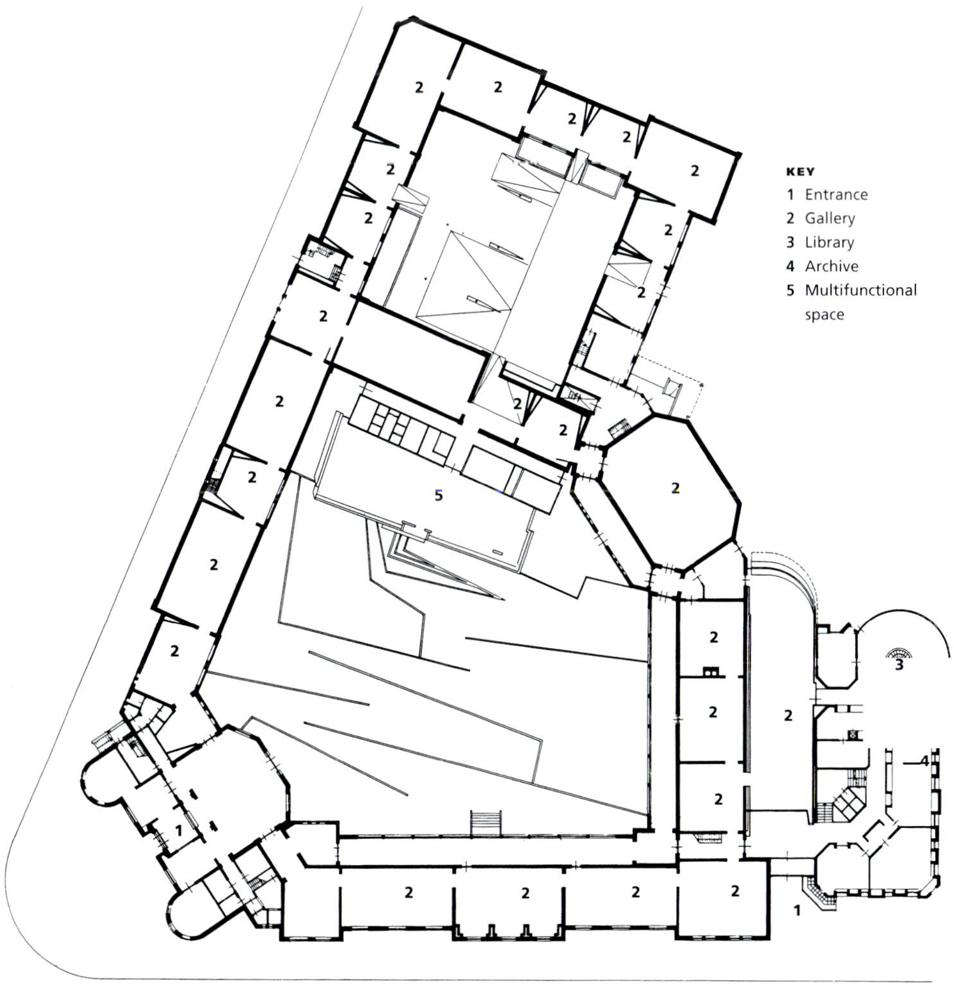

FLOOR PLAN

RIGHT: The new exhibition galleries present a studied composition of frosted glass and concrete. Light enters through a glazed roof and lightwells in a scheme which inserts a band of modernity through a heritage institution with skill and finesse.

4.11 kisho kurokawa
softopia japan center building
gifu, japan

This public complex to support multimedia enterprises in Gifu Prefecture has harmonious interiors which reflect the relationship between the advanced and the indigenous

ABOVE: Night view of the Softopia Japan Center showing low-rise and high-rise elements of the scheme. **RIGHT:** The ground-floor atrium lobby has a segment-shaped water feature mirrored by aeroplane-style aluminium eaves which puncture the façade. **PAGES 232–33:** View of tearoom from pavement.

EMERGING multimedia and information technology industries around the world tend to be based exclusively in metropolitan areas. Japan is determined to push such developments out into the regions and is supporting an infrastructure to make it happen. Kisho Kurokawa's Softopia Japan Center Building in Gifu Prefecture is an expression of this trend. It is a giant public complex dedicated to multimedia-related enterprises, which forms part of an entire 'eco-media city' and sits in a pool of shallow water as a symbol of the symbiosis with nature.

The relationship between information technology and eco-technology is one of Kurokawa's design themes, which he carries through with conviction. His building has two main parts: a high-rise block housing a host of administrative, research, restaurant, meeting, editing, training and gallery facilities; and a low-rise extension for large-scale events containing a seminar hall and an events hall. These two main elements are connected by an atrium lobby space which acts as an entrance hall; its aeroplane wing-style aluminium eaves, as part of the exterior brought inside, provide a modern counterpoint to paintings by Japanese artists which tell the story of old Gifu.

The atrium is just one of the many fine signature interiors in the scheme. Kurokawa's familiar trademarks range from complex spatial compositions which make intriguing play on the Japanese tradition of asymmetry to hard surfaces softened by unusual angles and textures. Two local lobbies within the tower reflect sunlight along optical fibres and feature stainless-steel sculptures. Kurokawa's love of material detail is what makes his environments come alive, no matter how vast in scale the public commission. Here, he uses only natural stone for those parts of his project that touch the earth; the higher up he goes in the high-rise, the lighter the materials become – from polished granite, to tiles, to aluminium and eventually alumite.

COMPLETED **February 1996**

COMMISSIONING CLIENT **Gifu Prefecture**

TOTAL FLOOR SPACE **35,940 square metres**

NUMBER OF LEVELS **15 (including two below ground)**

TOTAL CONTRACT COST **US $ 215 million**

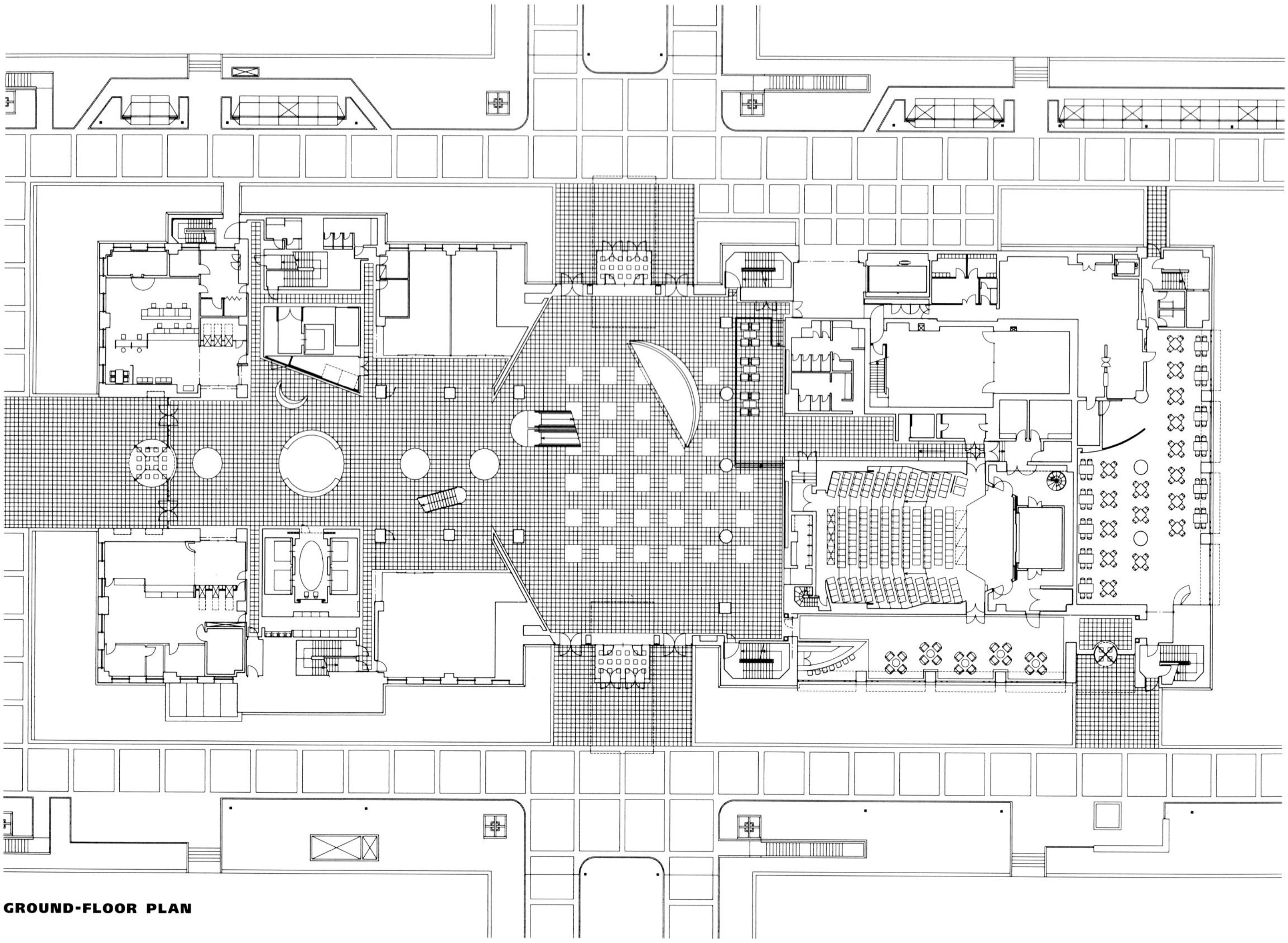

GROUND-FLOOR PLAN

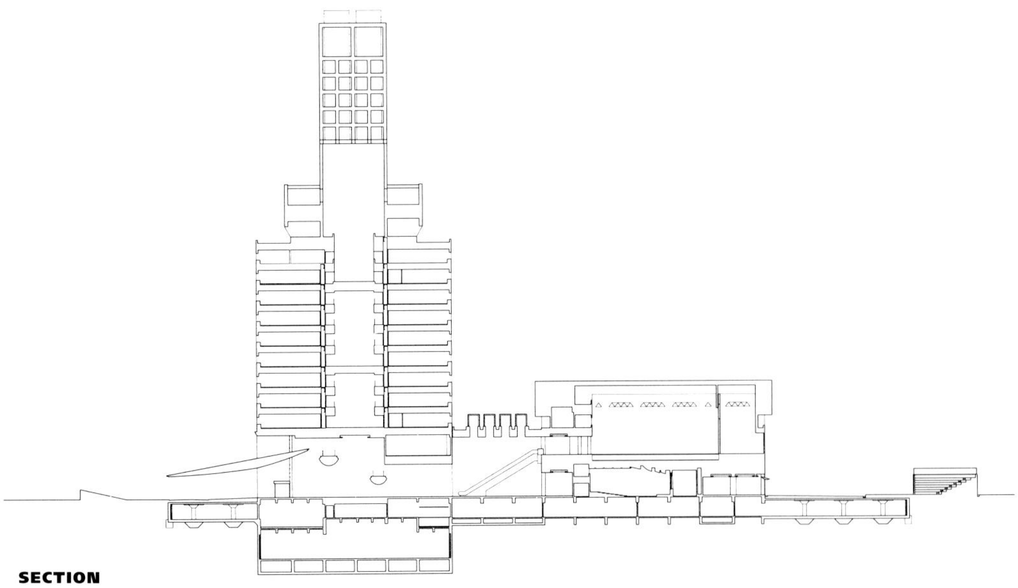

SECTION

RIGHT: Seventh-floor local lobby in the tower reflects sunlight along fibre optic cables. The stainless-steel sculpture is by Minami Tada.

4.12 thomas van den valentyn
schloss belvedere music college
weimar, germany

The insertion of a Modernist music school into a U-shaped, restored Baroque court is a stunning exercise in counterpoint, which reveals a subterranean concert hall of rare quality

BAUHAUS meets the Baroque in this scheme at Weimar, which inserts a newly built music school in a confident white Modernist style into the restored U-shaped court of the eighteenth-century Belvedere palace. As a large-scale exercise in counterpoint, this project by Thomas van den Valentyn with partner S. Mohammed Oreyzi for 130 music students can have few equals, as two different architectural traditions are respected at one and the same time.

The meticulous restoration of three wings of the palace to house dormitories, rehearsal rooms, administration and a refectory opening on to a sunken stone terrace, evokes the old inns of the eighteenth century. But the real attraction is the new school conceived as a tribute to the Bauhaus, which was based in Weimar under director Walter Gropius from 1919 to 1923. Viewed from the sloping park in which it sits so elegantly, the school has a Corbusian composition with three distinct layers: the stone foundations, the ground-floor glass insert and the 'floating' white roof.

The grey-green stone conceals a real interior jewel – an almost subterranean concert hall in raked arcades of concrete and wood, which is accessed by a spiral staircase, seats 300 and doubles as a gymnasium. An amphitheatre effect is amplified by an open-air theatre visible through glazing on the back wall that completes the oval shape. At the top of the structure, the white box houses a series of classrooms built in plywood with views over the park, and is supported on ten slender cylindrical pillars running through the ground floor. Internally, pine-clad wooden cubes have been placed randomly through the ground-floor level to create the idea of a small town with streets and alleys, enveloped by floor-to-ceiling glass.

COMPLETED **April 1996**

COMMISSIONING CLIENT **Deutsche Bank AG, Frankfurt**

TOTAL FLOOR SPACE **5,700 square metres**

NUMBER OF FLOORS **3**

TOTAL CONTRACT COST **DM 22.5 million**

ABOVE: View across the open-air amphitheatre and through the glass wall into the sunken concert hall, which completes the elongated oval shape.
BELOW: The sections show the relationship of the new music school to the Baroque palace building within the mature landscape.

SECTIONS

LEFT: Interior view of the raked concert hall, which doubles as a gymnasium. The open-air can be seen beyond the glass grid wall.

SITE PLAN

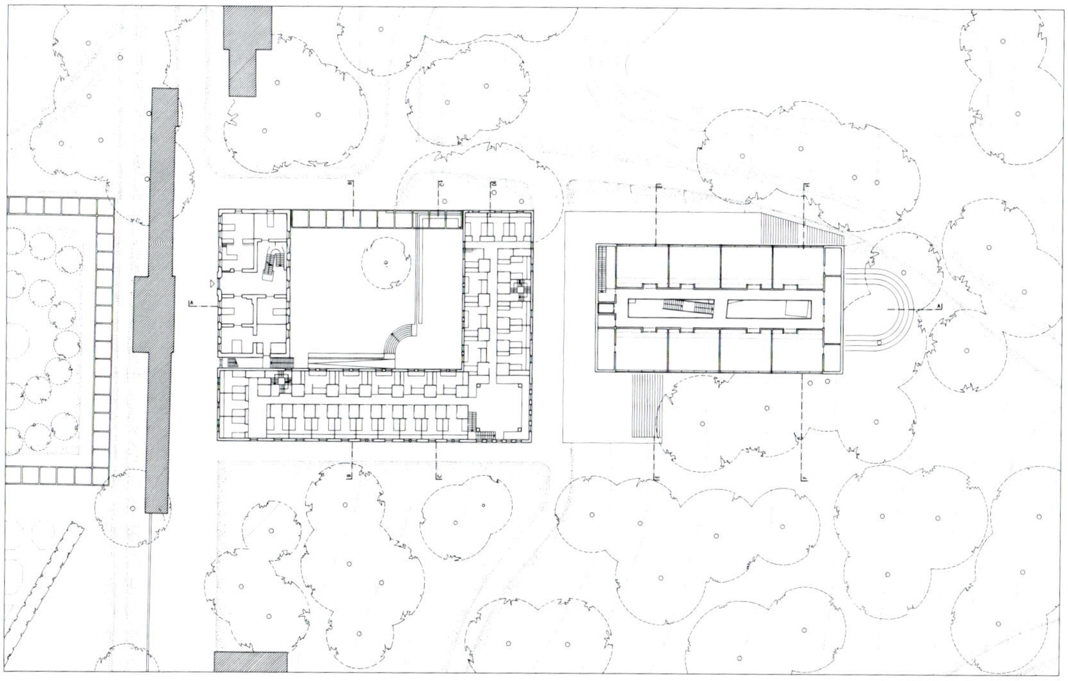

4.13 j.dubus & j.p.lott
palace of justice
evreux, france

A sculptural treatment of concrete in a new palais de justice, where a spiral staircase takes centre stage, marks a radical departure from the traditional symbolism of law court architecture

DUBUS & Lott's sinuous way with white concrete – a growing feature on the French architectural scene – is given ample expression in the old town at Evreux. Not only has the practice designed a new science faculty for the local university as a sweeping white curve, but it has also created an extension to the law courts on a cramped site in the heart of the town which achieves a similar modernist luminosity through its interaction of glass, curving shapes and the plasticity of concrete.

The architectural composition of the project produces a spectacular interior with a tightly wound white spiral staircase which pierces a large glass ceiling. This dominant feature sits in a dazzling atrium which is accessed via a walkway raised four metres above the floor, and immediately exposes a large part of the configuration of the building to the visitor. The eye is drawn skywards not only by the helix form of the staircase but also by pieces of sculpture by Benoît Luyckx, which diminish in size as they scale the full height of the sloping wall to the glazed roof.

The sinuous design theme is carried through S-shaped wooden benches and the curved sections of surrounding pillars and walls, as light enters the warm-hued interior spaces through various glass walls and ceilings. This is a scheme that unites legal facilities previously scattered across several sites in one building but gives each its own independent public and professional access. The ground floor is devoted to an industrial tribunal, the first floor to clerks' offices, the second floor to a court of commerce and the third level to the magistrate's court. The building is crowned by a library which offers panoramic views of a town on which Dubus & Lott have so clearly put their stamp.

COMPLETED **January 1996**

COMMISSIONING CLIENT **Ministry of Justice**

TOTAL FLOOR SPACE **5,000 square metres**

NUMBER OF FLOORS **6**

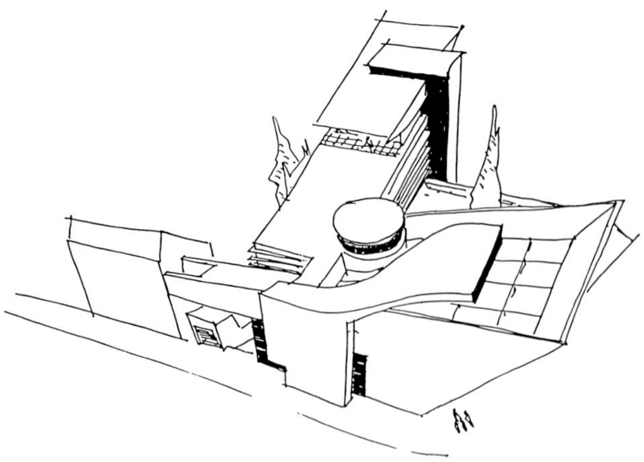

ABOVE: Axonometric sketch.
RIGHT: The tightly wound spiral staircase demonstrates the architects' plasticity with concrete in the main atrium space. It penetrates the building's glass roof.

BELOW: View of the central staircase from an upper level. **RIGHT:** Inside the main atrium, stone sculptures by Benoît Luyckx accentuate the height of the space by reducing in scale as they go up the concrete wall.

GROUND-FLOOR PLAN

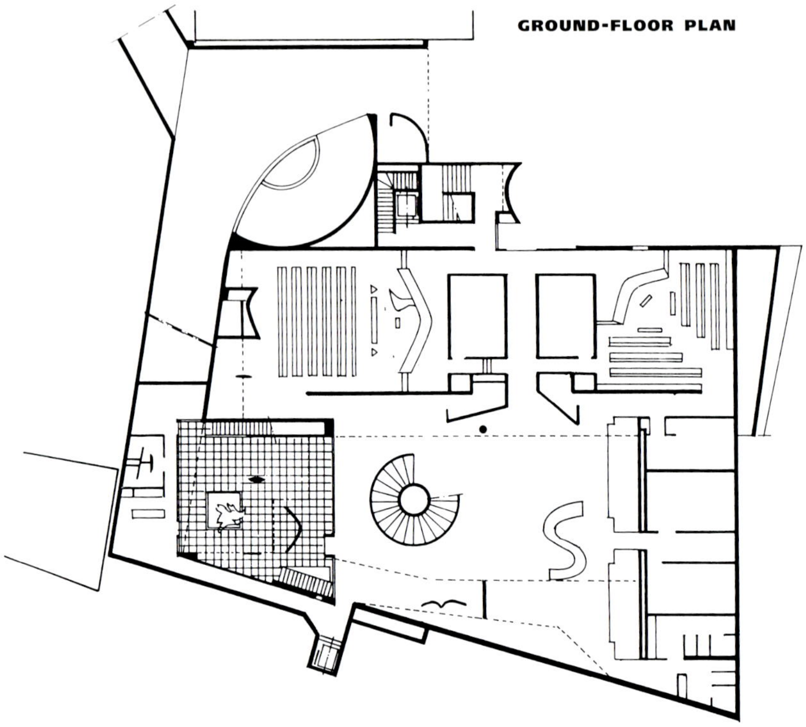

SECTION

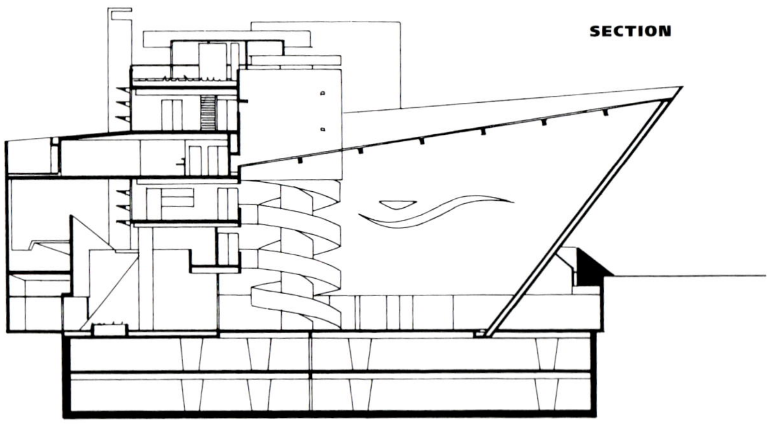

Anderson/Schwartz Architects
180 Varick Street, 15th Floor, New York, NY 10014, USA

Anderson/Schwartz is an award-winning, multi-disciplinary firm which has achieved international recognition for its innovative solutions to the workplace, often combining the straightforward simplicity of traditional building techniques with the complexity of more obvious and studied design. Frederic Schwartz and Ross Anderson received their Masters of Architecture degrees from Harvard University in 1978, having graduated from the University of California, Berkeley, and Stanford University respectively. Prior to founding their own company in 1984, Schwartz was Director of Venturi, Rauch and Scott Brown and Anderson Associate at MLTW/Turnbull Associates. They have both taught architectural design at Princeton, Harvard, Yale, Columbia, Pennsylvania and Miami Universities, as well as at North Carolina, Carnegie-Mellon and Parsons. Schemes include the much praised SMA Video and Production Facility; the Predictive Systems Offices, Reach Network and Isaac Mizrahi & Co. Headquarters. Recently completed work comprises a 50,000-square-foot New York magazine office interior, and residences on Long Island. In 1996, Ross Anderson opened his own company Anderson Architects.

Apicella Associates
9 Ivebury Court, 325 Latimer Road, London, W10 6RA, UK

Apicella Associates, formerly Apicella Associates Architecture and Design, was founded by Lorenzo Apicella in 1989. He studied architecture at Nottingham University, Canterbury College of Art and The Royal College of Art in London before moving to the United States to work for Skidmore Owings and Merrill. From 1986–9 he led the architecture and interior design group of the London consultancy Imagination, collaborating with clients such as Harrods, British Telecom, Forte Plc, Ford and British Steel. Apicella currently serves on the RIBA Awards Panel; he has been chairman of the National Awards jury on four occasions; and he has most recently served as an international juror for the American Institute of Architects' Awards in San Diego. He has taught widely within the UK and has been a visiting critic at Canterbury, London and Oxford. Apicella Associates' current projects range from a major office building opposite the Tate Gallery in London to a new range of furniture for a British manufacturer.

Architekturbüro Bolles-Wilson
Alter Steinweg 17, 48143 Münster, Germany

Architekturbüro Bolles-Wilson was founded in 1987 by Julia B. Bolles-Wilson and Peter Wilson, architects who had previously worked together in their own London-based practice, Wilson Partnership. Peter Wilson was born in Melbourne, Australia, where he first studied architecture. He extended his training at the Architectural Association in London where he was Unit Master from 1978–88. Julia Bolles was born in Münster and studied at the University of Karlsruhe. Postgraduate studies were followed by a teaching position at the Chelsea School of Art, which came to an end when she started working with Peter Wilson in 1980. Projects include: a government office in Münster (1991–5); an exhibition stand at the Osaka Expo' (1990); a waterfront and restaurant in Rotterdam (1995); the New City Library, Münster (1993); the WLV Office Building, Münster (1996); and the New Luxor Theatre, Rotterdam (1996–2000).

Bramante Architects
Teddington Wharf, Teddington, Middlesex, TW11 8BD, UK

Gabriele Bramante studied architecture at Kingston University, the Graduate School of Design at Harvard University and in Japan. Before setting up in private practice, she was Japan Correspondent for *The Architectural Review* and for two years she taught design at Canterbury School of Architecture. She also worked as design consultant for a German-based interior design company specializing in hotels, where she was responsible for the design of the leisure and sports facilities within hotel complexes. She has been highly acclaimed for her recent designs, most notably for the Citizens' Advice Bureau for which she has received the International Lighting Award from the LIF, the International Technical Excellence Award from the BIAT and the BBC Design Award.

Branson Coates Architecture Ltd
23 Old Street, London, EC1V 9HL, UK

Branson Coates was founded in 1985 by Nigel Coates and Doug Branson. Nigel Coates was born in 1949 and attended the Architectural Association where he was Unit Master from 1979–89. In 1983, he formed NATO (Narrative Architecture Today) with colleagues from the AA. The group published a magazine and exhibited the architects' work. Doug Branson graduated from the Architectural Association in 1975, after which he worked with DEGW. Before co-founding Branson Coates he worked in the Branson Helsel Partnership. BCA's early projects include the Caffe Bongo at Parco in Tokyo, as well as retail outlets for Katharine Hamnett, Jigsaw and Jasper Conran. Their work for these clients continues, but recent schemes also include the Silo art gallery building in Tokyo (1993) and the Nautilus and La Forêt restaurants at Schiphol Airport (1993). Currently they are occupied with a new 20th Century Gallery Building for the Geffrye Museum, in London, and a restaurant for Liberty, London. Branson Coates have designed exhibitions for Dunhill and the Pompidou Centre, and more recently 'Living Bridges' at the Royal Academy of London, as well as a touring exhibition of British public interiors for the British Council. Nigel Coates is also involved in furniture design (clients include SCP, Poltronova, Arredaesse and Bigelli).

Chadwick International
1a Birkenhead Street, London, WC1H 8NA, UK

Chadwick International is an architectural practice specializing in space management, design and operational consultancy. Andrew Chadwick, Principal of Chadwick International, trained at Cambridge University School of Architecture under Sir Leslie Martin and formed Hulme Chadwick & Partners in 1973. He was one of the early pioneers of the use of CAD in architecture which led to his interest in space planning and management. In 1987 he invented the Organisation Modelling technique for the establishment and manipulation of space requirements for major and complex organizations in a relocation project for Midland Bank. In 1990 Chadwick Group Ltd was formed when the American interior-architect Charles Pfister joined the company. The Chadwick Group Ltd has now renamed itself Chadwick International. In 1996, The Space Time Office for Andersen Consulting in Manchester won the DuPont Award for Innovation in Meeting Business Objectives.

Caulder Moore
The Coach House, 273A Sandycombe Road, Kew, Surrey, TW9 3LU, UK

Caulder Moore was founded in 1990 to specialize in commercial interiors. Their clients now include, in retail, companies such as Aquascutum, Whistles, Warehouse and Margaret Howell; and Luminar Leisure, Mercury Taverns, City Centre Restaurants and Rock Garden in the leisure area. The practice is becoming involved in projects outside of the United Kingdom working for clients such as Christian Lacroix. Their work has achieved a high level of commercial success and in 1985 the company won the retail category of the Design Effectiveness Awards for their collaboration with Warehouse; in 1986 they were a finalist for their Aquascutum interiors. They are currently working on a British flagship for Guess in Knightsbridge, London.

Design Shed
27 Fleet Street, Liverpool, LI 4AR, UK

Design Shed was founded in 1989 and today has three partners, Jonathan Falkingham, Miles Falkingham and Fiona Woodward. The company specializes in urban regeneration projects, designing complex mixed-use developments on restricted urban sites. Jonathan Falkingham is also the Mananging Director and founder of Urban Splash, a progressive property development company dedicated to the regeneration of derelict and neglected inner-city areas, and has involved Design Shed in numerous redevelopment plans. Major projects include: the Concert Square Apartment; bars and offices in Liverpool for which they received a RIBA Award for Architecture; and a schoolhouse in Trafford Park, Manchester, which was also recognized by the RIBA. Recent urban-planning and environmental design schemes number the Liverpool City Centre theming and Shaw Street Environmental Master Plan, both 1996.

Design System
Kenchiku Kaikan, 5-26-20 Shiba, Minato-ku, Tokyo 108, Japan

Design System was founded by a group of graduates taught by Dr Kiyoshi Seike, Professor at both the Tokyo Institute of Technology and Tokyo Art University, with the specific intention of designing 'beautiful architecture faithful to its function'. Though its origins go back to 1948, when Kiyoshi Seike opened his laboratory office at the architectural material laboratory at the Tokyo Institute of Technology, it only started as a corporation in 1968 with the commencement of the planning for Expo '70.

J. Dubus & J. P. Lott
2 rue Custine, 75018 Paris, France

The architects Jean Dubus (b. 1949, Paris) and Jean-Pierre Lott (b. 1962, Paris) founded their partnership in 1986. Since then they have worked extensively throughout France and in Spain, Algeria and Nairobi, and they are currently completing the French Embassy in Phnom Penh, Cambodia. Their practice deals mainly with large-scale public and educational facilities and recent schemes include the Lycée Polyvalent d'Osney and the Palais de Justice and a university restaurant at Evreux. Today they are working extensively in Evreux adding to their list of current schemes; these include a further extension of the university faculty, as well as their city law courts, the Palace of Justice.

Ecart
111 rue Saint-Antoine, 75004 Paris, France

Ecart was founded in 1978 by Andrée Putman (who left the company in 1997). Putman was born in Paris and studied music under Poulenc, before becoming first a journalist and later a design consultant for the mass-market chain Prisunic, and then co-founder of 'Créateurs et Industriels', which introduced the work of Issey Miyake and Jean Muir, among others, to France. The Ecart practice is divided into three specific disciplines. Ecart SA is the design office, specializing in interior and product design, varying from hotels to boutiques, corporate offices to private houses, and museums to governmental offices. Notable designs include the Office of the Minister of Culture (1984), Ebel Headquarters (1985), Morgans Hotel (1985), and the Im Wasserturm Hotel (1990). Ecart International re-edits furniture and objects by such designers as Eileen Gray and Mariano Fortuny and edits designs by Ecart SA (designers regularly used include Patrick Naggar, Paul Mathieu and Michael Ray). Andrée Putman licensing division designs objects distributed throughout the world, which include rugs, upholstery fabrics, tableware and bathroom accessories. Recent projects by Ecart SA number exhibition areas for the Cartier Foundation, Paris (1993); the Sheraton Hotel, Paris-Roissy (1994); the Bally Boutiques concept (1993–4) and the brand images of Baccarat and Swarovski.

Elliott & Associates Architects
35 Harrison Avenue, Oklahoma City, OK 73104, USA

Elliott & Associates Architects provide services which include master planning, architectural, landscape and interior design, retail-space design, image development, civil, structural, mechanical and electrical engineering, graphic and signage design, as well as product and lighting design. They work on a range of project types, which include retail offices, restaurants and residential through to Municipal, City, State and Federal Government schemes, museum and historic restorations. They have been awarded over 80 major local, regional, national and international awards and their work has been published widely.

Environment Design Institute
Mita Sonnette BLDG 3F, 1-1-15 Mita, Minato-ku, Tokyo 108, Japan

Mitsuru Man Senda (b. 1941 in Yokohama) was the Head of the Environment Design Institute between 1968 and 1984. He graduated from the Architectural Department of the Tokyo Institute of Technology in 1964 and worked for Kiyonori Kikutake Architects and Associates for four years. While he headed the Environment Design Institute, he gained a doctorate in engineering. He has held several teaching positions in Japan and today is Professor of Architecture in the Engineering Department of the Tokyo Institute. He has been given various prizes: in 1993 he was awarded the Architectural Institute of Japan Kazumigaseki Memorial Prize and Grand Expo Prize, Supreme Order of Merit for his Shinshu Expo Alpiko Plaza.

EEA Erick van Egeraat Associated Architects
Calandstraat 23, 3016 CA, Rotterdam, The Netherlands

Erick van Egeraat was born in 1956 in Amsterdam. He graduated from the Architecture Department of the Technical University of Delft in 1984. He co-founded Mecanoo Architects in 1983 where he worked until 1995 when he decided to set up his own practice. He has lectured at various academic establishments throughout the Low Countries and in Germany and more recently at the Royal Institute of British Architects (1995), the Junta de Sevilla (1995), the Oxford School of Architecture (1995); the Association for Architecture, Brussels (1995); and the Staatliche Akademie der Bildende Künste, Stuttgart (1996). He is an Honorary Member of the Bund Deutsche Architekten and has received national acclaim for his designs, being recommended for a design award in 1995 for the glass roof and boardroom of 'The Whale' in Budapest. His work has been the subject of numerous articles and reviews.

Fernau & Hartman Architects
2512 Ninth Street, No. 2, Berkeley, California 94710, USA

Fernau and Hartman was founded in 1980 by Richard Fernau (b. 1946) and Laura Hartman (b. 1952). They both have Masters of Architecture from the University of California, Berkeley, where they teach today. They have received awards for all their built projects and have earned reputations for their architectural design, interior design and technical innovation. Their work ranges from furniture and interiors to residential, commercial and institutional buildings. Recent schemes include the Von Stein Residence, collective housing for the Cheesecake Consortium, the Tipping Building, the f/X Networks Corporate Headquarters and the Nickelodeon Headquarters. Their work has been published both nationally and internationally.

Fitch Inc.
10350 Olentangy River Road, Worthington, Ohio, 43085, USA

The US company Fitch Inc. was originally founded as RichardsonSmith, a firm of industrial product designers, in 1959 by Dean Richardson and Dave Smith. Situated just outside Columbus, Ohio, it was located on an old horse farm, which is its Midwest offices today. Gradually RichardsonSmith began to diversify as the cycle of product development shortened and the value of integrated design strategies became more apparent. In 1982, Martin Beck, a partner in a Boston design firm was brought in to lead the company's transition from a product development group to a multifaceted design firm. The company worked with the London-based retail design group of Fitch PLC on various projects. In 1989 Fitch acquired RichardsonSmith. Today, Fitch PLC is a holding company for Fitch Ltd in London, Fitch S.I. in France and Fitch Inc. in the US. Fitch's US operations are organized into three sectors: product development, communications and environments. The environments group focuses primarily on store design. As well as Planet Reebok, it has designed prototype stores for Blockbuster Music, Blockbuster Games, Hush Puppies and Caribou Coffee Co.

Gensler
One Rockefeller Plaza, Suite 500, New York, NY 10020, USA

San Francisco-based Gensler & Associates was founded in 1965 by Arthur Gensler, JR (FAIA). They have offices throughout the USA and in Hong Kong and Tokyo, and have received more than 250 local and national design awards. The practice provides a broad range of services, including architectural design, interior architectural design, building and site evaluations, space planning, graphic design, signage design, product design and master planning. Clients include Apple Computer, Bank of America, Sony Pictures Entertainment Inc., the Walt Disney Company, General Motors and the Pepsi-Cola Company.

Michael Graves
341 Nassau Street, Princeton, New Jersey 08540, USA

Michael Graves was born in Indianapolis and received his architectural training at the University of Cincinnati and Harvard University. Since the formation of his practice in 1964 he has become an influential figure, in part responsible for moving urban architecture away from abstract Modernism towards more contextual and traditional themes. He has produced architectural designs for over 200 projects. Through his affiliated company Graves Design he has produced an extensive collection of furniture and consumer products, collaborating with manufacturers such as Alessi, Arkitektura, Swid Powell, Baldinger and Atelier International. Major architectural projects include the Walt Disney World Swan and Dolphin Hotels, Orlando, Florida; the Disney Company Corporate Headquarters, Burbank, California; the Crown American Offices; the Whitney Museum of American Art in Johnstown; a master plan for the Detroit Institute of Arts; the Denver Public Library; and the Clark County Library in Las Vegas. Current schemes encompass work in Japan and Taiwan, as well as the corporate headquarters for Thomson Consumer Electronics in Indianapolis; an office building for the Ministry of Culture in The Hague; the Pittsburgh Cultural Trust's Public Theater and condominiums on Miami Beach. Graves has designed the Life 1996 Dream House and has recently been selected as the principal designer of the US Courthouse Annex in Washington, DC. He is a member of the American Institute of Architects and has received many awards including 15 ***Progressive Architecture*** awards and nine American Institute of Architects National Honor awards. Graves is the Schirmer Professor of Architecture at Princeton University, where he has taught since 1962.

Daryl Jackson International Limited
Broadcourt, 43 Drury Lane, London, WC2B 5RT, UK

Daryl Jackson International Limited was established in the UK by Daryl Jackson and Richard Hywel Evans and today works in the UK, Italy, Germany and Hungary. Recently they have specialized in leisure and arts facilities with many of the completed projects receiving awards for their innovative approach. The company has offices in Berlin and in Australia.

Jestico & Whiles Architects
14 Stephenson Way, London, NW1 2HD, UK

The architectural practice of Jestico & Whiles was founded in 1977 by principals Tom Jestico, John Whiles, Robert Collingwood and Tony Ingram and today has offices in London, Glasgow, Prague and Munich. Preoccupation with lightweight structures and components can be seen in early industrial projects at Epsom (1979) and Waltham Cross (1982), while later schemes for Friends of the Earth, the Policy Studies Institute and research for the UK Department of Energy represent the development of Jestico & Whiles's approach to the concept of low-energy work spaces. Further projects include a science and technology park in Scotland and several inner-city industrial/office buildings, including Gallery Court, Stukely Street and Jockey's Fields. Current work numbers embassies and ambassador's residences in Latvia, Bulgaria and Bratislava; a major CrossRail station interchange, two hotels in central London and their largest project to date – Burrell's Wharf, a £28 million residential and leisure development on a Grade II listed site in London's docklands.

Kauffmann Theilig & Partner
Zeppelinstrasse 10, 73760 Ostfildern, Stuttgart, Germany

Dieter Kauffmann was born in 1954 in Sindelfingen. After graduating from the Fachhochschule of Augsburg in 1978, he worked for architects in Stuttgart before taking up an appointment with Behnisch and Partner in 1980 where he remained until he joined Heinle, Wischer and Partner. In 1988, he went into partnership with Andreas Theilig. Theilig was born in Stuttgart in 1951. After graduating from the Technische Hochschule in Darmstadt in 1978 he worked briefly for architects in Darmstadt before also joining Behnisch and Partners. He has lectured at the Fachhochschule in Biberach.

Ben Kelly Design
10 Stoney Street, London, SE1 9AD, UK

Ben Kelly Design was established in London in 1977 by designer Ben Kelly (b. 1949), who studied environmental/interior design at the Royal College of Art, graduating in 1974. Elena Massucco joined the practice in 1987, and Chris Cawte in 1991; key designers who have worked for BKD include Sandra Douglas and Peter Mance; all four are graduates of Kingston University's interior design course. Kelly's early individual projects include the Howie Shop (1977); work for Malcolm McLaren/The Sex Pistols; and Lynne Frank's first office. Ben Kelly's major designs number: the Haçienda nightclub and venue, Manchester; the Dry 201 bar and restaurant, Manchester; the 4AD record company headquarters, London; and offices for Rainey Kelly Campbell Roalfe, advertising agency, in London, as well as new offices for Lynne Frank. They have recently worked on the exhibition design for the 1996 BBC Design Awards and the Glasgow International Festival of Design 1996 Exhibition. They are currently working on a flagship store scheme for a major clothing company. Kelly has taught interior/3D design at Kingston University and acts as external assessor at Glasgow School of Arts. ***Plans and Elevations***, a book on the practice, was published in 1990 and BKD featured in 'Sublime: The Sol Mix' an exhibition on Manchester music and design, as part of the 'Door Window Staircase' exhibition, Kelvingrove, Glasgow (1992). The practice has won numerous awards for 'The Basement' in the Science Museum, London.

Makoto Koizumi
Makoto Studio, 2nd Floor, 2-2-34 Futjimidai, Kunitachi-city, Tokyo 186, Japan

Makoto Koizumi was born in 1950 in Tokyo. He started his design career with the Joint Centre Co. Ltd before founding his own practice in 1990. He specializes in the interior design of shops, showrooms, offices and residences. Recent projects include the Toppan Printing SP Plaza and IMUSE Showrooms (1994 and 1995); the executive offices for Toyo Ink; the Omuro craft shop and café and the Attitude boutique (1996). He also works on display, exhibition and furniture design. He is beginning to achieve considerable recognition within Japan and in 1996 alone received the C.S. Design Prize, the Nashop Lighting Contest Encouragement Prize, the Display Design Excellence Award and the J.C.D. Design Encouragement Prize.

Kengo Kuma & Associates
2-5-5 Minami Aoyama, Minato-ku, Tokyo 107, Japan

Kengo Kuma was born in 1954 in Kanagawa Prefecture and graduated from the University of Tokyo with an MA in Architecture. In 1985 he received an Asian Cultural Council fellowship grant and became a visiting scholar at Columbia University. In 1987 he established the 'Spatial Design Studio' and began to lecture at Japan's Women's University. Since 1994 he has been visiting critic at Columbia University. Kengo Kuma's designs have been exhibited internationally at the Venice Biennale in 1995, the Milan Triennale, the RIBA in London and an exhibition entitled 'Fluctuations Fugitives' at the Centre d'Art Contemporain de La Ferme du Buisson in Paris. Recent projects include the Noh Stage in Miyagi and River/Filter in Fukishima in Japan, as well as the Water/Glass Villa.

Kisho Kurokawa Architect & Associates
11F Aoyama Bldg, 1-2-3 Kita Aoyama, Minato-ku, Tokyo 107, Japan

Kisho Kurokawa was born in Nagoya in 1934 and studied architecture at Kyoto University. In 1960, while studying for a doctorate at Tokyo University, he formed the Metabolist Group, whose philosophy – closely linked with Buddhism – viewed urban architectural forms as organisms capable of growth and change, a belief which is echoed in his designs to date, most notably: the capsule pavilions at the International Expo 1970, Osaka; the Nagakin Capsule Tower, Tokyo (1972); and Sony Tower, Osaka (1976). Major projects include: the National Bunraku Theatre, Osaka; the Roppongi Prince Hotel, Tokyo; the Japanese-German Culture Centre in Berlin and the National Museums of Modern Art in Nagoya, Hiroshima and Wakayama. As well as his architectural works, he has designed distinctive furniture for Tendo and Kosuga and has exhibited in New York, Paris, London, Dublin, Moscow, Milan, Florence, Rome, Budapest and Sofia, and most recently at the Sackler Galleries at the Royal Academy of Arts 'Recent Works – 4 Museums' (1993). Kurokawa is a member of the Japan Institute of Architects and an Honorary Fellow of both the American Institute of Architects and the Royal Institute of British Architects. He has received international recognition for his work, being awarded the Japan Literary Grand Prize and citations of excellence from the AIA for his 'Philosophy of Symbiosis' in 1992. The following year he was presented with the Deutschen Naturstein–Preis for the Japanese-German Centre in Berlin.

MBM Arquitectes SA
Placa Reial 18, Pral., 08002 Barcelona, Spain

Josep Martorell and Oriol Bohigas studied together before founding MBM in 1951. David Mackay joined the partnership in 1962 and Albert Puig Domenech in 1986. Martorell was head of the architectural department of the Vila Olimpica, guiding the urban design of the scheme. Bohigas was head of the Barcelona School of Architecture from 1977 to 1980, at which time he became chief architect and planner of the first democratic government of the city. With a staff of around 25 the firm has handled over 300 architecture and urban planning and design schemes during the last 40 years, working in Mexico, France, Germany, The Netherlands, Italy, Scotland and Wales. Recent projects include the Olympic Village and Olympic Port in Barcelona and the main pavilion for Expo '92 Seville. The practice has taken part in numerous international competitions, frequently being awarded first prize. Recent projects include housing in Breda, The Netherlands (1995); Bite Avenue and Square in Cardiff (1994); urban-design studies for Edinburgh waterfront (1995), and urban-planning studies with new photovoltaic/thermal building components for the Directorate General, Science Research and Development – European Commission (1995).

Atelier Mendini
Via Sannio 24, 20137 Milan, Italy

Alessandro Mendini was born in Milan in 1931 where he studied architecture at the polytechnic. As well as directing the journal *Ollo*, he has published the design magazines *Casabella*, *Modo* and *Domus*. For many years he has been the theorist of avant-garde design, co-founding the Global Tools Group in 1973 as a counter-movement to established Italian design. In 1978 he started his collaboration with Studio Alchimia in Milan and developed the so-called 'Banal Design' which sought to change items in daily use into new and ironical objects – a notable example being the early version of the Proust Chair painted in a divisionist technique for the Bau.Haus Collection in 1980. In 1983 he became Professor of Design at the University of Applied Art in Vienna and was also made a member of the scientific committee of the Domus Academy. In the late 1980s he established the Genetic Laboratory for Visual Surprises, in order to research and question established ideas of taste and form. His own work covers architecture as well as furniture, product, tableware and interior design, and he is currently design adviser for Swatch and Alessi. Other clients include Zanotta, Fiat, Zabro, Driade, Poltronova, Elam and Abet Laminati. In 1990 he opened Atelier Mendini with his brother Francesco Mendini, designing projects such as the Groningen Museum, and with Yumiko Kobayasgu, the Paradise Tower, Hiroshima. Alessandro Mendini's work has been the subject of countless exhibitions and one-man shows throughout the world.

MET Studio
6–8 Standard Place, Rivington Street, London, EC2A OBE, UK

MET Studio is an award-winning design consultancy, specializing in exhibition and interior design for museum, corporate, government and leisure clients worldwide. The company was formed in 1982 and is led by Managing Director Alex McCuaig. Together with Museums Director, Deirdre Janson-Smith, and Leisure Director, Vic Kass, McCuaig supervises a team of concept planners, researchers, architects, interior, exhibit and graphic designers. MET Studio also works with modern artists and sculptors whose specially commissioned work is often integrated into projects. The Studio was awarded the 1995 Minerva Award for the Best Environment for its work on The Environment Theatre at the National Museum of Natural Science, Taiwan. In 1994 it won the Best Exhibition Award at the *DesignWeek* awards for its work on the Sciences of Life Exhibition for the Wellcome Trust in London and in 1996 MET won the same award for the Telecom World project in Hong Kong. 'Science for Life' was also named the Best Education Initiative at the 1994 IBM Museum of the Year Awards, as well as a receiving a Special Award for Lighting Design. Recent projects include an exhibition for Hong Kong Telecom; a travelling exhibition for the Wellcome Trust; the National Museum of Prehistory, Taiwan; The Evolution of Plants exhibit at Kew Gardens; the Electronic Theatre at the Science Museum, London; and the D&AD Festival Exhibition 1995 at the Saatchi Gallery, London.

Narud-Stokke-Wiig AS Architects
Radhusgaten 27, 0158 Oslo, Norway

Narud-Stokke-Wiig was formed in 1979 and is still run by its three founding members, Jorn Narud, Gudmund Stokke and Ole Wiig. The firm now employs over 50 people, 35 of whom are qualified architects. It deals with residential, corporate, cultural and leisure-facility design, as well as industrial buildings, laboratories, hospitals, schools and refurbishment. Their work has been widely published and exhibited, most recently at the Norsk Form, Oslo; the 1999 Information Centre, Glasgow; and the Royal Fine Art Commission for Scotland. Since its foundation the firm has won several competitions, prizes and awards, including the RIBA Architecture Award for Scotland and the Civic Trust Award 1981 for the City Art Centre, Edinburgh (1983); the Concrete Award for Elmholtveien 6; and the Nordic Sheet Award for Architects in 1994. Recently completed designs number the Control Tower, Oslo International Airport (1994); the Science Building at the University of Trondheim (1994); the Haukeland Hospital, Bergen (1995); the Regional Hospital in Trondheim (1995); and the Scottish Architecture and Design Centre, Edinburgh (1995).

Jean Nouvel et Associés
4 cité Griset, 75011 Paris, France

Jean Nouvel was born in 1945 in Lot, Garonne. He graduated from the Ecole National Supérieure des Beaux Arts, Paris, in 1971. His practice gained international recognition following the design of the Institute du Monde Arabe, Paris, in 1987. Other important projects include the Hotel-Restaurant St James, Bordeaux (1989); the cultural centre at Mélun-Sénart (1986); the renovation of the Opera House in Lyons (1990 competition award); the Cartier Foundation, Paris (1994); the Tour Sans Fin at La Défense, Paris; and the Galerie Lafayette in Berlin. Jean Nouvel continues to produce successful furniture designs collaborating with Ligne Roset, Ecart and other manufacturers. His architecture, which relies heavily on contemporary technology as a necessary means of expression, has been the recipient of many major design awards internationally.

John Outram Associates
44 Connaught Square, London, W2 2HL, UK

John Outram was born in India and spent his National Service as a pilot in Canada. Before studying architecture at the Regent Street Polytechnic and later at the Architectural Association in London, he toured the United States during the 1950s. He practised for a while in the Mediterranean and during his early career worked in the public and private sectors, undertaking a town-planning course and gaining invaluable experience through his involvement with the rebuilding of four Nash Terrace houses in Regent's Park. He started his own firm in 1973, and early works include the McKay Trading Estate at Poyle and the Pumping Station on the Isle of Dogs. His concern with materials and their ingenious usage is evident throughout his work. The Headquarters for Harp Heating clothed a glass 1960s building with brick 'robot' duct columns. In 1986 he developed a new form of concrete and in 1989 used masonry tiles and 'Doodlecrete' inlaid concrete on an office development in the City of London (on hold due to the recession). In 1991 Outram took part in the first Architecture Biennale, Venice. Along with James Stirling, Norman Foster, Richard Rogers, Michael Hopkins and Nicholas Grimshaw, he formed the British pavilion. As well as the Judge Institute, Cambridge, he has recently worked on the Computational Engineering Building at Rice University, Houston, Texas. He is currently working on a multifunctional complex in the centre of The Hague.

John Pawson
27–29 Whitfield Street, London, W1P 5RB, UK

John Pawson's designs explore space, light and materials and avoid stylistic mannerisms. He has worked in Spain, Japan and America as well as the United Kingdom and has won an international reputation for minimalist interiors. He was educated at Eton and worked in his family's textile mill in

Yorkshire before undertaking an extensive period abroad, travelling in India and Japan where he taught for four years. He studied at the Architectural Association in his early thirties. His designs range from art spaces to domestic interiors and from shops to restaurants and offices. Current projects include proposals for the Young Vic Theatre in London, a hotel in Covent Garden, as well as a number of private houses in America. His work has been published extensively, including a major monograph in 1996

Pentagram Architecture
204 Fifth Avenue, New York, NY 10010, USA

Pentagram Design was founded in 1972 in London and has since expanded to include offices in New York (1978), San Francisco (1986), Hong Kong (1994) and Austin, Texas (1995). Pentagram Architecture (US) was founded by James Biber in 1991 and specializes in residential interiors, restaurants, retail outlets, offices, health clubs and exhibition design. James Biber AIA graduated from Cornell University's College of Architecture, Art and Planning and worked for various American architectural practices before founding his own company in 1984. He has taught classes in Architecture at Cornell and Syracuse Universities, as well as at the Parson's School of Design. His designs have been recognized with major awards, from among others, the New York State Association of Architects and the New York Chapter of the American Institute of Architects. Projects for Pentagram Architecture include the newly opened Sullivan's Restaurant and Broadcast Lounge, New York, the Good Diner and Bolo. Clients number Disney Imagineering, Plus One Fitness and the Cooper-Hewitt National Design Museum.

Gaetano Pesce Ltd
543 Broadway, 5th Floor, New York, NY 10012, USA

Gaetano Pesce was born in 1959 in La Spezia, Italy, and studied at the architecture department of the University of Venice between 1959 and 1965. He is currently Professor at the Institut d'Architecture et Etudes Urbaines in Strasbourg, although he lives and works in New York and has an office in Paris. Pesce is known for his multi-disciplinary approach, and his work ranges from architecture to industrial design, exhibition design, drawing, sculpture, music, fashion and urban planning. He has worked for companies internationally such as Cassina, Italy; Knoll International, USA; and Vitra, Switzerland. Many of his works are in the permanent collections of major design museums, including the Metropolitan Museum of Art, New York; the Musée des Arts Décoratifs and the Centre Georges Pompidou, Paris; and the Musée des Arts Décoratifs, Montreal. For the Centennial of the Venice Biennale in June 1995 Pesce designed 10,000 one-off resin vases and in 1996 a major retrospective of his work was held at the Centre Georges Pompidou. Major works include the 'Organic Building', Osaka (1990–3), and the Chiat/Day offices, New York. Currently Pesce is working on a collection of affordable design objects for the home distributed under the Fish Design label.

Petzinka, Pink & Partner
Cecilienallee 17, Düsseldorf, D-40474, Germany

Petzinka, Pink & Partner was set up in 1994 by Karl-Heinz Petzinka and Thomas Pink. The practice has realized over 150 architecture and interior design projects for which it has received numerous awards in Germany and abroad. Karl-Heinz Petzinka was born in 1956 in Bocholt and studied architecture at the polytechnic in Aachen. From 1983–92, he was in practice with Jürgen Overdiek. He is Professor of Planning and Building Technology at Darmstadt. Thomas Pink was born in 1958 in Hamburg and also studied architecture at the polytechnic in Aachen. In 1987 he joined the partnership of Jürgen Overdiek and Karl-Heinz Petzinka.

Reichen & Roberts Architectes
17 rue Brézin, 75014 Paris, France

Founded in 1973, Reichen & Roberts received almost immediate recognition for their refurbishment of textile mills in northern France, as well as the conversions of La Grande Halle de la Villette and Le Pavillon de L'Arsenal in Paris. Their recent renovation of the Menier Chocolate Factory into the Headquarters of Nestlé France was awarded the MIPIM '96. Newly built schemes include the American Art Museum in Giverny, the French Embassy in Qatar and the Environmental Technology Centre in the Ruhr.

Rockwell Group
5 Union Square West, New York, NY 10003, USA

David Rockwell was born in 1956 in Chicago, from where he moved to Guadalajara, Spain. He took his BA in Architecture at the University of Syracuse and went on to study at the Architectural Association in London. He inherited his love of show business from his mother who was a Vaudeville star. The Rockwell Group is best known for its entertainment architecture and highly dramatic and spectacular interiors such as the Nobu, Vong, Monkey Bar in New York, as well as nearly all the Planet Hollywood restaurants. The company is also concerned, however, with residential, retail, mixed-use and commercial projects. They strive to complete unique interiors that mix the best of technology, entertainment and design and are experts in the use of high-tech video technology, handmade objects and special effects. Clients include the Walt Disney Company, CBS, McDonalds, Caesars World and Sony Theatres. Designs currently in progress or under construction include: the Official All Star Café at Time Square; Disney's Creative Palate Restaurant; the CBS Retail Store on Broadway; and a 190,000-square-foot entertainment complex for Forest City Ratner on West 42nd Street. The Rockwell Group is the recipient of numerous major design awards and its work has been widely published.

Philippe Starck
27 rue Pierre Poli, 92130 Issy-les-Moulineaux, Paris, France

Philippe Starck was born in Paris in 1949. He attended the Ecole Camondo to train as an interior designer but did not complete the course. He worked as a fashion designer for the Pierre Cardin furniture collection, then in the early 1970s he formed his own company making inflatable objects. The 1980s saw him designing avant-garde nightclub interiors, and he won recognition for his work on Les Bains and La Main Jaune, which were inspired by the science fiction of Philip K. Dick. After a period of activity in New York, he returned to France where he has since built up an international reputation and today runs his own intentionally small design company Starck Ubik. He has been responsible for major interior design schemes, including François Mitterrand's apartment at the Elysée Palace, the Café Costes, and the acclaimed Royalton and Paramount hotels in Manhattan, New York. He has also created domestic and public multi-purpose buildings such as the Headquarters of Asahi Beer in Tokyo. As a product designer he works for companies throughout the world, collaborating with Alessi, Baleri, Baum, Disform, Driade, Flos, Kartell, Rapsel, Up & Up, Vitra and Vuitton. His many awards include the Grand Prix National de la Création Industrielle. His work can be seen in the collections of the major design museums worldwide. Recent projects include: the Delano Hotel in Miami; the Mondrian hotel in Los Angeles; a new flat-pack, build-it-yourself wooden house, available through the Trois Suisses mail-order catalogue; as well as the Theatron nightclub in Mexico. Starck is currently artistic director of Thomson Consumer Electrics.

Studio Granda
Fjolnisvigi 2, 101 Reykjavik, Iceland

Studio Granda was founded in 1987 by Steve Christer (born in 1960) and Margarét Hardardóttir (born in 1959). They studied at Edinburgh University and the University of Newcastle upon Tyne respectively, and both later graduated from the Architectural Association in 1984. The City Hall at Reykjavik was their first completed project and resulted from a competition entry. Subsequent schemes have included private residences and landscaping for the City of Reykjavik, as well as numerous competitions for public buildings in the city. The partners have exhibited in Iceland, Germany, Norway, Switzerland, Austria and the United Kingdom. In 1996 they took part in the 'New Generation of the North' show at the Venice Biennale.

Shin Takamatsu Architect and Associates
36-4 Jyobadaiin-cho, Takeda, Fushimi-ku, Kyoto 612, Japan

Shin Takamatsu was born in 1948 in Shimane Prefecture, Japan. He trained at Kyoto University and in 1977 established the Takumi Design Office. He has held educational positions at Fukui Technical University, Osaka College of Art's architectural department and was Assistant Professor of the Kyoto Seika University until 1991. Shin Takamatsu Architect and Associates was founded in 1980, the Takamatsu Planning Office in 1988 and Takamatsu & Layani Architects Associates in Berlin in 1993. His work has received considerable acclaim both within Japan (he was given the Kyoto Prefecture Meritorious Cultural Service Award in 1994 and the Education Minister's Art Encouragement Prize in 1996) and internationally. Takamatsu became an Honorary Fellow of the American Institute of Architects in 1995. He has exhibited in Europe and the United States, having solo shows at the San Francisco Museum of Modern Art and the Aedes Gallery, Germany. Recent projects include large scale public buildings in Japan, such as Kunibiki Messe, Matsue.

TDO (Tsujimura Hisanobu Design Office)
501 Hoteiya-cho, Nijo-agaru, Fuyacho-dori, Nakagyo-ku, Kyoto 604, Japan

Born in Kyoto in 1961, Hisanobu Tsujimura graduated from interior design school in 1982. He established the architectural and interior design company TDO in 1995. In 1995 and 1996, he received the Japan Society of Commercial Space Designer Award.

Valerio Dewalt Train Associates
200 North Lasalle Street, Chicago, Illinois 60601, USA

Valerio Dewalt Train was founded over 30 years ago and deals with both new construction and renovations, specializing in corporate design, high-tech industrial buildings, laboratory and research facilities, retail schemes, cultural centres and multi-family housing. The principal-in-charge, Joseph M. Valerio received a Bachelor of Architecture at the University of Michigan and a Masters at U.C.L.A. He has received numerous design awards including four National AIA Honour Awards and twelve local AIA Awards. He is currently serving as President of the Chicago Architectural Club and is on the board of the Contemporary Arts Council. He has been responsible for many of the company's leading projects, including the apartment blocks in Arizona and California and a 400-seat restaurant in San Francisco. He is currently in charge of the mixed-use redevelopment of the Capitol area of Madison, Wisconsin, and overseeing the $200 million construction for US Robotics during their national and international expansion. Mark D. Dewalt studied at the University of Illinois and is currently working on a headquarters for Automatic Data Processing and a dormitory renovation at Elmhurst College. The third partner, Jack de Train, is President of Valerio Dewalt Train. He trained at the University of Illinois and at the University of Tennessee where he specialized in structural engineering. He worked for Skidmore Owings & Merrill where he was associate partner before moving to VDT. He is at present in charge of the interior remodelling of the John C. Kluczynski Federal Building and the construction of the five-storey office addition of US Robotics. He is a fellow of the American Institute of Architects.

Van Berkel & Bos Architectuurbureau
Weesperstraat 105, 1018 VN Amsterdam, The Netherlands

Ben van Berkel trained at the Rietveld Academy and the Architectural Association in London, receiving an Honours Diploma in architecture in 1987. He is a tutor at the Technical University in Delft and at the Academies of Architecture in Amsterdam and Rotterdam. Since 1990 he has been a member of the architects' panel of the Foundation for the Visual Arts. His practice is active in the fields of civil, utility and urban design, notable projects being the Erasmus Bridge over the River Maas, Rotterdam (1990–5); the extension and renovation of the State Museum Twente, Enschede (1992–5); the Stolen Health Centre, Amsterdam, begun in 1992; and a master plan for the Amsterdam Waterfront in collaboration with Rem Koolhaas, W. J. Neutellings, A. Geuze, C. Christiaanse and J. Gor. He has exhibited widely in Europe and the USA and took part in the 1991, 1993 and 1995 Venice Biennale.

Thomas van den Valentyn
Aachener Strasse 23, 50674 Cologne, Germany

Thomas van den Valentyn studied architecture at the Staatliche Kunstakademie in Düsseldorf and in Vienna with Hans Hollein. He has been in practice since the early 1980s and has completed numerous public and domestic projects in Bonn, Cologne, Hamburg and Weimar. Recent schemes include the Loggia zum Stadthaus (in progress), Bonn; the 'Dreiturm' High Rise (in progress), Cologne; the Juridicum Martin-Luther-Universität (in progress), Halle; and the Godesberger Allee, Bonn (1995–7). He has received national recognition in the form of various domestic prizes and his work has been published in the majority of German architecture magazines.

Rafael Viñoly Architects
50 Vandam Street, New York, NY 10013, USA

Rafael Viñoly was born in Montevideo, Uruguay. He studied architecture at the University of Buenos Aires and founded his own practice, 'Estudio de Arquitectura', with six associates. It quickly became one of the largest architectural firms in South America and by 1974 Viñoly had won over 50 competitions. He studied for a Masters degree and taught at the University of Buenos Aires until the military coup of 1974 when he left and organized an alternative architecture school. Viñoly went to the United States four years later as a guest lecturer at Washington University and then at the Harvard Graduate School of Design. He created his own firm the following year. His work ranges from private residences and retail interiors to university buildings, courthouses, performing arts centres and corporate headquarters. His largest project to date is the Tokyo International Forum, which was completed in 1996. Current projects include a sports stadium for Princeton University, a mixed-use office building in Beijing and the re-zoning of a 1.6 million square-foot development in Manhattan. He has received numerous awards, most recently the 1995 Medal of Honor AIA and the 1996 Excellence in Design from the AIA.

Von Gerkan, Marg & Partner
139 Elbchausee, Hamburg, Germany

Von Gerkan, Marg & Partner is one of the most successful architectural firms in Germany. Founder Meinhard von Gerkan was born in 1935 and studied in Berlin and Brunswick. In 1965 he began a collaboration with architect Volkwin Marg, and within the first year the team won seven first prizes in competitions, including one for the Berlin Tegel airport. The firm has been known as Von Gerkan, Marg & Partner since 1972, and it has won over 90 national and international competitions and received numerous awards. In 1974 Meinhard von Gerkan became Professor at the Technical University of Brunswick. Important projects include: airports in Moscow, Hanover, Stuttgart and Hamburg; the Convention Hall in Bielefeld; the New Fairgrounds Messe in Leipzig; and Zürich-Insurance, Hamburg.

Wickham & Associates Architects
199-205 Old Marylebone Road, London, NW1 5QP, UK

Wickham & Associates was established in London in 1971 by Julyan Wickham (b. 1942) who studied at the Architectural Association (1961–6), and worked for Edward Cullinan Architects. He has taught at many colleges in the United Kingdom and The Netherlands and was external examiner at Glasgow School of Art. Partner Tess Wickham (b. 1945) studied at the London School of Economics and worked as a designer for Pearce Marchbank and with Wickham, becoming a partner in 1981. Recent commissions have included urban studies and projects such as the passenger areas at the airport at Karaganda in Kazakhstan (1993–); the Bank Restaurant, London (1996); residential projects in Holland and London; and an urban study for the extension of Lelystad, in the Netherlands, which comprises a proposal for a mixed development of residential, commercial, retail, entertainment and parkland. They have exhibited their work nationally and have been published in architecture magazines.

Pep Zazurca
Eduardo Conde 50 301, 08034 Barcelona, Spain

Pep Zazurca was born in 1955 in Barcelona and qualified as an architect in 1979. In 1988 he won the competition for the Barc Carlos 1 in the Olympic Village in Barcelona, and in 1992 the competition for the Olympic hockey stadium in Tarrasa. He was awarded the Puig i Cadafalch prize in 1989.

Nickelodeon Headquarters
New York, USA

Architect and interior design: Fernau & Hartman Architects

Project team: Richard Fernau, Laura Hartman (principals-in-charge); David Kau (project architect); Turk Kauffmann, Scott Donahue (design team); Geoff Holton, Sarah Cunniff, Susan Stoltz, Erica von der Heyden, Chat Chuenrundeemol, Keith Dubinsky, Ariel Dunkel, Tania Davidge (project team). Client: MTV Networks. Associate architect: Kohn Pederson Fox Interior Architects. Main contractor: Lehr Construction Corporation. Structural engineers: Leichtman and Lincer. Consultants: Flack & Kurtz (MEP engineer); Shen Milsom & Wilke (acoustics).

Union Bank of Norway Head Office
Oslo, Norway

Architect and interior design: Narud-Stokke-Wiig AS Architects

Project team: Ole Wiig (partner-in-charge); Mirjana Grahovac (project architect); Tore Schjetlein (architect); Tom Holtmann, Mai The Nguyen, Ingvor Hoyland, Anne Tomberg. Client: Linstow Eiendorm AS, on behalf of the Union Bank of Norway. Main contractor: PEAB. Consultants: Berdal Stomme AS, Erichsen & Horgen AS, Berg-Nilsen & Reinertsen AS. Masonry and tiles: Rolf Holm AS. Steel structure: S. Langseth Sveiseverksted AS. Glass roof: Foga Fasad AS. Paintwork: M. Bratfoss AS. Stone mason: Naturstein AS. Parquet flooring: Bo Andren Norge. Partition walls and ceilings: Nor Partner. Steel stairs: Solberg Industrier. Glass walls: Oslo Glass and Vindu. Ironmongery: NT Moller Undall. Flooring: Asker Tapet and Gulvbelegg. Awnings: Solex AS.

Ustate US Robotics
Skokie, Illinois, USA

Architect and interior design: Valerio Dewalt Train Associates

Project team: Joseph M. Valerio (partner-in-charge); David R. Jennerjahn (project architect); Randall S. Mattheis, Nancy Willert, Michael Cygan, Louis Lovera, Mark Demsky. Client: US Robotics Corporation. Engineer: WMA Consulting Engineers (mechanical/electrical/fire protection). Furniture consultant: Desks, Inc. General contractor: Turner Construction Company.

Andersen Consulting
Paris, France

Architect and interior design: Chadwick International

Client: Andersen Consulting. Lighting: Artemide. Stonework and false floor: Ste DBS. Marble: Tredent. BET: Gectra. Mirrors: Guillaume Saalburg; Française du Verre. Furniture: Marcatre SNC; Orga System; Wilkhahn; Forum Diffusion. Movable partitions: Acoplan. Entrance carpet: CS Steel SA. Paintwork: 5PR. Ceiling: Ste PMG. Signage: Modulex.

Andrassy Boardroom
Head Office National Nederlanden and ING Bank, Budapest, Hungary

Architect and interior design: EEA Erick van Egeraat Associated Architects

Project team: Erick van Egeraat; Tibor Gall (project architects); Maartje Lammers (assistant architect); Astrid Huwald, Gabor Kruppa, Janos Tiba, Stephen Moylan, William Richards, Ineke Dubbeldam, Ard Buijsen, Miranda Nieboer, Harry Boxelaar, Axel Koschany, Tamra Klassen. Client: National-Nederlanden Hungary Ltd, ING Bank Budapest, ING Real Estate. Main contractor: CFE Hungary Epitoipara Kft. Management services: Pro Plan Kft. Quantity surveyor: Munk Dunstones Associates. Structural consultant: ABT Adviesburo voor Boutwtechniek bv. Mechanical and electrical consultant. Ketel Raadgevend Ingenieurs bv. Glass construction: Permasteelisa, Conegliano. Interior contractors: Van Gils projekten bv, Patella, Desseaux, Ketel projektservice. Lifts: Otis Hungary. Mechanical services: Air & Chaleur. Electrical services: VIV Siemens. Models: Henk Bouwer.

Design Offices, Pentagram Design Inc.
204 Fifth Avenue, New York, USA

Architect and interior design: Pentagram Architecture

Project team: James Biber (partner/architect); Michael Zweck-Bronner (project architect); Jim Cleary and Leslie Wellcott (assistants). Client: Pentagram Design Inc. Contractor: Bronx Builders. Structural consultant: Anchor Consulting. Textiles: Mary Bright Originals (curtains). Tabletops: Formica. Dividers: Forbo Industries. Floorcovering: Bentley Mills. Pendant light: custom made by Fabulux. Ceiling lights: Visa Lighting, LucePlan, Artemide. Paintwork: Benjamin Moore. Conference-room seating: Nuovo Melodrom. Conference-room lighting: Pentagram, fabricated by Stuber/Stone. Coat rack: Zero US Corp. Furniture: custom-made by Pentagram, fabricated by Vail Fixturing and Bronx Builders.

PolyGram International Offices
St James's Square, London, UK

Architect and interior design: Jestico & Whiles Architects

Project team: Tony Ingram, Tony Ling, John Wotton, Eoin Keating, Adrian Morrow, Amir Ramezani, Rachel Antelme, Alan Waterman, Anne Rowell. Client: PolyGram International. Project manager: Project Management International. Structural engineer: Price and Myers. Quantity surveyor: Wheelers. M. & E. Consultants: Rybka and Smith Ginsler & Battle. Acoustic consultant: Acoustic Design Limited. Contractors: Nico Construction (management). Subcontractors and suppliers: Philips (lighting); Elementer (ironmongery); Industrial Design; Hafele; Dorma; Duffy & Carr (structural strengthening and demolition); Matthew Hall (mechanical and electrical services); Midland Light Alloys (architectural steelwork in the conservatory); Critall (window replacement); Robseal (roof coverings); Sarnafil; Torr Stone (copings, stonework and external decoration); Staverton (specialist joinery); W. R. Leggott (handrails and balustrades); Pollards (Fyrespan) (entrance screens and architectural metalwork); Junckers (timber flooring); Nippon Electric (glass block walling); Nazeing Glass (glass block floor); Splinter Group (reception desk).

Ackerman McQueen Advertising
Tulsa, Oklahoma, USA

Architects and lighting design: Elliott & Associates Architects

Client: Ackerman McQueen Advertising. Collaborating lighting designer: Hunzicker Brothers. Contractor: Lassiter Richeg & Co., Inc. Electrical contractor: Jerry Buysse Electric. Lighting suppliers: Hale; Metalux, CSL; Sunnex; IPI; National Speciality Lighting; Sure Lites; Norbert Belfor, SLP.

Nestlé Headquarters
Noisiel, France

Architect and interior design: Reichen & Robert Architectes

Project team: Jacques Lissarrague (principal-in-charge), Florence Robert (landscape), Anne Carles-Stefano (interior design). Client: Nestlé France. Chief of works: Noisiel Building Department. Main contractor: Bovis SA. Contractors: GII (façades), OTH (electricity), Cortel (cabling system), Restoration Conseil (kitchens). Restoration of exterior: Pradeau & Morin and Lefaure. Head of exterior restoration: D. Lefevre. Consultants: Laurence Allégret and Michel Pironi (lighting); Socotect (acoustics); Dragon Rouge (signage). Flooring: Quillery & cie, Sementic, Fougerolle, Pierre & Pasquet. Metalwork: A.C.M.T. (interior); Goyer Talon P.M.B. (exterior). Exterior woodwork: Menuiserie de Flandre. Glasswork: Visama. Movable partitions: Someta. Ventilation: Sulzer Infra, Payet-Pluchet, Martet Mercier. Artists: Michel Boulanger, Sylvie Blochet, Dominique Bailly. Lighting suppliers: Trilux & Radian.

Chiat/Day Advertising Offices
New York, USA

Interior design: Gaetano Pesce/Pesce Ltd

Project team: Gaetano Pesce (principal and design); Kent Hikida (project architect); Olafur Thordarson V.P., Patrick Rannou, Douglas Bergert, Lisa Hill, Denise Ha (architectural team); Michael Schinelli, Zingg Avi Cohen, Darin Johnstone, Leonid Yentus, Joseph Sabel, Michael Whitney, Jason Tillman. Client: TBWA Chiat/Day Inc. Advertising. Contractors: Tony Pugliese/Paintcraft (custom interior painting and fabric wall finishes); Ruvolo & Di Maria (custom wooden tables); Metrospace (millwork); CTI (walls and ceilings); Versailles (upholstery); Metal-forms and Kraman (metal fabrications); Penguin (A/C mechanical); Alex Manuelle;

Fosdick/Bills. Consultants: JB&B (electrical engineering); Thorton Tomasetti (structural engineering); A&H (architectural); Siemens Rolm (telephone systems); Tri-Met (shop drawings).

House of Engineers
Herrenberg, Germany

Architect and interior design: Kauffmann Theilig & Partner

Project team: Stefan Rapp (architect-in-charge), Viet Dam, Thomas Weber. Client: H. & M. Wetzstein. Engineering services and technical equipment: Ingenieurgesellschaft für Haustechnik Wetzstein GmbH. Structural elements: Pfeffercorn & Partner. Exterior construction: Wolfgang Preuss; Weil der Stadt. Structural engineer: Ingenieurbüro für Bauphysik.

Citizens' Advice Bureau
Chessington, Surrey, UK

Architect and interior design: Gabriele Bramante

Project team: Gabriele Bramante (project leader), John Woodman and Paul Holden. Client: Kingston Citizens' Advice Bureaux Service. Contractors: Cleveland Stuctural Engineering Ltd (steel); Wormald Fire Systems (sprinkler intallation); Siemens plc (building management system); Siemens Lighting (interior lighting); Reggiani (exterior lighting); J. B. Riney & Co. Ltd (civil engineering); Reyhau Ltd (under-floor heating); Sarnafil (roofing contractor); Ashby & Horner Joinery and Interiors Ltd (interior joinery fit out); BMW AG Munich (locking systems); Technical Blinds Ltd (internal louvre blinds for roof glazing); Edwards Heating Ltd (Mechanical and Electrical); Tadcaster Building Limestone (stone flooring); Jandor (glazing). Quantity surveyor: Davis Langdon & Everest. Structural engineers: Whitby & Bird. Fire engineering: Ove Arup & Partners/Arup Fire. Suppliers: Kronospan (MDF doors); Elementer Industrial Design Ltd (ironmongery); Pilkington Glass Ltd (glazing); Kingspan Insultation Ltd (roof insulation).

Water/Glass Villa
Atami City, Japan

Architect and interior design: Kengo Kuma & Associates

Project team: Kengo Kuma (project architect); Kenichi Hosomura, Takaaki Ando. Client: Bandai Co. Ltd. Main contractor: Takenaka Corporation. Structural engineers: N. Takata & Associates. Mechanical engineers: Kawaguchi Mechanical Engineering and Yamazaki Electric Engineering. Lighting consultant: T. Konishi & EPK. Steel manufacturer: Kakuto Corporation.

Oxo Tower Wharf Restaurant
London, UK

Architect and interior design: Apicella Associates

Project team: Lorenzo Apicella, Hilary Clark, James Robson, Jane Sheidow, Matthew Clare. Client: Coin Street Community Builders. Main contractor: Barlow Shopfitting. Project management and quantity surveyor: Turner & Townsend. M. & E. Engineer: Cundall Johnson & Partners. Café tables: Inecasis, supplied by Conran Contracts. Café chairs: Series 7, supplied by Atrium. Wooden tables and benches: Dee Gaind, manufactured by Handley and Applin. Flooring: Contract Flooring Sales. Slate flooring: Burlington Slate. Specialist services: Tricon Food Consultants.

Sheraton Hotel
Roissy, Paris, France

Interior design: Ecart

Client: I.T.T. Sheraton. Hotel design, construction and interior layouts: Martinet Architecture. Lessor: Aéroports de Paris. Design of interchange module: TGV/RER Stations. Builder: C.B.C. Heulin Construction. Consultants: Impedance SA (acoustics); Aartill (lighting); Restauration Conseil (kitchens). Room layout: Chantiers Baudet SA. 5.20 level layouts: Lambro Contact Ltd. Decorative metalwork and light fittings: L.C.S.D. Rails, drapes, net curtains, bedspreads: Soutumier. Room furniture: Durlat. 5.20 level furniture: Laval. Business armchairs: Ecart International.

Ricordi Café
Kyoto, Japan

Architect: TDO (Tsujimura Hisanobu Design Office)

Project director: Hisanobu Tsujimura. Client: Shigeo Mashiro. General contractor: Masamune Kenchiku Co. Ltd. Furniture: Moon.

1996 QE2 Refit
global

Architect and interior design: MET Studio Ltd

Project team: Alex McCuaig (Managing Director); Chris Cawte (project manager); Jane Sharpe (project coordinator); Peter Mance and Murray Jervis (senior designers); Phil Holbrook (designer). Client: Cunard Line, New York. Main contractor (shipyard): A. & P. Appledore (Southhampton) Ltd. Yard subcontractor: CLC Marine Ltd; Trimline International Ltd (bathrooms and Yacht Club and Lido modification); Ocean Interiors Ltd (Mauretania Restaurant, Princess Grill and Britannia Grill). Direct contractor: International Interiors (dance floor, carpeting, blinds and curtains in Casino).

1994 QE2 Refit
global

Architect and interior design: MET Studio Ltd

Project team: Alex McCuaig, Chris Cawte, Joseph Mitchell, Vic Kass, John McNeece, Mark Hilferty, Tony Dougdlae, Erol Aziz. Interior design: McNeece Ltd. Client: Cunard Line Ltd. Contractors: Vlohm & Voss AG, Mivan Marine, CLC Marine. Lighting: DHA Design Services. Acoustics: Sandy Brown Associates. Seating: Englender Furniture Ltd; Kesterport Fabric by Baumann Dekor. Carpet: Brintons. Lighting fixtures: Mivan Ltd, Erco, Oldham, G. H. Montage. Paint: Zolatone. Glass map: Livermead Art Glass. Partitions in the Lido Restaurant: Forbo-Resopal.

Tapika Restaurant
950 Eighth Avenue, New York, USA

Interior design: Rockwell Group

Project team: David Rockwell (principal); Niels Guldager (project manager); Alice Yiu, Ed Bakos, Ger Lambert, Chris Smith. Client: Peter & Penny Glazier. Contractor: Lotus Equities, CTP. Fabric: GP Baker for Lee Jofa; Sonia's Place; Henry Calvin Fabrics. Plaster: Fred Martin, Visions in Plaster. Leather: Edelman. Blue art glass: F. J. Gray Glass. Photographic framing: Soho Galleries. All metal work: Sanchez/Nitzberg Inc. Woodwork/upholstery: Concord Woodcraft. Vestibule collage and wheat wall: Surfacing Arts. Curtains: Carla Weisberg. Lighting: Focus Lighting. Silver dollar and Jay Dusard sepia photographs: Duggal. Brick wall treatments: Modeworks.

Bargo
Glasgow, Scotland, UK

Architect and interior design: Branson Coates Architecture

Project team: Doug Branson; Nigel Coates (design direction); Allen Bell, Tony Burley, Mick Haley, Geoff Makstutis, Gerrard O'Carroll, John Paul, Oriel Prizeman, Simon Vernon Harcourt. Client: Bass Taverns/Tennents. Contractor: Dimension Shopfitting Ltd. Structural engineer: Rennick Partnership. Quantity surveyor: Gordon Hall Grayson & Company. Planning supervisor: Young and Gault. Graphic identity: Branson Coates. Chairs and tables: Nigel Coates, supplied by Omniate.

Sony Theatres Lincoln Square
New York, USA

Architect and interior design: Gensler

Project team: T. Michael Darner (project director); Robert Green (design director); David Fridlund (project manager); John Scouffas (project designer); Steven Adams (designer). Client: Sony Theatres. Architect of record: Schuman, Lichtenstein, Claman, Effron Architects. Building architect: Kohn Pedersen Fox Associates. Construction manager and main contractor: Lehrer McGovern Bovis Inc. Acoustic consultant: Shen Milsom & Wilks. Lighting consultant: Gallegos Lighting Design. Structural engineer: Robert Rossenwasser Associates. Mechanical/electrical/plumbing engineer: James Cooper and Associates. Graphic designer: Gensler. Mural design: Robert Green of Gensler. Muralists: Evergreene Painting Studios. Sculptors and ornament: Hayles and Howe Plasterers.

Niseko Higashiyama Prince Hotel Annex
Niseko, Japan

Architect and interior design: Design System; Kiyoshi Seike (architect).

Client: Seibu Golf Corporation. Interior design: Design System, Kazuhide Takahama, Studio 80, Q Designers. Structural engineering: Structure Planning Laboratory. Main contractors: Taisei Kensetsu, Takasago Netsugaku Industries, Saikyuu Industries, Koudensha.

Bank Restaurant
London, UK

Architect and interior design: Wickham & Associates Architects

Project team: Julyan Wickham (main designer); Tim Pitman (job architect); Pedro Chavez, Dawn Hammond, Rod Heyes, Rupert Hardcastle, David Taylor and Tess Wickham. Client: Marchthistle Ltd. Main contractor: Pat Carter Constracts Ltd. Quantity surveyor: E. C. Harris. Structural engineers: Dewhurst Macfarland & Partners. Services engineers: Fulcrum Eng. Partnership (conept); Atelier 10 (production). Kitchen installation/consultants: Hansens Kitchen Equipment Ltd. Kitchen range: Bonnet. Kitchen ventilation: Vianen Kitchen Ventilation UK Ltd. Mechanical contractor: ACE, Air Cool Engineering. Electrical contractor: ICA, Inner City Electrical (London) Ltd. Refrigeration: Williams Refrigeration Ltd. Joinery: Becher Joinery. Specialist steelwork: Rod Smith (bar stools, champagne stands); Nevill (stainless-steel bar rails, handrails, rigidized panels); Design Fabrication (steel on chandelier). Upholstery: Ease & Co. Glasswork: F. A. Firman (Harold Wood) Ltd. Murals: Pola Wickham. Sculpture: Richard Cowdy.

Theatron
Mexico City, Mexico

Interior design: Philippe Starck. Architect: Baltazar Vez.

Client: Grupo Hostemex. Lighting: Isometrix.

Cannon Sports Club
City Branch, Cannon Street, London, UK

Architect and interior design: Daryl Jackson International (UK)

Client: Cannons Sports Clubs (UK). Contractor: Lelliott/APS Construction Management. Structural engineer: Atelier Ten. M. & E. engineer: Atelier Ten. Interiors consultant: Jenkins Group. Resin floor: Surtech. Metalwork: Aynsley Metalwork. Glazing: Hubbards, MGA. Wood floors: Wallis Wood Floor. Services: H. Page. Yacht duct: Sailspar. Specialist lighting: Box Products. Fabric screens: Ullman. Swimming pool: London Swimming Pools. Joinery: Charles Barrett. Squash courts: Prospec.

Cannons Sports Club
Covent Garden Branch, London, UK

Architect and interior design: Daryl Jackson International (UK)

Client: Cannons Sports Clubs (UK). Main contractor: Holloway White Adam (aerobics hall). Structural engineer: Atelier One. Services engineer: Atelier Ten. Construction management: Cannons (changing rooms, pool, membership office). Changing room fit-out: Charles Barrett. Specialist joinery and stairs: 15M. Fabric roof: Landrell/Aura Fabric Engineering. Mirrors: Warner Glass. Wood floors: Wallis Wood Floors. Stone carpet: Fleurit. Ceilings and partitions: Hatmet. Lighting: Staff; i Guzzini; Erco. Services: A.J. Engineering.

Galerie Lafayette
Friedrichstadt Passagen, Quartier 207, Friedrichstrasse/ Französischestrasse, Berlin, Germany

Architect and interior design: Jean Nouvel et Associés

Project team: Jean Nouvel (project control); Barbara Salin, Laurence Daude, Judith Simon, Viviane Mortean (project architects); Olga Bauer, Franca Comalini, Hiram Duyvestijn, Vincent Hubert, Jean-Louis Maniaque, F. Marzelle, Frédéric Neubauer, Walter Kruse, Nicole Weber, Judith Simon, Xavier Lagurgue, Wolfgang Kruse, Wolfgang Keuthage, Mathias Raasch, Judith Simon, Stacy Eisenberg, Said Fahrat, Nathalie Miegeville, Christina Sewerin, Alexandre Vaucher, Niki Van Osten, Beth Weinsten (assistant architects). Client: Euro-Projekt Entwicklungs GmbH. Structural engineer: Ove Arup & Partners and Polonyi & Fink GmbH. M. & E. engineer: HL Technick AG. Façade: IBS Schalm. Security engineer: Institute Lehmann. Graphic design: Sabine Rosant. CAD design: Antoine Assi and Mounir El Hawat. Quantity surveyor: Tollyard GmbH.

Ricci Store
Bold Street, Liverpool, UK

Interior design: Design Shed

Project team: Miles Falkingham, James Weston. Client: Goodman International. Main contractor: M. Rose Builders. Glazing contractor: O. J. Taffinder. Steelwork: Central Steel Fabrication. Glazed bricks: E. B. International. Specialist joinery: SJS. Lighting: ERCO. Flooring: Crucial Trading Co. Tiles: Swedecor. Picket gate: Bolton & Brady. Shelving: Reglit. Furnishings: Aram Designs.

Zumtobel-Staff Showroom
Lemgo, Germany

Architect and interior design: Architekturbüro Bolles-Wilson

Project team: Prof. Julia Bolles-Wilson and Peter L. Wilson; Jim Yohe (project architect). Client: Zumtobel-Staff. Lighting concept: Licht Köln. Lighting: Zumtobel-Staff. Local subcontractors. Furniture: Staff's furniture workshop.

Swatch Store
Via Montenapoleone, Milan, Italy

Interior design: Atelier Mendini

Project team: Alessandro Mendini, Francesco Mendini (project directors); Alex Mocika, Andrea Balzari. Client: Swatch AG, Biel CH. Main contractor: Lisar SpA. Opus Romano mosaic: Bisazza.

Jigsaw
New Bond Street, London, UK

Architect and interior design: John Pawson

Project team: John Pawson, Vishwa Kaushal, Enzostefano Manola, Anthony Thistleton, Simon Dance, Alejandro Fernandez, Niall Maxwell. Client: Jigsaw (Robinson Webster Holdings Ltd). Main contractor: RBS Shopfitters. Structural engineer: S. B. Tietz & Partners. M. & E. engineers: Ian Mackay Associates. Lighting: Isometrix.

Ronda Store
Barcelona, Spain

Architect and interior design: Pep Zazurca

Client: Ronda SA. Interior design: Mar Ruiz. Graphic design: Ruiz & Company. Architect: Francesc Morres. Construction: 'Relluc' – Jordi Rosinyol.

Eickhoff Store
Düsseldorf, Germany

Architect and interior design: Petzinka Pink & Partner

Project team: Karl-Heinz Petzinka, Thomas Pink, Mark Hellman, Claudia Hirsching, Andreas Jablonski, Michael Kircher, Mirwaiss Mussa, Mechthild Offner, Gerda Rotteveel, Roswitha Sporr and Barbara Wallraff. Client: Eickhoff-Königsallee GmbH & Co. Shopfitters: Meyerfeldt. Electrical engineers; Elan Elektroanlagen GmbH. Wooden flooring: Thoren. Electrical consultant: Elan Elektroanlgen GmbH. Glazing: Conzen GmbH. Heating and ventilation: Gladen; Kruse; Hein. Staircase and balustrade: Iven & Kirchdorfer GmbH. Artwork: Kohne GmbH. Exterior natural stone: Marmor May GmbH. Carpets: Mewes GmbH. Shutters: Meyerfeldt. Elevator: Schiffer GmbH. Linoleum: Tapeten Passage GmbH. Curtains: Vedder GmbH.

Mahogany Hair Salon
London, UK

Interior design: Caulder Moore

Client: Mahogany. Main contractor: Bridport Shopfitters. Furniture: Viaduct. Chairs: Takara Belmont. Backwashes: Welonda.

Bumble & Bumble Hair Salon
New York, USA

Architect and interior design: Anderson/Schwartz Architects

Project team: Ross Anderson (partner-in-charge); M. J. Sagan (associate in charge); Stephen O'Dell (project architect); Caroline Otto, Jago van Bergen, Paul Henderson, Todd Stodolski, Luis Zufiaur, Aaron Bentley. Client: Bumble & Bumble. General contractor: Alliance Builders Corporation. Structural engineer: Gilsanz Murray Steficek. Mechanical engineer: Electro Mechanical Technical Group. Interiors consultant: Corey Delaney. Lighting consultant: Rick Shaver. Light fixtures: Stonce, Killark, Halo, Alinea, Elliptipar, Adjusco, Lamar. Flooring: Stoneclad (acrylic cement floor); FritzTile (terrazzo tile); Town & Country – distributors (bamboo flooring); Foribo (linoleum flooring). Hardware: Schlage Lock Company. Paint: Benjamin Moore Paints. Furniture: g/Directions (third-floor waiting area seating and coffee table); Anderson Architects/Imaginary Road (third-floor waiting-area bench table); United Chair/Design Tex (office chairs/fabric); Sol y Luna (make-up area chairs). Window shades: Window Architecture. Filing cabinets: Office Speciality. Sinks: Takara Belmont. Steamer trunk fabrication: Shoufany Custom Woodworking. Robot fabrication: Uwe Trauman. Custom-tinted plaster: Beriah Wall. Blackboard: Ay-won. Green acrylic: Lexan. Fibreglass panels: Alpha-one. Wire mesh: Kentucky Metal Products.

Toppan Network Lounge
Tokyo, Japan

Interior design: Makoto Koizumi

Client: Toppan Printing Co. Ltd. Production: Toppan Printing Co. Ltd (Toshio Takeda). Direction: Toppan Printing Co. Ltd (Norio Hiki, Akira Takenawa). Lighting: Ushio Spex (Shoichi Kumasaka). Installation: Toppan Academia Group.

Planet Reebok
New York, USA

Interior design: Fitch Inc.

Client: Reebok International. Collaborator: C.I.T.E. Design New York (graphic elements and coordination of project). Touchscreen window: Planet Interactive. Lighting consultant: Lighting Management. Fixture manufacturer: PAM International. Standard lighting elements: Lightolier. Custom lighting elements: Windsor. Flooring: Amtico.

Glass Hall, Tokyo International Forum
Tokyo, Japan

Architect and interior design: Rafael Viñoly Architects

Project team: Rafael Viñoly, Jay Bargmann, Jim Herr, Harris Feinn, Sandra McKee, Charles Blomberg, Naomi Sato. Client: Tokyo Metropolitan Government; Tokyo International Forum. Architectural consultants: Masao Shiina Architects and Gendai Kenchiku Kenkyujo. Structural engineer: Structural Design Group and Co. Ltd. Mechanical engineer: P. T. Morimura & Associates. Consultants: Theater Workshop (theatre); Lighting Planners Associates (lighting); Yamaha Acoustic Research Laboratories and Jaffe Acoustics Inc. (acoustics); John A. Van Deusen & Associates Inc. (mechanical transportation); ALP Designers Inc. (landscape); Boundary Layer Wind Tunnel Laboratory (wind tunnel); Institute of Industrial Science (climate analysis). Quantity surveyor: Futaba Quantity Surveying Co. Ltd.

The Supreme Court of Iceland
Reykjavik, Iceland

Architect and interior design: Studio Granda

Project team: Margrét Hardardóttir, Steve Christer, Ásdís Ágústsdóttir, Sólveig Berg Björnsdóttir, Jóhann Einarsson, Margrét Hardardóttir, Haraldur Helgason. Client: The Icelandic State. Main contractor: Ármannsfell. Structural engineers: Línuhónnun. Mechanical engineers: Almenna Verkfrædistofan. Electrical engineers: Rafteikning. Landscaping consultant: Hafsteinn Haflidason. Project management: Framkvaemdasysla rikisins (State Building Agency). Acoustics: Verkfrædistofan Önn. Carpentry: Trésmidjan Borg; Trésmida Armannsfells. Copper cladding: K. K. Blikk ehf. Doors and wood flooring: Innidir. Electrics: Rafsel. Furniture: Epal ehf; Grein ehf; A. Gudmundsson ehf (office). Paintwork: Arnar Öskarsson. Steelwork: Stalprydi; Sudulist; Jarnsmidja Ódins Gunnarssonar; Vélsmida einars Gudbrandssonar; Vélsmida Konráds Jónssonar. Plastering: G. E. Verktakar. Signage: Merking. Sound system: Nyherji hf. Sheet-flooring: Solvi M. Egilsson. Terazzo flooring: Húsprydi. Wooden flooring: Beykir. Suppliers: Teppaland (carpets); Hardvidarval (linoleum); Glertaekni (glass); Straumur ehf (shelving); Z-brautir og gluggatjöld (roller blinds); Epal ehf; Penninn hf (furniture).

Aichi Children's Centre
Aichi Prefecture, Japan

Architect and interior design: Environment Design Institute & Fujikawa Hara Associate. Project architect: Mitsuru Senda.

Client: Aichi Prefecture. Structural design: Mutsurou Sasaki Structural Planning Institute. Building equipment: Nobuo Nakahara (a professor emeritus of Nagoya University), Environment Equipment Planning. Graphic designer: Shin Matsunaga. Construction: Kumagaya/Taikei/Sinwa Construction J.V. Air conditioning: Sin-nihon Air Conditioning/Fujima Construction J.V.

Judge Institute
Cambridge, UK

Architect and interior design: John Outram Associates

Project team: David Bass, Natasha Black, Anthony Charnley; Wendy Dellit (project architect for conservation); Iona Foster, Felna Fox, Rebecca Granger, Elizabeth Gregory, Bill Gregory, Timothy Hall, Nicola Hem, Raida Kassim Bench, Sally MacKay; Glen Millar (project architect for the castle); Jean Murphy, Nina Noor; John Outram (project architect for the design), Huw Owen (project architect on site); Amir Ramezani, Jeremiah Sheehan; Alan Smith-Oliver (project architect coordinator). Client: Faculty of Management Studies Cambridge University. Carpet, cork tiles: A1 Flooring. Steelwork: BBB&WW. Architectural metalwork: Coles. Plaster tiles: G. Cook & Sons. Plasterwork: John Venn Plastering. Façade restoration: Collins & Curtis. Concrete staining: Construction Cosmetics. Replacement windows and curtain walling: Corfe Joinery. Metal windows to curtain wall: Crittall. Stone column restoration: Coulsons Restoration. Gallery marble floor: Diespeker. Junckers floor: Durabella. Timber balustrades, seating boxes: East Chapel. Brickwork: Grosvenor Brickwork. Mechanical services: Haden Young. Façade restoration: Holden Conservations Services. Glazing: Ipswich Glass. Gallery landings: Richard Lees Steel Decking. Joinery: Piper Products. Decoration: Qualco. Gallery timber ceiling: Swift Horsman. Structural steelwork: William Sharp. Electrical installation: Sotham Engineering Services. Erected pre-cast concrete: Stone Developments.

Banyoles Municipal Theatre
Banyoles, Spain

Architect and interior design: MBM Arquitectes SA

Project team: Josep Martorell, Oriol Bohigas, David Mackay, Jeroni Moner; Lluis Pau (interior design). Client: Town Council of Banyoles. Main contractor: Sitvisa. Acoustic systems: Higini Arau. Fittings: Projecte y Gestio Industrial. Graphic design: Nuria Duran. Economic planning: Edetco. Technical management: Jaume Pallars.

Neue Messe
Leipzig, Germany

Architect and interior design: Von Gerkan, Marg & Partner

Project team: Prof Volkwin Marg (project director); Hubert Nienhoff; Kemal Akay (project manager); Beata Sturm, Christiane Hasskamp, Monika Scharrer; Veronika Kruch (east entrance); Nyna Bergfeld, Gabriele Köhn; Jutta Hartmann-Pohl (west entrance); Björn Bergfeld, Wolfgang Balbach, Suzanne Bern, Christina Harenberg, Almut Schlüte, Miriam Dank, Fulvio Melle; Klaus Courmont (exhibition halls); Armin Wittershagen, Uwe Friedrich, Annette Kersig, Robert Stüer; Jane Schmahl (pavilion restaurants); Ulrich Weigel, Gisbert v. Stühlpnagel, Bernd Gossmann, Yasmin Balbach, Jochen Köhn, Michael Pohl, Aristide Hamann, Birgit Rith; Tom Naujack (congress centre); Christian Hoffmann, Hubert Hirsch, Dirk Kahlig, Elisabeth Menne, Clemens Dost, Ben Dieckmann, Fernanda Barbato, Monika Kaesler, Thomas Behr (administration building), Angelika Juppian, Petra Kauschus; Heike Bteuler (open-air utilities); Dieter Rösinger, Ursula Köper, Annette Löber, Verena von der Brincken; Wieland Freudiger (interior fittings and furniture); Franz Lensing; Marco Bartusch (metal construction, escalators, lifts and locks); Reinhold Weiten; Hubercus v. Dallwitz (technical coordination); Jochen Köhn and Robert Stüer (computer services); Ines Buchin; Annett Kretzler (administrative support); Rolf Niedballa, Uwe Grahl, Hans-Peter Bentike, Andreas Ebner, Peter Krüger, Roland Lauer; Kerstin Mahler (bill of quantity). Client: Leipziger Messegesellschaft MbH. Project management: IRW Ingenieurbüro Rauch und Wiese. Structural engineer of steel-glass hall: gmp in cooperation with Ian Ritchie Architects/Civil Engineering: Obermeyer Albis-Baupla; RWT, Institut für Stadtplanung. Information systems: Atelier Mac Kneissel. Façade consultant: PBI, Klaus Glass; Ing-Büro Wronn. Natural stone consultant: Ing-Büro Pinck. Technical systems: HL-Technik; Ebert-Ingenieure. Structural design: Ing-Büro Polonyi & Partner; Ing-Büro H. Haringer. Insulation: Von Rekowski-Wolff. Acoustics: Akustik-Ing-Büro Moll, Ing-Büro Knothe. Shell and steel construction: Wayss & Freytag AG, Stahlbau Mauen GmbH (exhibition hall); Mero Raumstruktur GmbH; Glasbau Seele GmbH (glass hall); ARGE Messcturm, Stock GmbH; Stahlbau Illingen GmbH (construction tower); Techno-Metall GmbH; ARGE Seele/Friess (administration and congress centres). Façade construction exhibition hall: Fassadensysteme; Kulkwitz; Koldt GmbH. Façade glazing and sun-protection systems: Rheinhold & Mahla GmbH, Leipzig. Support free steel stairs: Hark GmbH & Co. KG. Gallery railings: ARGE Schultz/Dahme; Metallbau Gayger. Metal and glass door structures: Breitenbach GmbH. Movable partition walls: Hüppe Form GmbH. Panorama lifts: Tepper-Aufzüge GmbH & Co. KG. Natural stone cladding: Kiefer-Reul-Teich GmbH. Concrete ashlar construction/flooring materials: Betonsteinwerk Uetze GmbH. Steel work: Arnold GmbH; Friedricksdorf/ Ts Metall und Werkzeugbau GmbH. Landscaping: Wehberg; Schmidtke. Mature trees: Bruns-Pflanzen Export; Lorenz von Ehren. Furniture: Kayenburg Linear Einrichtung. Carpentry and interior fittings: Lindner AG; Ohning Innenausbau GmbH; Stöppler Innenausbau – Möbel Anfertigung; VHB Vereinigte Holzbau-berriebe GmbH & Co.

Meteor Plaza
Shimane, Japan

Architect: Shin Takamatsu Architect and Associates

Project team: Shin Takamatsu, Kyoko Mochizuki and Shigeto Abe. Client: City of Mihonoseki and Shimane Prefectural Government. Main contractor: Takenaka Corporation. Structural engineer: Yamamoto-Tachibana Architects & Engineers. Mechanical engineer: Architectural Environmental Laboratory. Museum design and planning: Shin Takamatsu Architect and Associates; MSI Japan; Office Hayashi; Jeugia Corporation. Mechanical/electrical/ structural: Daidan Corporation; Shimane Electronics; Sanko Kucho Co. Ltd.

Denver Central Library
Denver, Colorado, USA

Architect: Michael Graves

Project team: Karen Nichols (senior associate); Tom Rowe (senior associate/project architect); John Diebbol (senior associate); Mary Yun, Meryl Blinder, Keoni Fleming, Andy McNabb, Saverio Manago, Stephanie Magdziak, Jane Maybank, Carole Nicholson, Brian Pinkett, Karin Rhae, Pamela Carter Rowe, Kirsten Thoft, Andrea Wang. Architect of record: Klipp Colussy Jenks DuBois Architects P.C. Project team: Brian Klipp (directing principal); Cornelius (Kin) DuBois (principal/ project architect); Otis Odell (associate project architect); Peter Incitti; Garey Dickenson (project manager); Laureen Ferris, Juana Gomez, Brett Linscott, Wayne Pierce, Tom Siebert, Diane Travis. Interior design: Engel/Kieding Design Associates Inc. Client: City and County of Denver Department of Public Works. Construction manager: Hyman/Etkin Construction. Structural and civil engineer: SA Miro, Inc. Mechanical engineer: The Ballard Group. Associate mechanical engineer: John L. Altieri. Electrical engineer: Gambrell Engineering. Lighting consultant: Clanton Engineering, Inc. Graphic design: Weber Design Partners. Kitchen design: Thomas Ricca Associates. Soils engineering: Aquirre Engineering. Surveyors: Kelly Surveying Associates, Inc. Lighting: NeoSource (custom); Columbia; Edison-Price; Kurt Versen; LiteControl; GE Lamps (standard). Custom furniture: Blanton & Moore; Craftwood; Transline. Landscape design: Badgett and Coover-Clark Architects. Acoustics: David L. Adams and Associates. Elevator consultant: Lerch, Bates & Associates.

The Basement, Science Museum
Exhibition Road, London, SW7, UK

Interior design: Ben Kelly Design

Project team: Ben Kelly (project leader); Helen Abadie (project architect); Bill Shorten, Kevin Brennan, Angela Kyriacou, Jonathan Williams, Kirk Le Voi (design team). Client: The National Museum of Science and Industry UK). Contractors: Bilfinger and Berger UK Ltd (main contractor); Platt and Davis Ltd (electrical); Allied Mechanical Services Ltd (mechanical); Southern Metal Fabrication (structural steelwork); Southdown Construction (architectural metalwork); Selcourt Ltd (flooring). Structural engineer: Dewhurst MacFarlane and Partners. M. & E. Consultant: Andrew Sale Associates. Quantity surveyors: Keogh Edwards Partnership. Art consultant: Clare Cumberlidge. Artist (floor design): Tim Head. Graphics and signage: Assorted Images. Shop fitters and joiners: Varbud Construction Ltd; A. Davies and Co. (shopfitters) Ltd; Davis Howarth Jacob. Terrazzo: WB Simpsons and Sons Ltd. Reclaimed Burmese Teak: Victorian Wood Works. Floor finish: Marmoleum Dual, Forbo Nairn. Glass blocks: Luxcrete. Recycled plastic sheet: Made of Waste. Aluminium cladding: Gooding Aluminium. Floor and wall tiles: Langley London Ltd. Glazed bricks: Gilson Ceramique Architecturale EB (International). Glazed blocks: Trenwyth Astra Glaze. Pendant and bulkhead lights: J. and G. Coughtrie Ltd. Terrace lights: Marlin Lighting Ltd.

Rijksmuseum Extension
Enschede, Holland

Architect and interior design: Van Berkel & Bos Architectuurbureau bv

Project team: Ben van Berkel (project architect); Harrie Pappot (project coordination); Joost Hovenier (project leader); Hugo Beschoor Plug, Pieter Koster, Peter Meier, Martin Visscher, Jan van Erven Doren, Serge Darding, Arjan van Ruyven. Client: Ministry of Housing and Construction Dep. Project Management, The Hague. Contractor: Punte bv, Enschede. Technical consultants: Ministry of Housing and Construction, The Hague; Dep. of Design and Technique: A. H. Wiecherink bv, Enschede (technical installations, air-conditioning and heating); Peutz & Associes bv (acoustic consultants). Landscape architect: Lodewijk Baijon.

Softopia Japan Center Building
Gifu, Japan

Architect and interior design: Kisho Kurokawa Architect & Associates

Client: Gifu Prefecture. Main contractors: Takenaka; Dainippon; Giken; Tsuchiya; Usami Corporation. Structural engineer: Gengo Matsui & Musa & Hoshino Architect and Engineer Inc. Mechanical engineer: Sogo Consultant. Acoustics: Nagata Acoustic Inc. Terrazzo blocks: Sekigahara Stone Company. Glass fibre wall and EG wall: Nitto Boseki Co. Ltd. Optical fibre: Laforet Engineering. Elevators: Mitsubishi Electric Corp.

Schloss Belvedere Music College
Weimar, Germany

Architect and interior design: Thomas van den Valentyn

Project team: Thomas van den Valentyn, Mohammad Oreyzi (project architects); Beate Borghoff, Isabelle Sak, Angela Ader, Rüdiger Meissner, Christoph Merten. Client: Deutsche Bank AG, Frankfurt. Building and project management: Harms & Partner Ingenieure. Foundations: Stefan Polonyi. Lighting consultant: Licht-Kunst-Licht. Landscaping: Martin Diekmann, Hanover.

Palace of Justice
Evreux, France

Architects and interior design: J. Dubus & J.P. Lott

Client: Ministry of Justice. Technical control: Apave Normandie. Art work: Benoît Luyckx. Programming: Medial. General contractor: Sogea Nord Ouest. Exterior stone cladding: A.C.F.M. Metalwork: Dewilde et Artestrat. Glasswork: Zenith. Exterior woodwork: Diter. Interior woodwork and fixed furniture: J.P.V. Shelving: Tixit. Parquet: Piederrière. Plumbing: 3B. Heating: Rineau. Electrical contractors: Cegelec; G.T.C. Cofratel Signatel. Paintwork: Morin. Furniture: Dubus & Lott (Castelli; Alo; Knoll). Signage: Marcel Signaletique.

INDEX OF ARCHITECTS, DESIGNERS AND PROJECTS